THE SOCIAL COST OF FUEL CYCLES

Report to the UK Department of Trade and Industry
(Department of Energy)

by

The Centre for Social and Economic Research on the
Global Environment
(CSERGE)

FINAL REPORT

SEPTEMBER 1992

LONDON : HMSO

The views expressed in this publication are those of the authors and do not necessarily reflect those of the Government or the Department of Trade and Industry

THE SOCIAL COST OF FUEL CYCLES

This report has been prepared by:

David PEARCE

Camille BANN

Steven GEORGIOU

Centre for Social and Economic Research
on the Global Environment
(CSERGE)

CSERGE
University College London
136 Gower Street
London WC1E 6BT

PREFACE AND ACKNOWLEDGEMENTS

This report is a literature survey, not original research. Where possible, and in the time available, we have however drawn out some of the findings in an effort to derive preliminary estimates of social cost 'adders' for UK fuel cycles. The resulting estimates are <u>illustrative</u> only. A full research programme is needed to obtain more credible estimates.

Many people have helped in the preparation of this report. We wish to thank especially the staff of Nuclear Electric and the Energy Technology Support Unit (ETSU), Harwell for help and guidance. Special thanks go to Nick Eyre of ETSU, and John Robb of the National Radiological Protection Board. We would also like to thank Ross Ferguson of Newcastle University for sharing his own research results, and members of the EC - US Department of Energy long term study of the social costs of fuel cycles. Finally, Jo Pieris bore the brunt of most of the typing with extraordinary patience and skill. Catherine Cronin, Janet Roddy, and Hyper Typer also worked wonders with the word processing.

DWP
CB
SG

CSERGE May 1992

CONTENTS

SOCIAL COST OF FUEL CYCLES

SECTION ONE:

EXECUTIVE SUMMARY

1   PURPOSE OF THE REPORT

This report was commissioned by the UK Department of Energy. Its purpose is to <u>survey the available literature</u> on the monetary estimation of the social costs of energy production and use. We focus on the social costs of <u>electricity production</u>.

The report is not intended to convey original research, nor could original research have been carried out in the time available. Nonetheless, the report does take various estimates of social cost and shows how they might be converted to monetary 'social cost surcharges' or <u>externality adders</u> in a UK context. It is also important to appreciate that the literature surveyed is on the <u>monetary</u> costs of fuel cycles. This literature is itself very large and very diffuse. There is in addition an even larger literature on the 'physical' environmental and human health impacts of fuel cycles. Some of this literature is the basis for the monetary estimation, but a great deal of additional work exists on physical impacts which has not been used to derive monetary impacts. Indeed, most of it is not in a form that permits monetary estimation. This physical literature is not surveyed in this report. The extent to which this imparts bias in the results is not known.

An externality adder is a surcharge that may be added to the marginal private cost of electricity in order to reflect the non-market damages or benefits that a given electricity-generating technology creates.

Examples of such damages might be environmental impacts from energy-related air pollution, the risk of major accidents in mines or power stations, any subsidies paid to a given fuel cycle, and military expenditures for the protection of overseas oil supplies. An example of a benefit may be the energy security that a fuel source confers because the fuel cycle is 'indigenous' -i.e. does not rely on geographically external sources of supply. Note that the imposition of an adder on energy sources involving risks of supply automatically allows for the energy security benefit of indigenous sources. It is not legitimate to confer a benefit on indigenous sources while at the same time adding a cost to non-indigenous sources: this would be double counting.

The basic rule for determining whether an adder exists or not is that a cost or benefit occurs which cannot legitimately be said to be included in the prevailing market cost of the electricity generated by the given fuel technology.

Adders may therefore arise for two basic reasons: (a) because of <u>environmental damages</u> and (b) because of <u>non-environmental externalities</u> such as subsidies. We adopt the terms environmental externalities (EEs) and non-environmental externalities (NEEs) to cover these different effects. Hence:

$$\text{Externality Adder} = \text{EEs} + \text{NEEs}$$

The externality adder needs to be seen in the context of the theory of social cost pricing. The fundamental requirement for the optimal pricing of energy is that prices should reflect the full social costs of production and use. The relevant formula is:

$$P = MC + MEC + MUC$$

where P = the optimal price of electricity

MC = marginal cost of generation

MEC = marginal external cost, i.e. the externality adder = EE + NEE

MUC = the marginal 'user' cost, designed to capture the cost in the future of using up a unit of a non-renewable resource today.

Note that MEC and MUC are added to the <u>cost</u>, not the <u>price</u> of electricity. MEC and MUC could be added to price only if prices were initially equal to marginal private costs. In practice, prices diverge from marginal costs for various reasons. First, if there are non-competitive markets, prices will be higher than marginal private cost. In general, externality adders should still be added to private costs, however. This is because separate industrial policy should be aiming for the removal of the non-competitive market distortion. On occasion, however, a regulatory agency may decide that the 'over-pricing' due to the market imperfection broadly offsets the 'under-pricing' due to the neglect of the externality. The second reasons for prices to diverge from costs is that there may already be a policy on the externality in question. These points are important when <u>making use</u> of externality adder estimates.

Consider, for example, a technology which, on private cost criteria, costs more than other technologies, but which carries with it certain environmental and energy security benefits. Governments may choose to 'subsidise' this technology because of its environmental and security benefits. In terms of <u>prices</u>, the comparison is between

$$p_i = mc_i - mb_s - mb_e$$

and $$p_o = mc_o$$

where p = price, mc = marginal cost, mb_s = marginal security benefits, mb_e = marginal environmental benefits, i = the 'beneficial' technology and o = the polluting, 'insecure' technology.

If prices have already been adjusted - through explicit or implicit subsidies - then it is not legitimate to add externality surcharges to the <u>prices</u> of the more polluting, less secure fuels. On the other hand, it is always correct to add surcharges to the <u>costs</u> of polluting fuels provided prices have not been adjusted on other fuels.

This issue affects the way in which NEEs are added to EEs. If NEEs (e.g. subsidies) are designed to capture environmental benefits it would be double-counting to credit the 'clean' technology <u>and</u> simultaneously debit the 'polluting' technology. In terms of the previous example, it would be <u>wrong</u> to adjust prices as follows:

$$p_i = mc_i - mb_s - mb_e$$

$$p_o = mc_o + mc_s + mc_e$$

2

where mc_s and mc_e are marginal security and environmental costs respectively.

In general, then, the rules are:

   i)   add any externality cost to the marginal private costs;
   ii) deduct any externality benefit from costs;
   iii) avoid double-counting where any non-environmental externality is in fact an accounting adjustment to reflect true externalities.

The report concludes with some estimates of environmental externality adders that may have relevance for the UK.

For the reasons to be discussed below, these highly provisional figures must not be taken to be accurate measures of externality adders. They are intended to be illustrative only. The justification for attempting even a broad-brush indicator of externality adders is that their relative scale provides some guidance on the further work that is needed if externality adders are to be refined and made more credible.

The uses to which such a survey might be put are many, but these are not the primary focus of the report. Since social costs arise at all stages of the fuel cycle for each energy source, the approach has been one of investigating impacts either at each fuel cycle stage, or seeking EEs and NEEs that already allow for complete fuel cycle impacts.

2   THE FUEL CYCLES

The fuel cycles under consideration are:

   conventional coal-fired systems without gaseous emission control
   modern coal fired stations (PF + FGD)
   oil fired systems without FGD and low NOx burners
   combined cycle gas turbines
   new nuclear energy (PWR)
   wind energy
   landfill gas
   geothermal energy
   tidal power
   hydro-electric power
   wave energy
   solar energy (photovoltaics and thermal)
   coal-fired combined heat and power (CHP)

It also seems sensible to add:

   municipal solid waste plants.

Orimulsion is excluded from the review, but any fuel cycle is relatively easily evaluated in the future provided emission factors are known.   Advanced coal-burning techniques (fluidised bed combustion (FBC) and integrated gas combined cycle (IGCC) are not dealt with separately owing to the absence of comprehensive emission factors for the UK. However, SO_2 reduction with IGCC would be of the order of 99% compared to 90-91% for PF + FGD. The SO_2 externality would therefore be lower.

However, the literature on social costs is not so conveniently organised. It is not always possible, therefore, to relate the literature directly to the fuel cycles above. Far and above the most work has been done on the coal-fired cycle and on nuclear electricity.

A fuel cycle is taken to mean the complete set of activities associated with the production of a unit of electricity. For example, in the case of nuclear power the cycle includes the mining of the uranium ore through to fuel fabrication, power generation, reprocessing, waste disposal and plant decommissioning. It also includes the impacts of constructing the power plant. While transmission is common to all forms of electricity, transmission impacts will vary according to the relationship between the source of power and the end consumer. Some power sources are constrained as to location - wind to open, windy areas; nuclear to coastal sites; wave to offshore sites. For completeness, however, these costs should be estimated if possible. In practice, what can be said is determined by the available literature. As yet, the social costs of transmission (aesthetics of overhead transmission and possible electro-magnetic field health effects) have not been estimated. In the same way, the health impact literature does tend to allow for power plant construction, but other impacts from plant construction tend not to be estimated. Again, therefore, caution must be exercised when interpreting the figures given in this report.

3   ENERGY CONSERVATION

Energy conservation is often called the 'fifth fuel'. The full report devotes a separate chapter to conservation. Conservation will have some negative externalities, especially in connection with the manufacturing processes involved in making insulation material. Conservation may also increase the level of exposure to indoor air pollutants. Typically, the social cost literature provides little information on these costs. But conservation also avoids damage in so far as it precludes the requirement for new energy sources. Thus the adders associated with new energy sources become benefits to energy conservation. Once again, however, it is not legitimate to list conservation as a fuel cycle and credit it with avoided damages if those damages are at the same time debited to the other energy sources. This would be double counting. Proper social costing of energy sources would, of course, encourage more conservation. Note that the precise way in which conservation results in avoided damage depends on how conservation measures affect the merit order of electricity supply. It might be the case that conservation would have as an effect the keeping in existence of old, higher pollution plant. This effect would need to be offset against pollution from a new plant to get a net estimate of avoided damage. This would require systems modelling. The social cost literature appears not to have addressed this issue (see Chapter 13 of the full Report). Conservation also avoids any externalities associated with transmission.

4

4   HOW MIGHT EXTERNALITY ADDERS BE USED ?

While the use to which externality adders might be put is not the prime focus of this report, it is helpful to set out briefly the alternatives for their use. In particular, some uses will require that the estimates of absolute size of adder be accurate. Others require less accuracy in that the rank order of technology by adder is adequate.

There are three basic ways that adders may be used:

(a)   Ranking with Grandfathering

This approach involves requiring electricity utilities to rank only new capacity by social cost and to introduce them accordingly. Existing plant is not affected (hence 'grandfathering'). Moreover, there is no requirement to charge the social cost in electricity tariffs. The adder is used to rank social desirability. Clearly, however, the use of adders in this way will affect system cost if the lowest social cost technologies are not also the lowest private cost technologies. Ranking with grandfathering need not involve wholly accurate estimates of adders, although utilities may well dispute even a ranking if they feel the adders are wholly non-credible.

(b)   Taxation with Grandfathering

In this approach the adder is actually charged to new capacity only. The premium on accuracy in estimating adders is much greater.

(c)   Complete Emissions Adder Taxation

In this approach all sources of generation - new and old - are taxed by the appropriate adder.

The use of externality adders is most widespread in the USA. To date, however, only the first approach - ranking with grandfathering - has been used. A detailed overview of the US regulatory situation with respect to adders is given in Annex 2 of the full report.

5   ESTIMATING ADDERS: BASIC PROCEDURE

The way in which adders are standardised is through two basic measures:

(a)   'emissions' (E) per unit of electricity generated or delivered: for example, grams of sulphur dioxide per kWh;

(b)   monetary damage (D) per unit of pollutant concentration: for example, £s of building corrosion per tonne SO_2 deposited (the ambient concentration, C).

If the emission - concentration function is known, then it is technically possible to calculate:

$$(\pounds D/C)(C/E)(E/kWh) = (\pounds D/kWh)$$

which gives a direct estimate of the externality adder in terms of money values (pence) per kWh. Subject to the caveats in Section 1, these adders may then be added to the private cost of generation.

In practice there are a great many complications. Many studies measure damage ($\pounds D$) but do not relate it to concentrations or emissions. Some relate damage to concentrations but do not cite emissions. Some relate damage to emissions without considering the E-C link. Very few studies deal with a single plant, so that what is measured is actually some _average_ damage estimate for all existing sources. Relating damage to hypothetical new plant is thus hazardous on the basis of the available literature. Only a major research activity can identify the probable value of marginal damage. It requires, for example, consideration of an hypothetical addition to total system capacity and identification of the associated emissions, concentrations and damage. In contrast, most of the existing literature looks at damage done by, say, a specific air pollutant to crops, forests, health in general. What emerges, then, is an average damage estimate from existing sources, not a marginal damage estimate from new sources. A research project to identify marginal damages is under way as part of the United States Department of Energy - European Commission joint project on fuel cycle evaluation, due for completion in 1992/1993 - see Annex 1 of the full report.

Once again, these caveats must be borne in mind when interpreting the estimates. Chapter 2 of the full report provides a detailed discussion of these issues.

6   EMISSION FACTORS

In order to estimate air pollution impacts, it is necessary to have emission factors for the fuel cycles. The factors set out below are based on those provided by the Energy Technology Support Unit at Harwell. ETSU's estimates are the most complete and the only ones available for the UK on a fuel cycle basis. Fuel cycle estimates for the USA are available for some cuel cycles, otherwise they tend to relate to generation only. Consultations with other experts suggest a general consensus on the ETSU estimates. The ETSU estimates relate to complete fuel cycles excluding plant construction. However, as discussed later on, it is possible to obtain some 'adders' which incorporate power station construction impacts.

Emission Factors for UK Fuel Cycles

(grams emissions/kWh)

Cycle	SO2	NOx	Part	GHGs as Cequ
Old Coal	14	5.3	0.16	352
New Coal	1.2	2.7	0.16	296
Old Oil	16.4	2.5	0.16	300
Gas	0.5	0.9	?	139
Nuclear	0	0.2	0	14
Landfill	0.5	0.9	?	139
Waste	4.1	2.7	6.4	?
CHP	0.6	1.3	0.08	150
Renews	0	0	0	0

New oil may be compared directly with new coal. The oil figures quoted here exclude any FGD plant.

[GHGs = all greenhouse gases in grams carbon equivalent; CHP at half values for new coal; waste values are highly dependent upon type of plant and composition of waste. See Chapter 3 of the full Report for further discussion and description of fuel cycles.]

Other impacts, such as radiation and health, are treated separately below (see Chapter 4 of the full report).

7   THE MEANING OF EXTERNALITY ADDERS

Since this report deals with the monetary value of damage done it is important to understand what these measures reflect.

A monetary measure reflects the willingness to pay of individuals to avoid damage or to secure an improvement in quality of life. In turn, willingness to pay (WTP) reflects individuals' preferences for or against some change in the state of the environment, or risks to health etc. It is also possible to elicit a willingness to accept compensation for tolerating environmental damage or some risk to health and life. This WTA measure should, in theory, not differ much from the WTP measure. But in practice they do differ, often by large amounts with WTA exceeding WTP. Since, theoretically, there is no particular reason to use WTP rather than WTA, the use of one estimate rather than the other will influence the size of the externality adder. There is at present no consensus within economics on the reasons for the apparent disparity between WTA and WTP. However, for fuel cycle evaluation purposes the differences may not matter too much. First, both WTA and WTP measures have been used to derive 'values of a statistical life' (see below) and these values are pooled in the resulting values used in this report. In the USA WTA estimates for a statistical life appear to be greater than WTP estimates, but for UK and Europe there appears to be little difference. Since our focus is on the UK, the 'pooling' of WTA and WTP measures for health makes little difference. Second, the WTA/WTP disparities seem best documented for situations in which species are threatened. Generally, energy sources do not threaten species existence so that the nature of the disparity may not be as significant for energy-related environmental impacts.

When using the monetary measure approach to social cost, then, some quite explicit value judgements are being used.

The first is that people's preferences count, i.e. it is wholly legitimate to allocate resources within an economy according to what people want as revealed in their behaviour in allocating their incomes.

The second value judgement involves accepting that preferences, when measured by willingness to pay, reflect the prevailing distribution of income. Willingness to pay is affected by ability to pay. This may seem unfair compared to a rule that each person's 'vote' should be counted equally.

In respect of the first value judgement it is of course the case that many decisions in society are not responsive to what people want. Schooling is not determined by what pupils want. Many other decisions have to do with moral obligation, duty, and the public good, rather than with an aggregation of single individuals' votes. The defence of the first value judgement is that (a) not being responsive to what people want is non-democratic, and (b) that moral concerns frequently show up in expressed preferences. But, of course, societies have always reserved the power to allocate some resources for 'merit goods' and may also believe that public goods - goods that are consumed jointly by many people without a diminution of supply (such as air quality) - should be publicly provided if individuals' preferences understate their true preferences (the 'free rider problem'). Understatement of true preferences for environmental quality may arise in the context of the methodologies used to elicit preferences. For example, 'contingent valuation' procedures involve asking people to state their willingness to pay for environmental quality. If the respondent believes that, although he or she states bid below their 'true' valuation, others will nonetheless state high positive bids, then the environmental quality in question may still be provided. If it is impossible to exclude any individual from the benefits of the environmental quality (as is the case with true public goods), then the individual understating their true value of the good will be a 'free rider'. Contingent valuation studies have typically not shown this free rider behaviour to be significant. On the other hand, it is not easy to tell if revealed values in hypothetical contexts are equivalent to true values if the respondent was actually asked to pay. The state of the art does not yet enable us to determine the extent of this 'hypothetical bias', but there is some suggestion that contingent valuation studies overstate true preferences.

The second value judgement means that those with higher incomes tend to get a higher weighting in the determination of externality adders. This is how market systems work. In estimating externality adders we are therefore mimicking the market. Technically, the adders could be re-estimated by adjusting the values to those that would arise if everyone had the same income. Such adjustments are complex, but have been done in the past. No such adjustment is made in this report. One defence of this, apart from the complexity, is that the pricing of energy ought not to be used as the means to influence decisions about what is, or is not, a fair distribution of income. That is, if WTP seems 'unfair' then the proper approach is to modify income and wealth taxation to secure whatever the fair distribution of income is.

The reliance on preferences is important for at least three other reasons.

The Absence of Markets

First, the externality adders frequently relate to <u>non-marketed</u> effects. There is no obvious market in clean air, for example. This means that techniques have to be developed to find out what people's WTP for the non-marketed effect actually is. This is the <u>valuation issue</u>. A number of very well developed techniques exist for eliciting non-market values, notably:

contingent valuation - based on asking people for their WTP

contingent ranking - based on inferring values from expressed rankings between alternatives

travel cost method - based on inferring the demand for the characteristics of a site from the travel expenditures undertaken to reach that site

avertive expenditures - based on inferring WTP from monies spent to avoid damage

dose-response methods - based on estimating linkages between a pollutant (the dose) and damage to, say, health or crops (the response) and then valuing that damage at either a ruling market price or a further inferred price (such as the 'value of a statistical life')

risk compensation - based on finding the sums of money that labour markets (or other markets) implicitly compensate for risks, e.g. higher wages in risky occupations

hedonic pricing whereby property or land prices are analyzed to see the extent to which they capture variations in the characteristics of that land and property. For example, a polluted area should have lower house prices relative to a non-polluted one.

All these techniques have analytical foundations in the pure theory of consumer demand. None is problem-free, but an extensive empirical and theoretical literature exists on their use. It is these techniques that are used to obtain the money damage figures for <u>environmental</u> externality adders. Non-environmental externalities are usually estimated differently - see later.

Risk Perception

The second issue arising from the reliance of externality adders on preferences concerns the perception of risk. If the logic of WTP is pursued, then individuals' WTP to avoid risk must be taken into account, even if experts consider the risk to be negligible. Failure to treat values based on perception would, of course, offend the basic value judgement underlying damage valuation. But this means that if people behave as if a risk was 1 in 100 when, in terms of 'objective' risk (measured by actual occurrences per time period of operating experience) it is 1 in 1,000,000, the higher valuation arising from the higher risk would enter into the externality adder. The obvious way in which this affects fuel cycle valuation is in the context of nuclear accidents, although it can also be relevant to natural gas terminal explosions, oil rig disasters and major coal mining disasters. Hence this topic is treated separately below.

Discounting the Future

The third issue arising from reliance on preferences is that people have preferences for the time-incidence of damage and benefit. Generally, we suppose that individuals prefer damage to occur later and benefits to occur sooner: there is a fundamental 'impatience' in individual wants. As it happens, recent research is revealing some quite strong exceptions to this. For example, many people seem to exhibit a concern to have greater resources allocated to the future in order that they may feel secure in their older age. Nonetheless, economics works on the general presumption that people discount the future, i.e attach a lower weight to the future than to the present. On the basis of the first value judgement underlying monetary valuation, the analyst is obliged to honour the existence of discounting. If preferences count, then preferences for the present over the future must count too. The underlying discount rate should reflect individuals' preferences for the present over the future. But investment also takes place because it yields a higher flow of consumption benefits than does consumption. This is due to the productivity of capital. This capital productivity also explains the existence of positive discount rates since, by putting resources aside today, they yield rates of return based on the net productivity of capital.

This discounting behaviour affects fuel cycle evaluation. If some of the damage is long-lived or occurs well into the future, then discounting will downplay that damage and the resulting externality adder will be correspondingly small. Indeed, if the damage is a long way into the future, discounting will tend to make that damage negligible, even if it is very large.

Many people, including many economists, find this discrimination against the future unacceptable. The view taken here is that it is not legitimate to reject positive rates of discount simply because they seem intertemporally unfair. This amounts to asking that the discount rate serve two conflicting purposes - intertemporal efficiency and intertemporal fairness. If intertemporal fairness is a social objective - as most people would agree it is - then it should be dealt with by policies dedicated to achieving it (e.g. inducements to savings behaviour, constraints on depleting overall stocks of resources etc.) rather than by attempting to manipulate energy investment decisions alone. This argument is similar to the one about WTP and income: adjusting investment decisions directly is not an efficient way to achieve a fair distribution of income, neither is it an efficient way of securing 'sustainability' and intergenerational fairness. Put another way, both equity concerns should determine the overall

10

context of energy decision-making. Chapter 18 of the full report discusses the discounting issue in detail.

As far as the externality adders in this report are concerned, the discount rate does not play a significant role. This is because the damages done by emissions, for example, are not 'located' in any specific period of time. Some of the damage estimates are annualised from present values of damage - i.e. an estimate of damage over time is re-expressed as a value per year. Some are estimates of damage per year from per annum emissions. All damage is then expressed per kWh/per year. If one was evaluating a <u>new power station</u>, these per annum damages would need re-expressing as present values to be compared with the other costs and benefits of the power station. However, a new power station would <u>add</u> damage to <u>existing</u> damage from the first year of its operation. Hence the per annum figures estimated in this report can be thought of as incremental annual damages, although, as noted previously, the estimates are not <u>ideal</u> estimates of marginal damage. Finally, if a new power station is being appraised, some allowance would need to be made for the time-lag between emissions and damage. Damage does not occur instantaneously in the case of health or forest impacts.

We have dwelt on the philosophical underpinnings of externality adders because if the basic philosophy is not accepted then neither will the resulting empirical estimates of adders be accepted. In our view, the basic philosophy is sound, or, at least, is as sound as any alternative.

Transferability

A major issue in valuation - perhaps <u>the</u> major issue at the moment - is how to determine the extent to which valuations derived in one context can be applied to other contexts. If damage is, say, £X per gram of pollutant in situation A, can this value be 'transferred' to situation B ? The general answer at the moment is that we do not know. Major research efforts are under way to determine the conditions for transferability of values. A pre-requisite is what is known as <u>meta-analysis</u> whereby existing estimates of the values of a particular impact or asset are subjected to statistical analysis to explain why they vary. This procedure of 'explaining the variance' may enable a central estimate to be obtained, together with indicators of how that central estimate will vary with local conditions. To date, there have been very few meta-analyses (see Chapter 14 in the full report). Those that have been undertaken - for recreation and for air pollution values from hedonic price studies - are very promising.

8   THE ADDERS: HEALTH

Voluntary and Involuntary Risk

The valuation of health impacts of fuel cycles is complicated by the fact that some risks are voluntarily assumed and some are not. For example, if a coal miner's wage already contains some premium to reflect the riskiness of the occupation, it is not then legitimate to <u>add</u> accident costs to the price of coal as a 'health adder'. Essentially, some or all of the health impact is 'internalised' in the price of coal and hence in the price of coal-fired electricity.

The so-called 'value of life' literature (see below) confirms that some risk elements are internalised by labour markets. Unfortunately, there is no way of telling if the risk is wholly internalised. Moreover, it is not an easy matter to determine whether all labour markets function so as partly or completely internalise risk, or whether only some do. The issue is important because there is evidence to suggest that involuntary risk is valued far more highly than voluntary risk. That is, if we incorporate all accident and health risks in health adders we may be overstating the adder because of internalisation. But if we omit all occupational health risks because of a belief that labour markets fully internalise risk, then the adder will understate social costs to the extent that the omitted risks are unperceived and hence involuntary. At the moment, there appears to be no easy way of resolving this issue.

The procedure used in this report is to count all health damage as being 'non-internalised'. While this imparts an upward bias in the estimates, there are reasons to suppose that there are downward biases arising from (a) an inability to capture easily the morbidity damages, and (b) the use of wage-risk premia in the estimates of the 'value of a statistical life' (i.e. being based on voluntary risks these values may understate involuntary risk damage).

We have no way of determining how much bias this imparts to the estimates used here. As far as coal and oil are concerned, however, the accident/disease mortality data suggest it is public health effects that are most important, not occupational losses. Since public health effects are not affected by the wage-risk internalisation argument, the bias should be small.

The 'Value of a Statistical Life'

A critical component of health adders is the value of a statistical life (VOSL), often misleadingly termed the 'value of life'. The VOSL measures the WTP for a reduction in the risk. Estimates are obtained from wage-risk studies, from contingent valuation approaches (i.e. asking for the WTP to reduce risk), or from implied market behaviour with respect to risky goods (e.g. pesticides) or risk-reducing goods (e.g. seat belts).

Reviewing the various estimates in some 80 studies suggests the following valuations (see Chapter 4 of the full report):

Value of a Statistical Life

(£1991 million)

	UK/Europe	USA
Wage-Risk	2.0-2.5	2.5-3.9
CVM	2.9-4.5	1.0-1.8
Market	0.5-2.4	0.7-0.8
Total	1.8-3.1	1.4-2.0

The resulting value appropriate for the UK would appear to be around £2 million, and this value is used throughout the analysis in this report.

Valuing Morbidity

Whereas there are numerous studies for the value of a statistical life, there is very little evidence on the value of morbidity. Clearly, valuations will vary with the type of illness and disease, its duration, the associated anxiety, and so on. The state of the art in valuation simply does not yet permit the use of generalised 'values of a symptom day' and far more research is needed. Some limited morbidity adders are used here and are taken from PACE [1990] as follows (translated to p/kWh):

oil and coal : 0.12 p/kWh
gas : 0.04 p/kWh

Nuclear power morbidity is treated separately, see below.

Fuel Cycle Risk Factors

The approach adopted in this report is to take risk factors <u>for complete fuel cycles, including construction - where available</u>, and apply a VOSL of £2 million per life lost. Note that this ignores any internalised risk due to wage compensation. The total risk factors are shown below together with the resulting 'life adders'. These life adders <u>exclude</u> major accidents.

Risk Factors for Fuel Cycles
and 'Life Adders'
(Health and Accident Costs)

Cycle	Lives Lost per GW year			Adder p/kWh
	Occupational	Public	Total	
Coal	1.1	8.5	9.6	0.32
Oil	0.8	8.0	8.8	0.29
Gas	0.5	0.2	0.7	0.02
SolarPV	1.0	2.0	3.0	0.07
SolarTH	1.0	1.1	2.1	0.10
Wind	1.0	0.2	1.2	0.04
PWR	0.3	0.05	0.35	0.01
Hydro	1.0	.01	1.01	0.03

Note that risk factors are not available for some fuel cycles. Moreover, these estimates conceal quite significant ranges. The data come from a synthesis of a great many sources and reflect the source author's (Fritzsche [1989]) judgements. Note also that the health damage from coal will vary with the type of coal-fired power station. New stations will typically have lower <u>public</u> health costs due to lower emissions of particulates, SO2 and NOx. The impacts shown in the table above are for the whole fuel cycle, and unfortunately do not discriminate between 'old' and 'new' coal to allow for differential pollution impacts.

Nuclear Power Hazards: Routine Radiation

A large literature exists on the health impacts of nuclear power, primarily because of sustained environmental campaigns against civilian nuclear power. The result is that the health and accident impact of nuclear power is better studied than the other fuel cycles. Moreover, there is some attempt at standardising the health impact valuations, notably for routine radiation risks through the work of the UK National Radiological Protection Board. At the time of writing the NRPB is revising its approach to these valuations, but they currently suggest that a 'man sievert' should have a value of £40,000. Importantly, this figure can be shown to link well with the VOSL figure of £2 million. In one part of the nuclear industry (BNFL) a figure of £100,000 per man sievert has been used.

Adopting this range of £40 - 100,000 per man-sievert, and exposure levels of some 16 man Sv per GW year for the UK nuclear fuel cycle (inclusive of mining) produces a valuation of 0.01-0.02 p/kWh for routine radiation damage.

Nuclear Power Hazards: Accident Risks

Valuing accident risks is particularly controversial for nuclear power. This is because the few nuclear accidents that there have been have been particularly traumatic, notably Three Mile Island in the USA and, especially, Chernobyl. Moreover, radiation is perceived as an 'insidious burden' by many, due to its delayed impacts and its invisibility. If we recall that one of the main purposes of an externality adder is to place a surcharge on <u>new</u> plant, then the relevant risk of accident is that for a new plant, not existing plants. If, on the other hand, the adder is applied to complete emissions charging, <u>existing</u> plant risk factors are relevant since the adder would be designed to affect the merit order of using all plant. Since our terms of reference apply mainly to new plant we concentrate on risks for new plants.

The 'objective' risk versus risk perception issue now turns out to be important. Consider the objective risk of a nuclear power plant accident in the UK. Taking <u>design</u> risk factors for new PWRs such as that planned for Hinkley Point, and multiplying by the £2 million VOSL gives a 'nuclear accident adder' of 0.0000125 p/kWh, which is negligible. However, these risks are for accidents in which tens or hundreds of deaths occur because of the one accident. There is evidence to suggest that people do not value risks of 'group' accidents in the same way as they value individual deaths. Indeed, casual empiricism suggests this is so since of the many road deaths each year those that are reported by the media tend to involve only multiple deaths. This suggests that there should be some multiplication factor for 'group accidents' reflecting 'disaster aversion'. But just what the factor is is open to debate and there appears to be no consensus in the literature.

The number of exceeded fatal cancers per reactor year for a degraded core accident are taken from NRPB as reported in Ferguson [1991]. These give the second row in the table below (f for frequency, N for number):

14

$f =$	10^{-8}	10^{-9}	10^{-10}	10^{-11}
$N =$	11000-35000	46000-150000	110000-350000	180000-580000
fN^2	1-12	7-22	4-12	1-3
$300fN$	0.03 to 0.11	0.01 to 0.05	0.003 to 0.01	0.0005 to 0.002
$f.N^{3/2}$	0.01 to 0.07	0.01 to 0.06	0.004 to 0.02	neg to 0.004

The last three rows show how various 'disaster aversion' functions might be used to reflect the fact that society tends to weight group losses more heavily than single deaths. The 'square rule' (row 3) is suggested by Ferguson [1991] but he notes that it is not based on empirical studies. Ferguson states that the relevant UK risk perception studies do not exist to enable selection of empirically based functional forms for 'disaster aversion'.

Ferguson concludes that 'the risk of low probability, high consequence PWR accidents may be valued comparably with as much as about twenty individual deaths per reactor year'. At £2 million per statistical life, this would produce an adder of £40 million, or 0.67p/kWh across 6000 million kWh p.a. Closer inspection of the table above shows that 20 is an upper estimate. An average of 8 might be preferred. 8 deaths x £2m = £16m across 6000m kWh per GWyr would give 0.27p/kWh.

Row 4 in the table above uses a disaster aversion function suggested by Rocard and Smets (R-S) [1991]. Self-evidently, the R-S rule gives higher values for 'damage' up to a value of n=300. After that, the R-S rule gives lower damage values compared to the square function rule. If one reworks the above table with f.300N instead of the square rule, then the lives lost are very few, the highest value would be £0.21 million and the lowest a thousand £ or so. At £0.2m the adder would be negligible at 0.0033p/kWh, and at £1m it would be 0.016p/kWh. Rocard-Smets claim that their function is derived from work by Bohneblust in Switzerland and Germany and Hubert in France. But they also caution that the factor of 300 could be a factor of 1000 which would raise the upper estimate of the adder to, say, 0.01 to 0.05 p/kWh. Whereas R-S has some empirical foundation, Ferguson's proposed square rule has none. On the other hand, R-S is linear in n and this seems to offend the general intuition in the risk aversion literature. Looking at non-linear functions, we illustrate a further possible function of n to the power 3/2. This produces similar small adders to the R-S rule.

Overall, then, a 'disaster aversion' adder remains very uncertain. Use of a square function could make the adder as high as 0.67p/kWh, but the square function has no apparent empirical basis. Use of a Rocard-Smets function, which is linear in the number of people in the group accident, produces adders of 0.02p/kWh and perhaps as high as 0.05p/kWh. The issue is unresolved in the absence of fully fledged risk perception studies for the UK.

As far as nuclear accident costs are concerned, the health damage costs noted here do not take into account any property and output losses, nor any other economic costs of land sterilisation.

It is also important to note that 'major accidents' occur in other fuel cycles, notably with coal (mining accidents), oil and gas (offshore disasters, gas terminal explosions), and hydropower (dam bursts). **Owing to the absence of a suitable literature, these impacts have not been estimated in the current exercise.**

9   CROPS

A detailed assessment of the role of conventional air pollutants in crop damage has been completed by the USA's National Acid Precipitation Assessment Program (NAPAP [1991]). The NAPAP conclusions are that there is no evidence linking acid precipitation to crop damage, but that <u>ozone</u> reductions in the range of 10-25% would produce 'significant' increases in crop yields in the range \$0.7-1.7 billion. Ozone concentrations develop from NOx emissions. A rough indicator of an adder can therefore be derived from the NAPAP study by dividing the total damage by the tonnage of NOx reduction implied by the 10 and 25% hypothetical reductions. In 1987 the USA emitted some 19.5 million tonnes of NOx.[1] If the NAPAP range of damage is avoided by 10-25% reductions in these emissions, then damage avoided is some \$360 per tonne, or some 0.02 p/gram. One US review (PACE [1990]) suggests an adder of 1 US cent per 1lb emission, or 0.0013 p/gram NOx, very much less than the implied NAPAP figure. Applied to the emission factors in Section 6 above, these two estimates would imply adders of:

		PACE [1990]	NAPAP [1991]
'old' coal	:	0.007 p/kWh	0.10 p/kWh
'new' coal	:	0.004	0.05
oil	:	0.003	0.05
gas	:	0.001	0.02
CHP	:	0.002	0.03
Nuclear	:	zero	zero

Since the NAPAP damage figures are the latest and most authoritative, we adopt them. Their applicability to the UK depends on (a) the transferability of the dose-response functions, and (b) the relationship between US crop prices and world prices (i.e. the closer US prices are to world prices, the more valid the use of the approach.)

---

[1] See Economic Commission for Europe, <u>Strategies and Policies for Air Pollution Abatement: 1990 Review</u>, United Nations, New York,1991.

10   FORESTS

NAPAP [1991] reviews the evidence for forest damage. NAPAP implicates <u>ozone</u> in forest damage, but, on the information available (a benefit of $18-40 million for a 2% reduction in ozone in the South-East of the USA), it is not possible to derive an estimate of a 'forest adder'. The International Institute for Applied Systems Analysis (IIASA) has carried out an extensive economic impact study for Europe (Nilsson [1990]). For the United Kingdom the IIASA study estimates commercial and recreational damage of some $1.17 billion p.a. (including Ireland). This would suggest damage of around 0.06 g/SO2 or adders as shown below:

'old' coal	:	0.84 p/kWh
'new' coal	:	0.07
oil	:	0.98
gas	:	0.03
CHP	:	0.03
Nuclear	:	zero

However, the IIASA findings are disputed in terms of the dose-response functions used. They may be upper bounds, and we have no reliable way of estimating the lower bound.   More detail is provided in Chapter 6 of the full report.

In the case of acid rain impacts damage is, of course, 'imported' and 'exported'.   This complicates the interpretation of externality adders since they are estimated by looking at damage per tonne of <u>deposition</u>, regardless of the source of the deposition.   The adder therefore relates to <u>UK emissions</u> only in so far as those emissions are responsible for UK damage.   Strictly, as far as UK damage is concerned, each tonne of UK emission should be debited with the damage done by the <u>fraction</u> that is deposited in the UK.   Each tonne of <u>imported</u> deposition should then be surcharged in the country of origin according to damage done in the UK.   And each tonne of emission <u>exported</u> from the UK should be debited with the damage done in the receiving country.   While such adjustments are feasible they have not been made in this report: i.e. each tonne of emission is treated as if it causes the same amount of damage regardless of where it falls.   In so far as some depositions are <u>not</u> to land, this procedure will overstate the surcharge on emissions.

11   BIOLOGICAL DIVERSITY

Most energy resources are not directly implicated in the reduction of biological diversity, although water acidification is directly implicated in reductions in fish stocks and other water-based wildlife. Some energy sources will also <u>displace</u> wildlife which may not have alternative suitable habitats. One such study of the potential <u>Mersey Barrage</u> used contingent valuation to find the 'existence value' of people for conservation of the migratory bird habitat of the estuary, a habitat that would be displaced by the barrage. The analysis suggests a possible adder of 8.0 p/kWh if the existence values are extrapolated across 22 million households (see Chapter 7 of the full report). This is clearly an exaggeration since extrapolation of sample values to the entire nation tends to be valid only for unique heritage assets (e.g. a Grand Canyon or a Kakadu wilderness), but even if 10% of all households exhibited a WTP revealed by the contingent valuation study, the adder would be 0.8p/kWh, or some 10% on the expected average cost of Mersey Barrage electricity.

Contingent valuation studies of preferences for species loss are quite extensive. There appears to be some consistency in the per-household valuations that emerge, but few of the contexts relate in any way to fuel cycle impacts. One Norwegian study (Navrud [1989]) offers some basis for a 'water quality adder' based on Norwegian WTP to restore fish stocks in Norwegian lakes and rivers. Non-use values of some 390 N.Krone per household per annum for the benefits of a 30-70% reduction in SOx depositions in Norway would translate into a damage cost of around 0.03-0.06 p/gram SO2, or adders as follows:

'old' coal	:	0.42-0.84 p/kWh
'new' coal	:	0.04-0.08
oil	:	0.49-0.98
gas	:	0.01-0.02
CHP	:	0.02-0.04
Nuclear	:	zero

However, given the absence of other studies through which the zero-order reasonableness of a biodiversity loss figure can be tested, no adder is reported in the final analysis.

12 BUILDINGS AND MATERIALS

A number of studies exist on the economic cost of buildings and materials damage from air pollution. The various estimates are discussed in detail in Chapter 8 of the full report. The results suggest unit emission damage costs in pence per gram for SO2 as follows:

Study	Materials	Resident Buildings	Historic Buildings	Hshold Soiling	Total p/gram
USA [1990]	0.003	0.044			0.047
GER [1990]	0.009-0.014	0.053-0.094			0.062-0.108
NETH [1990]	<---- 0.043- ----> 0.092		0.013-0.021		0.056-0.113
NOR [1988]	0.011				0.011
DEN [n.d.]	0.035				0.035
U.K.[1990]		0.189	0.040		0.229

The UK figure (estimated from ECOTEC [1990]) is significantly higher than the other estimates which, allowing for the different coverage, are reasonably similar. On the other hand, the UK study has the advantage of a fairly extensive assessment of the stock of buildings at risk. Offsetting this, the methodology is not very firmly based in the principles of WTP.

If the UK figures are adopted, the adders become:

'old' coal	:	3.21 p/kWh
'new' coal	:	0.27
oil	:	3.76
gas	:	0.11
CHP	:	0.13
Nuclear	:	zero

There must be some doubts, however, about the size of these figures.

13   NOISE NUISANCE

Noise nuisance is not typically associated with fuel cycles, although some concerns have been expressed about noise from wind farms. Studies of traffic and aircraft noise using the hedonic price approach do suggest remarkably consistent adders. However, no reliable study was found which could be used to estimate noise impacts from power stations or other parts of the fuel cycle.

14   GLOBAL WARMING DAMAGE

Since the burning of fossil fuels contribute to the accelerated greenhouse effect, global warming damage needs to be debited to coal, oil and gas. Other fuel cycles should be debited according to any greenhouse gas emissions during the construction phase. Unless transportation requirements are very different between fuel cycles, GHG emissions from road and rail transportation of fuels will not significantly affect the size of the resulting adders. In terms of the available literature this report provides estimates of the 'global warming adder' for all parts of the fuel cycle other than plant construction.

On the basis of work by Nordhaus [1991] and Cline [1992] the damage done by a tonne of carbon equivalent of greenhouse gases is estimated to lie between £5.8 and £17.3. The range reflects estimates of damage ranging from 1% of 'gross world product' (GWP) - i.e. the world's GNP - and 3% of GWP. Applying these valuations to the GHG emission factors for the various fuel cycles produces the following adders (including Mortimer's [1991] quoted estimates of 4.3 g.C/kWh for hydroelectric power and 3 g.C/kWh for wind energy):

'old' coal	:	0.21 - 0.61 p/kWh
'new' coal	:	0.17 - 0.51
oil	:	0.17 - 0.52
gas	:	0.08 - 0.24
CHP	:	0.08 - 0.25
Nuclear	:	0.01 - 0.02

```
Hydro       :      neg  - 0.01
Wind        :      neg  - neg
```

Note that these figures exclude any 'catastrophic' costs from global warming. That is, they assume that the damage from global warming (e.g. property loss from sea level rise) occurs as a continuous, predictable function of the rate and level of warming. But many scientists argue that global warming damage is likely to be discontinuous, i.e. it will have thresholds. Beyond certain levels and rates of warming, damage might increase suddenly due to ecosystem collapse, changes in gulf streams and so on. While such discontinuities are disputed, a sensible procedure would be to add an insurance premium to the adders shown here, this premium reflecting society's willingness to pay to avoid the uncertain costs of any catastrophic event. No adjustment is made here since the current state of the art does not permit any reasonable guess at what this premium would be.

The low adder for nuclear power reflects the low emission factor. There is a debate about the validity of such factors - see Donaldson and Betteridge [1990] and Mortimer [1991]. This debate centres on two issues: (a) CO_2 emissions from the plant construction and decommissioning phases of nuclear power plants, and (b) differences of view about the extent to which low grade uranium ores would have to be used if nuclear power expanded substantially. Since the immediate concern is with the adders for new power plants in the UK in the next decade or so, the second concern is not relevant.

No allowance has been made for the former, but since we are interested in the relative size of adders across fuels, the error in omitting construction impacts is likely to be very small indeed[2].

15   LAND, WATER, VISIBILITY

The literature of energy-related land contamination, water impacts and visibility impacts is extremely limited. Loss of biodiversity through acidification of waters is dealt with under biodiversity. No estimates of land contamination damage were found, although costs of mitigating such damages exist for the USA. Mitigation costs are not, however, damage costs since it cannot be assumed that it is worthwhile undertaking the mitigation expenditures (see Chapter 2 of the full report for a discussion).

USA estimates of the damage done through visibility impacts are available. The basic problem is that their transferability to the UK context is extremely doubtful. Essentially, such values will reflect local preferences. For the record, PACE [1990] settle for the following visibility damage figures:

TSP :   83 cents/lb = 0.11 p/g

---

[2] Mortimer [1991] quotes fuel cycle emission factors for a new PWR of around 13 g.C per kWh. This apparently includes construction impacts. The actual emission figure used here is 14 g.Cequ -i.e. including all GHGs. Unless methane emissions are substantial, this suggests further that only a negligible error is involved.

SO2:   14 cents/1b = 0.02 p/g

NOx: 17 cents/lb = 0.02 p/g

(TSP = total suspended particulates.)   For a modern coal plant these damages would translate to 0.02 p/kWh for TSP, 0.02 p/kWh for SO2 and 0.05 p/kWh for NOx, a total of 0.09 p/kWh. We have chosen not to report any visibility adder for the UK. Similarly, no estimates are reported for water.

16   USER COSTS

A user cost arises when the use of a resource today necessarily precludes its use in the future. The clearest case in which user costs will arise is with exhaustible resources - use of a unit today precludes its use tomorrow. Potentially, then, user costs could arise in the context of oil, gas, coal and uranium. However, 'user cost adders' as surcharges to the price of electricity would be justified only if it can be argued that existing market forces fail to take account of user costs in the future. The object of adders is that they should be added to the private cost of production. No attempt has been made to estimate user costs, although some past UK estimates are reviewed in the full report.   As far as energy prices in the UK are concerned, there appears to be a consensus that user costs are already reflected in market prices.

17   NON-ENVIRONMENTAL EXTERNALITIES

Environmental externalities are not the only source of 'adders'. It is important to discover is a fuel is subsidised through other forms of expenditure. For example, coal mining is subsidised in a number of countries. Nuclear power research and development costs are often borne in part by central government, and so on. Other non-environmental externalities (NEEs) are more complex. We summarise some of the findings of the literature below.

Energy Security

Governments widely perceive that interruptions to the supply of oil, or oligopolistic price rises, have harmful effects on the macro-economy. There is fairly extensive evidence to support this perception. In part, measures to protect oil supplies against such 'price hikes' result in expenditure which does not show up in the price of oil. Hall [1991] has analyzed this phenomenon in the context of US military expenditures in the Middle East. He estimates that, in 1985, military expenditures resulted in a $7 per barrel subsidy to oil, or, to put it another way, there is a 'security adder' of $7 that should be added to the domestic price of oil to reflect this expenditure which otherwise would not have to take place. In terms of oil-fired electricity this would add around 1.4 USc/kWh = 0.8 p/kWh. No such study appears to have been carried out for European countries.

Nuclear Liability

In the event of a nuclear accident the liability of the nuclear power industry for the damage done by the accident is limited through the 1965 Nuclear Installations Act. However, it would be double counting to debit nuclear power both with the higher insurance premium that would result in the event of full liability and the adder for nuclear accident costs. the approach taken here, then, is that the accident cost adder already accounts for this effect. Chapter 17 discusses these NEEs in more detail.

Other factors giving rise to potential NEEs in the UK are (a) the Non-Fossil Fuel Obligation (NFFO); (b) R&D subsidies, and (c) subsidies to coal. Clearly, taxes and subsidies affect costs, but they tend to vary between countries and over time within any one country. If the object is to estimate NEEs for a future generating plant it is important to assess what tax and subsidy systems will be in place at the time that new plant is commissioned. Even then, what appear to be NEEs may in fact be governments' way of compensating for environmental externalities. For example, nuclear power may be subsidised in order to gain the benefits of energy security, as discussed at the beginning of this executive summary. This is one view of the existing structure of the NFFO in the UK. Other subsidies may have little to do with encouraging a particular fuel to be used in electricity generation - e.g. subsidies to the UK coal industry which are mainly aimed at cushioning the social costs of restructuring the industry.

For these reasons, NEEs are not separately estimated in this report.

18   SUMMARY EXTERNALITY ADDERS FOR THE UK ELECTRICITY SECTOR

We now draw together the estimates of the various adders. **Once again, it is important to emphasise the illustrative nature of the figures. Much research needs to be done to firm-up the figures and, ideally, new plant adders require estimation of damages from first principles using an hypothetical plant location in the UK.**

The Table below shows our 'best' estimates for the adders. It is not possible to say when they are marginal damage estimates and when they are average estimates. By and large, however, averages dominate.   It is important to understand that the figures relate to 'stylised' cases.   In practice, power stations vary in efficiency, fuel sources vary in pollution-content, and so on.   There is therefore a spectrum of adders for existing and projected power stations.

Environmental Externality Adders
(p/kWh)

Fuel Cycle: EEs	Old Coal	New Coal	Oil	Gas		PWR	Sol	Win	Hyd	CHP
Health										
-mortality	0.32	0.32	0.29	0.02		0.01	0.07	0.04	0.03	0.03?
-morbidity	0.12	0.12	0.12	0.04		0.01	-	-	-	0.06
-disaster	NE	NE	NE	NE	(a)	0.02-0.05	NE	NE	NE	NE
					(b)	0.27*				
Crops	0.10	0.05	0.05	0.02		NE	NE	NE	NE	0.02
Forest+	0.84	0.07	0.98	0.03		NE	NE	NE	NE	0.03
Biod	NE	NE	NE	NE		NE	NE	NE	NE	NE
Builds	3.22	0.28	3.77	0.11		-	-	-	-	0.14
Noise	NE	NE	NE	NE		NE	NE	NE	NE	NE
GHGs x	0.40	0.34	0.35	0.16		0.01	-	-	0.01	0.17
Visib	NE	NE	NE	NE		NE	NE	NE	NE	NE
Water	NE	NE	NE	NE		-	-	-	NE	NE
Land	NE	NE	NE	NE		NE	NE	NE	NE	NE

[Notes: underlined figures are negative; *(a) uses the Rocard-Smets function which is linear in the number of people affected; (b) takes the 'square function' estimate for risk aversion and the value of a group accident; x takes the average of the range for GHG damage; - means zero; NE means not estimated and probably positive; + indicates that the upper bound has been used.]

For landfill gas the EEs will tend to correspond to the values for natural gas.

For geothermal and wave power it has not proved possible in the time available to secure an overall adder profile.

For tidal a potential biodiversity adder of 0.8 p/kWh may be considered, although there is considerable uncertainty about this figure.

For <u>conservation</u> there is some evidence to suggest an adder of 0.01 to 0.02 p/kWh for the externalities associated with insulating materials and indoor pollution exposure problems. Note that the component EEs have not be aggregated. The reasons for this are (a) that some of the adders are inter-related. SOx emissions, for example, may actually <u>reduce</u> global warming damage; and, more importantly, (b) a number of the impacts have not been estimated due to the absence of a suitable literature. Totals would, at this stage, tend to give the impression that figures are 'firm' when in fact they omit several possibly important impacts.

Finally, it is important to look at the 'non-estimated' externalities. Disaster costs for oil, coal, hydro and gas have <u>not</u> been estimated, but will be positive and this may well affect the EE picture. Neither biodiversity nor noise is expected to be significant, but there may be some land contamination externalities for coal. Public perception of the nuclear waste disposal issue may also not be captured in the health adders for nuclear power - the same issue of perceived and objective risk arises.

19   RECOMMENDATIONS FOR FURTHER WORK

A substantial 'externality adder' exercise is taking place already in Europe under the EC-US DOE programme due for completion in 1992/1993. The critical issue of transferability is part of that programme. Other programmes of work on this in the USA are more likely to produce state-of-the-art conditions under which transferability can be assured. Is there any virtue, then, in the UK pursuing a further programme of research ?

The US-EC programme is highly focused on the coal cycle and nuclear power. The nuclear power focus also tends to be contained within Europe. It is not at the moment (February 1992) clear that this programme will produce a comprehensive benefit-cost approach to nuclear power.

We suggest, therefore, the following priorities:

1   A full evaluation of the economic impacts of 'acid rain' making use of the existing programmes of work in the UN ECE, the newly commissioned work by the World Bank for Eastern Europe, and the existing critical loads programme in the Department of the Environment. It is of fundamental importance that any research team investigating these issues have environmental economists as an integral part of the team. A considerable part of the 'adder' literature derives from studies where no consideration, or inadequate consideration, has been given to the proper measure of damage.

2   A full evaluation of the damage costs from global warming including an appraisal of the potential 'non-linearities' in damage due to potentially catastrophic or discontinuous events. Some work is progressing on this in the UK at University College London. Such a programme should be linked to 1 above in order to capture the interlinkages between CO_2 and 'traditional' pollutant control (Pearce [1992]).

3   An investigation of the dose-response relationships for human health, primarily for

morbidity. A mixed team of epidemiologists and economists is required. An attempt should be made to replicate the two stage multiple regression approaches that have been used in the USA. It is important to observe that the UK has virtually no rigorous studies in this area. Cross-sectional data are required on mortality and morbidity such that these data can be related to factors likely to affect morbidity and mortality: age, dietary habits, smoking, income, race, pollution levels, etc. Such a study would be expensive and would, ideally, need to control for indoor pollution exposure as well.

4   A detailed review of the accident costs - 'routine' and 'major' of each fuel cycle based on full life cycle analysis. This requires a combination of fuel cycle expertise, such as that at ETSU, with researchers experienced in mortality statistics, i.e. demographers, epidemiologists.

5   For other impacts areas, notably crops and forests, it is hoped that the EC-US study will suffice.

6   The existing buildings damage studies still lack economic rigour. It may be hoped however that work under way in the DoE will contain a greater economic component.

7   The UK needs to monitor closely, and participate in, progress in research into transferability of values. This is an integral part of the US component of the EC-US study.

19   REFERENCES

[Comprehensive references are given in the separate bibliography to the full report].

Cline, W [1992], The Economics of Global Warming, Institute for International Economics, Washington DC.

Donaldson, D and Betteridge, G [1990], 'Carbon Dioxide Emissions from Nuclear Power - a Critical Analysis of FOE 9', ATOM, February, 18-22.

ECOTEC [1990], Identification and Assessment of Materials Damage to Buildings and Monuments by Air Pollution, Birmingham.

Eyre, N [1990], Gaseous Emissions due to Electricity Fuel Cycles in the UK, ETSU, Harwell, March.

Fritzsche, E [1989], 'The Health Risks of Energy Production', Risk Analysis, Vol.9, No.4, 565-577

Lockwood, B [1992], The Social Costs of Electricity Generation, Report prepared for the Parliamentary Office of Science and Technology, CSERGE, London and Norwich (forthcoming).

Mortimer, N [1991], 'Nuclear Power and Global Warming', Energy Policy, Jan-Feb, 76-78

National Acid Precipitation Assessment Program (NAPAP) [1991], The Cause and Effects of Acid Rain Precipitation, NAPAP, Washington DC.

Nilsson, S [1991], European Forest Decline: the Effects of Air Pollutants and Suggested Remedial Policies, IIASA, Laxenberg.

Nordhaus, W [1991], 'To Slow or Not to Slow: the Economics of Global Warming', Economic Journal, July.

PACE [1990], Environmental Costs of Electricity, Oceana Publications, New York.

Pearce, D W [1992], 'The Secondary Benefits of Greenhouse Gas Control', Centre for Social and Economic Research on the Global Environment, University College London

SOCIAL COST OF FUEL CYCLES

SECTION TWO:

REPORT TO THE

UK DEPARTMENT OF TRADE AND INDUSTRY

CONTENTS

PART 1: FUEL CYCLE EVALUATION

A Note on Measurement Units Used in This Report

Calculation of externality adders in terms of money per unit of electricity is subject to considerable confusion owing to the different units used in the literature. We have adopted the following conventions:

1. Wherever possible we have used the metric weight system, i.e. grams, kilograms and tonnes. US data tend to be in US pounds and (short) tons, where 2000 lbs = 1 ton. Since 1lb = 0.4536 kg, 1 US ton= 0.907 tonnes. Or 1 tonne = 2205 US lbs.

2. Sulphur (S) is converted to sulphur dioxide (SO_2) by multiplying by 2, i.e. $SO_2 = 2S$

3. 1 tonne carbon (C) = 3.67 tonnes carbon dioxide (CO_2).

4. 1 tonne nitrogen dioxide as nitrogen (N) = 3.3 tonnes nitrogen dioxide (NO_2)

5. 1 tonne nitric oxide (NO as N) = 2.1 tonnes nitric oxide (NO)

6. 1 kWh = 3.6 MJ, 1 GJ = 10^3.kWh/3.6 1kWh = .0036GJ

Currency conversion and price escalators are taken from World Bank, World Tables 1991, World Bank, Washington D.C. 1991

CHAPTER 1 INTRODUCTION

1.1 Purpose of the Report

It is widely argued that the production and consumption of energy involves forms of environmental damage and benefits, and non-environmental costs and benefits, which are not adequately reflected in the price of energy in the market place. As such, energy markets are distorted: resources are over-allocated to those energy sources which fail to have either full social costs reflected in the price, and under-allocated to those sources which have low damage and high unpriced benefits.

While there is an extensive literature on the environmental impacts of energy productions and use, it is important to determine the relative importance of the unpriced or under-priced effects in question. Two ways of doing this are:

> a] environmental impact assessment (EIA) which describes and measures, as far as possible, the impacts without putting them into common units. Judgement is then exercised about the implications for encouraging or discouraging energy sources;

> b] social cost measurement whereby the impacts are 'monetised' and re-expressed as 'pence-per- kilowatt hour (kWh)'. The figure for pence/kWh is added to the true private costs of energy (hence 'externality adder') to give a social cost expression.

This report is concerned with the latter - social cost measurement - and refers to EIA only in as far as it is a step on the way to full cost measurement.

The aim of the report is:

> to survey the literature on energy social costs in the context of electricity production;

> as fas as possible, to elicit the consensus about the resulting 'externality adders';

> to highlight any gaps in knowledge.

1.2   The Fuel Cycles

As far as possible, the report focuses on finding adders which are relevant to the following fuel cycles:

Conventional coal-fired systems with and without flue gas desulphurisation [FGD] and low NOx burners.

Advanced coal burning techniques: fluidised bed combustion [FBC] and integrated gasification combined cycle (IGCC).

Conventional oil fired systems with/and without flue gas desulphurisation and low NOx burners.

The combined cycle gas turbine.

Nuclear energy with pressurised water reactors [PWR].

Wind energy.

Generators using landfill gas.

Geothermal energy.

Tidal energy.

Hydroelectric power.

Wave energy.

Solar energy.

Industrial and district combined heat and power (CHP).

Waste incineration

1.3 From Damage Cost to Externality Adder

Damage costs are expressed in various ways, e.g. aggregate willingness to pay (WTP) to improve visibility, WTP per household to conserve a resource, etc. Where such measures are credible, a further stage of analysis is required to translate such measures into externality adders. This section sets out a brief example, taken from PACE[1990] to show how this is done. This is for illustrative purposes only.

PACE [1990] estimates the following externality adder figures for the major fuel technologies:

Fuel Technology	Externality adder cents/kWh(1989$)
Older coal-fired boiler burning 1.2% sulphur coal	5.7
AFBC with same heat rate and burning 1.1% sulphur coal	2.8
Natural gas-fired steam plant	1.0
Residual oil fired boiler burning 1% sulphur oil	5.8
Nuclear Power	2.9
Solar	0-0.4
Wind	0-0.1

These are 'starting point' values - ie PACE regards them as minima - because many relevant costs are excluded and the studies from which the values are derived are often of too uneven quality for the figures to be regarded as accurate cost estimates.

Fuel technology externality adders are derived as follows:

The 'starting point' values for the specific pollutants, SO_x, NO_x, particulates and CO_2 were first arrived at by reviewing the costing studies of the damage caused by these pollutants to the impact categories human health, materials, vegetation and visibility.

From the studies reviewed a value of the damage per pound weight of emission caused by each pollutant to each impact category was chosen which most reasonably represented the range of values in the studies reviewed, considering the locations at which the studies were performed, their documentation and a judgement about their thoroughness.

As an illustration, for SO_2 the following external damage costs were chosen:

Impact Category	Externality Adder $/lb (1989$)
Health	
Mortality	1.72
Morbidity	0.05
Materials	
Corrosion	0.12
Crops	0
Visibility	0.19

Total starting point value	2.03

To further illustrate, consider the mortality figure. A study by ECO Northwest et. al. (1987) provided the starting point value for mortality effects of $ 1.72 lb/SO_2 and morbidity effects of $0.05 lb/$SO_2$. A dose-response approach was used to estimate the relationships between sulphur dioxide emissions and human health. Using a value of statistical human life estimate of $4m [89$], a morbidity value of $400,000, and annual sulphur dioxide emissions of 24,040 ton year. [i.e. 48 080 000 lbs] the values are obtained as follows:

Response	[1] Incidents No.	[2] Unit Values 89 $	[3] Damages Due to SO_2($)	[4] $lb SO_2
Mortality	20.7	4 000 000	$82 800 000	1.72
Morbidity	5.9	400 000	$2 360 000	0.05

[3] = [1]X[2]

[4] = $\dfrac{\text{\$ damages due to SO2}}{\text{48 080 000lbs/}SO_2\text{ yr emissions}}$

To arrive at externality costs expressed in costs per kWh the pounds of each pollutant emitted per kWh for each technology must be ascertained: i.e. emission factors are required. PACE [1990] uses the following emission factors for a coal-fired steam plant:

Emissions Factors for Coal-fired Steam Plants

Heat rate BTU/kWh 10,000
Coal sulphur content 1.2%

SO_2:	lb/SO2/kWh	1.8×10^{-3}
NO_x:	lb/NOx/kWh	6.07×10^{-3}
CO_2:	lb/CO2/kWh	2.09
Part:	lb/TSP/kWh	3.0×10^{-4}

The PACE procedure for computing damage per kWh generated and delivered is as follows:

The following is computed for <u>each</u> pollutant of each technology.

$$\frac{\$}{lb} \cdot \frac{lb}{mmBTU} \cdot \frac{kWh}{BTU} \cdot \frac{1}{(1-L)} \cdot \frac{1}{10^6} = \frac{c/kWh}{delivered}$$

Thus for each pollutant from an average coal boiler using 1.2% sulphur we have

	[A]	[B]	[C]	[D]		

SO_2: $[2.37] \cdot [1.8] \cdot [10,000] \cdot \dfrac{1}{1-0.15} \cdot \dfrac{1}{10^6} = 0.1430$

NO_x: $[0.81] \cdot [0.607] \cdot [10,000] \cdot \dfrac{1}{1-0.15} \cdot \dfrac{1}{10^6} = 0.0058$

Particulates:

  $[1.19] \cdot [0.15]^1 \cdot [10,000] \cdot \dfrac{1.18}{1-0.15} \cdot \dfrac{1}{10^6} = 0.0210$

CO2: $[0.0068] \cdot [2.09] \cdot [10,000] \cdot \dfrac{1.18}{1-0.15} \cdot \dfrac{1}{100} = 0.0168$

  0.0677

  = c/kWh delivered 0.068

where

[A] = Damage per lb of pollutants derived from valuation studies as described above

[B] = lbs emissions per mmBTU input

[C] = Heat rate BTU | kWh

[D] = Marginal energy losses, L=15%

1.4 Uncertainties in Externality Adders

How much reliance can be placed in the estimates of externality adders ? Unfortunately, some of the sources of uncertainty are still being researched. This is especially true of the issue of transferability -the extent to which valuations derived in one context can be applied to wholly separate contexts (e.g. from one site to another site) - and the estimation of dose-response functions. Dose response functions are essentially physical in nature and rely upon epidemiological and other scientific observation. In neither case is there any accepted relationship. The relationship between air pollution and human health, for example, is very much disputed, as is the link between air pollution and buildings damage, forest damage, and so on. The final source of uncertainty lies in economic valuation, i.e. the choice of a monetary measure which is then applied to the 'response', e.g human health damage.

These three sources of uncertainty combine to make the estimation of externality adders very difficult. Nor is the degree of uncertainty known: it is not possible to say that certain estimates have a 90% probability of being correct, for example. The new science of meta-analysis (Chapter 14) will help to reduce uncertainties by seeking explanations for variations in economic values. Meta-analysis will also help determine the extent to which derived values can be transferred to other contexts.

Our judgement, however, is that the main sources of uncertainty do not lie in the economics. They lie in the underlying dose-response relationships. The remit of this report is to investigate the monetary estimates of damage, not the even larger literature on dose-response functions. That would require a major undertaking of the kind envisaged in the US-EC social costs of energy programme currently (1992) under way. Moreover, inspection of even some of the dose-response literature shows that much of it is not in the form of estimates that can be subjected to economic analysis. 'Damage' in this literature may show up as leaf loss in trees or impairment of breathing function. Unless leaf loss can be translated to tree mortality, and breathing impairment to a working day lost or some other measure of restricted activity, it is extremely difficult to translate the dose-response estimates into economic magnitudes of use for estimating externality adders.

It follows that the estimates that are provided in this report need to be treated cautiously. They are 'first guess' estimates. We do believe, however, that further research will refine these estimates into usable figures for policy purposes.

1.5 How Might Externality Adders Be Used ?

The basic purpose of an externality adder is to alter the 'price' of a given form of electricity generation so as to reflect better the true costs of that generation. But there are several options for applying the adder. They are:

> (a) ranking with grandfathering. This is the weakest form of use and involves electric utilities ranking new capacity by social cost (i.e. system marginal cost plus the adder) but without actual pricing being affected. That is, utilities use the shadow prices to influence their choice of new capacity without a tax being applied to new capacity,

nor to existing capacity. This approach is used by a number of regulatory commissions in the USA (see Annex 2);

(b) taxation with grandfathering. Under this option existing capacity is not taxed, but new capacity is.

(c) complete emissions taxation. Under this option all sources, existing and new, are taxed by the adder.

As we shall see, the choice is important because existing generating capacity tends to be markedly more polluting than new capacity. Complete emissions taxation will therefore make significant differences to existing capacity, perhaps leading to wholesale retirement of plant.

NOTE 1. PACE presents two emission factors for particulates [3.0×10^{-4} and 0.15] since in this section we are more interested in methodology PACE's original figures are used although the inconsistency is noted.

CHAPTER 2 THE THEORY OF SOCIAL COST

2.1 The Concept of Externality

For any given energy service there will be certain <u>externalities</u> which are not reflected in the equilibrium market price of that energy service. A negative <u>externality</u> (external cost) arises when:

  a) the production and/or consumption of the energy services causes losses of <u>wellbeing</u> (welfare and utility) to some third party;

  b) that loss goes uncompensated by market processes.

Positive externalities involve third party gains in wellbeing that are <u>unappropriated</u> by the creator of the externality. When externalities are present the allocation of resources in the economy will be <u>inefficient</u>[1]. It follows that both the total amount of energy produced and consumed will be inefficient if externalities are present. When externalities vary by the type of energy resource, and they will do, then the <u>mix</u> of energy sources will also be inefficient.

The regulatory process <u>internalises</u> some of the externalities associated with energy. By 'internalisation' we mean that third party losses of wellbeing are compensated for by the creator of the externality, or are reduced through preventive measures. Thus a flue gas desulphurisation (FGD) plant might be installed in order to reduce acid rain emissions which damage third party wellbeing. In Figure 2.1 MAC shows the marginal cost of <u>abating</u> acid rain emissions; MDC shows the marginal <u>damage</u> (external) cost- i.e. losses in wellbeing due to the externality. A move from point X to point Y is justified because MAC < MDC for this move. The shaded area is the <u>internalised externality.</u>

In fact, it pays society (but not the polluter) to increase abatement to point Z where MAC=MDC. Beyond Z society incurs more costs than the benefit from damage reduction. The externality that remains (OZB in Figure 2.1) is the <u>optimal externality.</u>

2.2 Externality Pricing

The dominant reason for measuring the externalities associated with energy production and use is to secure some insight into the 'optimal' structure of energy sources required to meet a given demand for energy. The requirement is that energy should be supplied at <u>least social cost</u>. Such a mix of energy sources could be achieved in two ways:

  a) 'command-and-control', whereby regulations are placed on the production/consumption of energy so as to internalise externality;

  b) 'pricing' whereby each energy source will be taxed to reflect the externality.

Economic analysis suggests that (b) is preferred since it secures the mix at minimum aggregate compliance cost to society and acts as a continuous spur to technological change (Tietenberg [1990]) Pearce, Markandya and Barbier [1989]; (Stavins [1988,1990]).

In terms of Figure 2.1, the aim would be to set a tax equal to t. As long as t > MAC it will pay the polluter to adopt abatement technology. Clearly, t > MAC to the right of Z and t < MAC to the left of Z. If t is set exactly equal to MAC=MDC at the optimum, the tax will secure the optimal level of externality internalisation.

Under the polluter pays principle (OECD [1975]) it is generally assumed that the polluter pays the tax on all externality, not just the 'non-optimal' externality. The relevance of this is that measurement of social costs is very likely to reveal the existence of externality. What is observed, however, may be the _optimal level of externality. Regardless of this, it will, on the polluter pays principle, remain correct to charge a tax on the optimal level of externality (Pezzey [1988]).

2.3 Measuring Externality

2.3.1 WTP and WTA

Strictly, all externality should be measured by seeking one of the following:

    a)   society's willingness to pay (WTP) to avoid externality;
    b)   society's WTP to secure reductions on externality;
    c)   society's willingness to accept compensation for damage done;
    d)   society's (WTA) to forgo a benefit.

Figure 2.2 shows how these concepts might be illustrated. Since the various concepts correspond exactly to the four measures of consumer surplus introduced by Hicks [1943], the presumption is that they will not diverge. Willig [1976] shows that this ought indeed be the case. In practice, WTA measures for environmental quality often show up as being very much larger than WTP measures even after allowing for 'income effects'[2]. This issue is discussed further below. Its relevance for the social costs of energy is that the size of externality measure may well vary according to which measure, WTP or WTA, is chosen. This issue is addressed in more detail in Section 2.4.

2.3.2. Control Costs and Damage Costs

Figure 2.3 shows the context for valuation of energy related externality. For any given fuel cycle there will be various forms of technology and abatement measures. These will determine _emissions which are then transported to an emission point (area) where they 'dose' the receiving area, causing an impact (damage), the value of which is determined by WTP/WTA.

The valuation stage relates to the link between physical damage and its re-expression in terms of WTP or WTA. Figure 2.3 encapsulates the damage function approaches to valuation. Provided the various measures of WTP and WTA do not diverge significantly (see Section

2.4) this approach is adequate for current purposes. For example, some WTP measures are obtained by looking at 'avertive expenditures' - e g insulation against noise, medical expenditure etc. These appear not to be immediately relevant to the damage function approach since they are expenditures to avoid damage. However, a WTP measure to avoid damage could be applied to an estimate of damage done provided the relevant measures are not expected to vary much.

The methodologies for valuing externality are numerous. Annex 3 outlines the main approaches. Two general approaches to energy social cost evaluation may be discerned in the literature:

     a) approaches based in the valuation of damage done;
     b) approaches based on the costs of averting damage.

This distinction is important since approach (b) is widely used to approximate damage which should, technically always be measured by approach (a). An example is Gottinger [1991] in which the costs of controlling power station emissions are used sometimes to indicate the value of external costs due to those emissions. The implicit error in this approach is illustrated in Figure 2.4. There it is shown that, unless the level of control is optimal, use of control costs to measure damage costs will under- or over-estimate true damage costs.

Control costs are, however, widely used to estimate the externality associated with energy use. It is therefore worthwhile investigating the conditions under which it is legitimate to use control costs for the purpose. Partial justification lies in using the marginal control costs to achieve a predetermined standard. Suppose, for example in Figure 2.4 that the regulating authority sets E_2 as the standard. Then implicitly, the authority is assuming either that the damage function is like MDC; or that factors other than damage done are determining the standard. If the former, then there is some justification for using E_2d as the measure of (marginal) damage.

Clearly, if the true damage is E_2c, then the argument above is not correct - i. e. the regulatory authority has set the wrong standard in terms of efficiency criteria. At best, then, use of control costs to measure damage contains the potential for significant error. In the subsequent empirical survey, therefore, we indicate whether the literature uses control costs or damage costs.

2.4 Issues in Valuation

Given that the aim is to secure estimates of damage cost and translate them into externality adders a number of issues arise.

2.4.1 Imposed and Voluntary Risk

Observing the presence of damage does not necessarily imply that externality exists. The most notable and relevant example of this concerns health and mortality risks in energy extraction and production. Consider, for example, the case of accidents.

Apart from the difficulties of ascribing the mortality and incapacities to electricity production, there is an additional problem of determining whether the risks giving rise to the accidents are accounted for in the wages paid to workers in the relevant industries. If the risk is perceived and accepted voluntarily by the worker in question, then the value of the risk can properly be determined through an hedonic wage equation. This is indeed how most so-called 'values of life' are determined
[see Chapter 4].

If the risk is voluntarily assumed, however, and there is evidence that the risk premium is incorporated in the private costs of energy production and use, then there is no case for adding such values to the private costs of electricity generation. The externality has been internalised into the private cost structure of the industry. In terms of the social cost of energy calculation, occupational accident costs would be irrelevant if this process of internalisation could be judged to be present.

Two issues arise:

(a)   to what extent are occupational health and accident risks truly internalised into wage systems ?

(b)   if they are so internalised, can the values of risk increase be transferred to contexts in which risks are not voluntarily borne ?

Chapter 4 addresses these questions

2.4.2 Willingness to Pay vs Willingness to Accept

Section 2.3 indicated that several measures of individuals' valuations might be used in social cost measurement work. Economic theory suggests that these measures, essentially compensating and equivalent variations measures of consumer surplus, should not diverge by very much - no more than 10% - provided income and wealth effects are small (Willig [1976]). In practice, however, significant variations have been found when using questionnaire (contingent valuation) approaches to valuation. Willingness to accept (WTA) has been found to exceed willingness to pay (WTP) by factors of 2-7, and in one case 16 (see Table 2.1). Since, by and large, payment of compensation for environmental loss would make only small additions to an individual's wealth, income and wealth effects are likely to be small and hence cannot account for differences in valuation. Some other factor is therefore at work. Alternatively, the sources of evidence are themselves faulty.

Those who believe the issue is one of design and measurement error focus on the inherent problems of contingent valuation surveys, especially the hypothetical nature of the experiments. As Table 2.1 suggests, however, the WTA/WTP disparity exists even for experiments involving real exchanges. Moreover, recent work has suggested that the biases in CVM are not as significant as previously thought. It seems clear that experimental design has something to do with the disparities (Coursey et al. [1987]), particularly if uncertainty is included in the choices faced by respondents - it is well known that behaviour under uncertainty may offend the expected utility model[3]. Experiments in which respondents have only a quick 'one shot' at the answers to questions may also result in high disparities which are reduced when a learning process is introduced. But it appears not to account for all the disparity. WTA and WTP are likely to converge the closer is the context to a 'mature market setting' (Coursey et al. [1987]), but diverge the further the issue is from market contexts (e.g. paying for species conservation). Since some authors also believe that CVM works least well the less familiar is the respondent with the 'object' being valued, there is likely to be a strong divergence for valuations derived from CVM studies of 'unfamiliar' objects.

The alternative viewpoint is that there is an <u>endowment effect</u> whereby individuals have <u>loss aversion</u>, valuing reductions in a given set of resources more highly than equivalent increases (Kahneman and Tversky [1979]). Effectively, the valuation function is 'kinked' about the existing level of resource endowment (income). This is the underlying idea of <u>prospect theory</u> in which valuations have more to do with perceived change of status than with the absolute quantities of goods gained or lost. Moreover, the <u>way</u> in which decisions are made can matter as much as the outcomes of the decision. WTA questions for example may imply for the respondent some sense of relinquishing an implied entitlement. The two forms of exchange - gain and loss - are not perceived as being equivalent.

The relevance for the social costing of energy is potentially formidable. (There are also fairly dramatic implications for the underlying analytics of microeconomic theory. Effectively, indifference curves are no longer 'completely reversible' - i.e. the curve varies depending in which direction one travels (Knetsch [1989], [1990], Kahneman, Knetsch and Thaler [1990]). If WTA genuinely is several times larger than WTP, and if there is no particular reason to justify using WTP rather than WTA, then social costs could be two or maybe even ten times larger under a WTA regime. Since the validity of the disparities between WTA and WTP is currently hotly disputed there is little option but to report valuations according to whether they are WTA or WTP, and note the difference. There is no consensus on WTP/WTA disparities: it remains a debated issue. The significance of the debate for <u>energy</u> externality adders is, however, probably not substantial. Thus, the estimates of the 'value of a statistical life' are derived using <u>both</u> WTA (wage-risk) and WTP (contingent valuation) approaches. As Chapter 4 shows, disparities in values of statistical lives derived by these different means are not large. The major WTP/WTA disparities relate to wildlife preference valuation, and these are not of major importance for fuel cycles. Dose-response approaches tend to be used for crops, forests and buildings damage, and the use of market prices to value the responses involves an implicit WTP measure. How far WTA approaches would produce significantly different estimates is not known.

TABLE 2.1
SUMMARY OF WTP/WTA DISPARITIES (US $)

Study	Means			Medians		
	WTP	WTA	Ratio	WTP	WTA	Ratio
Hypothetical Surveys						
Hammack and Brown(1974): marshes	247	1044	4.2			
Sinclair (1978): fishing	35	100	2.9			
Banford et al. (1979)						
Fishing pier	43	120	2.8	47	129	2.7
Postal service	22	93	4.2	22	106	4.8
Bishop and Heberlein (1970): goose hunting permits	21	101	4.8			
Rowe et al. (1980): visibility	1.3	3.5	2.6			
Brookshire at al. (1980): elk hunting*	54	143	2.6			
Heberlein and Bishop(1985): deer hunting	31	513	16.5			
Real exchange experiments:						
Knetsch and Sinden (1984): lottery tickets	1.3	5.2	4.0			
Heberlein and Bishop (1985): deer hunting	25	172	6.9			
Coursey et al.(1987) taste of sucrose octa-acetate†	3.4	4.7	1.4	1.3	3.5	2.6
Brookshire and Coursey (1987): park trees††	10.1	56.6	5.6	6.3	13.0	2.1

*Middle- level several used in study
† Final values after multiple iterations
†† Average of two levels of tree plantings
Source:Kahneman, Knetsch and Thaler [1990].

2.4.3 Average versus Incremental Values

Social cost estimates can be prepared on two ways:

a)   by looking at the <u>existing</u> 'portfolio' of energy sources and deriving an average social cost per kWh;

b)   by looking at a <u>planned</u> investment capacity (hypothetical or real).

Many valuation studies relate to existing capacities. The resulting average values will <u>not</u> be directly transferable to marginal capacity changes if:

i)   the new capacity embodies changes in technology which alter the configuration of emissions through 'end-of-pipe' investments and improved fuel consumption

ii)   the averages relate to mixes of technology which are not replicated in expanded capacity.

These problems are largely overcome by using "money values per tonne emissions" as indicated in Chapter 1. Thus, if SO2 does £1 per tonne damage, such a figure can be applied to the relevant emissions for a new technology. This is the approach used here. However, it conceals a further problem. The average damage figure will reflect prevailing, or past, emissions and concentrations. If new capacity <u>adds</u> to existing concentrations then damage may be <u>higher</u> per tonne emissions than is implied by the average figure. The issue is complicated further by the fact that the estimated adder may relate to <u>past</u> concentration levels and concentration may have <u>fallen</u> since the estimate was obtained.

These cautions need to be kept in mind when evaluating <u>the policy</u> relevance of social cost measures. The relevant measures for the purposes of this report will be ones which can be applied to new capacity, but invariably no adjustment is made to capture the marginal rather than the average damage.

Figure 2.7 illustrates the divergences that may arise between marginal and average values. Similar issues arise with resource loss valuation. Many studies value the environmental <u>asset</u> in question, not changes in the size of the asset.

2.4.4 The Transferability Issue

External cost tends to vary by <u>location</u>. The damage done by acid rain, for example, varies according to the point of emission. An area with a lake or heritage building is likely to show more damage 'per tonne' of emission than say, an area of rocky soils with no high value land use. Moreover, studies of localised damage are not likely to be undertaken for <u>every</u> situation in which there is pollution damage. It follows that it would be highly desirable if values from one study could be transferred to other areas. The extent to which this is justified is the <u>transferability</u> issue.

There are two possible 'transfers':[4]

   a)   transferring <u>unit values</u>- e.g. a value for a day's recreational experience;

   b)   transferring <u>a damage function</u> -e.g. applying a regression linking damage to source in one area to another area with changes in the relevant parameters.

It seems fair to say that the transferability issue is only just now being addressed in the literature. Transferring unit values could be legitimate if the <u>source</u> population shares very close characteristics with the <u>target</u> population. Thus, a recreation - day may be worth £X in location A, and recreation days in location B could also be reasonably valued at £X if B has similar income characteristics to A, similar competing opportunities for recreation, and so on.

Transferring <u>functions</u> is perhaps more acceptable. This has the advantage that localised data can be inserted into the function. In Figure 2.5, for example, the observation of the function shown is used to generate a damage estimate for site A. But site B has a different emission level and the relevant damage can be read off the damage function. This approach was used in one major sulphur oxide study (OECD[1985]). Notice however, that transferability of functions should account for potential <u>thresholds</u> (discontinuities). Assuming the function is xBy, A will mis-state values in the reference environment if, in fact, the function has a discontinuity and appears as xBYZ.

In both the unit values and function case, some <u>average</u> from various studies might be used. For example, unit values of V_1, V_2 V_3, from three studies might be averaged such that [V_1+ V_2+ V_3 +]/3 is the value used in the 'new' context; or some function which approximates the average of several functions might be used. By and large, the literature suggests that, where possible, <u>functions</u> which have readily discerned site characteristics are to be preferred (Cantor <u>et al</u>. [1990]). Some attempts have been made to secure 'meta-functions' - i.e. functional forms which bring together many studies and which attempt to explain their results (Smith and Kaoru [1990])- see Chapter 14.

Clearly, transferability is a complex issue and the problems are not resolved in the literature. The main challenge lies in knowing what adjustments to make to estimates from a studied environment when they are transferred to a <u>reference</u> environment. Variations include:

   -      regional   differences: e.g.difference   in   broad   availability   of recreation sites;
   -      site differences: e.g. differences in pollution levels
   -      differences in individuals: e.g. variations in income

The degree of transferability is summarised in Figure 2.6.

Other issues of transferability are:

   a)   <u>scaling</u>: i.e. adjusting values in the source environment for differences in receptor status in the reference environment: eg. non- use values in A, with a population of X are applied to site B, population Y, such that B's values become Y/X times those of A;

b)   aggregation: it may not be possible to add up transferred values. As an example, a value in site A may not be added to a transferred value in site B if there are reasons for supposing that, if valued separately, the B values would be affected by the A values. This is the familiar 'framing' problem - i.e. if may not be possible to add separate WTPs since, if presented with all valuation possibilities, respondents will alter valuations of sites presented separately. Indeed, aggregate values may be affected by the order in which individual valuations are made.

Cantor et al. [1991] distinguish the following aggregation problems:

a)   Aggregation Across Infrastructure: even if electricity generation impacts are additive across site A and reference site B, the associated 'infrastructure' (raw materials etc) impacts may not be equivalent.

b)   Aggregation Across Same 'Endpoints' at Different Locations: an endpoint refers to the agent receiving the impact (humans), or the receiving asset (e.g building, lakes). The issue is whether a value derived for one asset can be aggregated across many assets: e.g. can a recreational benefit at site A be added to a recreational benefit at site B? The possible result is that aggregation of this kind will overstate total benefits.

c)   Aggregation Across Different Endpoints: the issue here is whether values for different endpoints - e.g. water quality and air quality -are additive. Hoehn and Randall [1982] show that aggregation will underestimate benefits (damage) if the goods are complements. Aggregation overestimates if they are substitutes. The presumption is that substitution is a more likely case. One apparent solution to this problems is to use a technique which values the composite of all endpoints - eg. for air pollution this might be soiling, health impacts, visibility etc. The hedonic property price method is attractive in this respect. However, problems arising in this context are:

i)   the composite valuation obscures the component parts of the value, making transferability difficult, if not impossible. Freeman [1982] for example, takes an arbitrary proportion of estimated house price depreciation to reflect amenity losses which can then be added to separately derived estimates of health damage etc;

ii)   it is not always clear which endpoint damage is being captured by the house price method since it depends on perception of 'what matters' by householders. Few house price studies contain separate perception valuations.

For these reasons hedonic property price (HPP) methods are regarded by some as being generally unsuitable for energy social cost evaluations (Cantor et al. [1991]). This may be a somewhat harsh judgement. The HPP method appears very suitable for valuing noise nuisance, but noise nuisance, in turn, is less relevant to energy social cost evaluation.

Another endpoint aggregation issue concerns health impacts of pollutants. A single pollutant (eg. ozone) may cause variable symptoms (aggravated chronic conditions, eye irritation, headaches). Is the value for avoiding a day of multiple symptoms the same as the sum of the values of avoiding a day of each symptom separately? Krupnick [1991] analyses this as a problem of jointness and separability. If both conditions are present than there is an aggregation problem. Krupnick concludes that the evidence on jointness in not clear, whilst the evidence on separability suggests it does exist (value of a day of X symptoms are less than the value of X days of each symptom). Assuming separability therefore overstates benefits.

d) Aggregation Across Individuals
    The issue here is whether separate valuation by separate individuals can be aggregated to obtain a social value. This is one of the eternally debated issues of welfare economics, i.e the 'interpersonal comparison of utilities'.

Benefit and cost estimation tends to be carried out in a context whereby it is possible to compare states of the economy in which some people are made better off and some are made worse off. This comparison is enabled by the use of the Kaldor-Hicks compensation test whereby if gainers hypothetically compensate losers, net social welfare is deemed to have increased. A stricter welfare economics based solely on Paretian considerations would deny that social welfare has increased in such circumstances. If some people are better off and others are worse off, such states are said to be 'Pareto non-comparable' because of the alleged impossibility of making judgements about the relative welfare of different human beings: the so called problem of 'interpersonal comparisons of utility' (IPCU). the position taken here is the Kaldor-Hicks one which overcomes the IPCU problem by arguing that individuals can judge their own welfare gains and losses and can translate them into meaningful measures of compensation or willingness to pay, permitting aggregation across different social states to take place.

Finally, transferability may be impaired if the damage done has different causes in the original and reference location, That is, people's valuations may be affected by the factors giving rise to damage, so that valuation of similar damage varies by cause. This may be especially true if individuals believe causal factors involve something they regard as unethical.

2.4.5 Information and Valuation

A number of contingent valuation studies have shown that valuation will vary according to the amount of information available (Schulz [1985], Semples et al. [1986]). Typically, the more information is provided, the higher the values elicited. The problem for fuel cycle evaluation, then, is to determine which are the 'correct' values - those with or without full information. There are no simple answers to this question. Technically, since information is not costless, there is an optional level of information and it might therefore be argued that valuations should be elicited at the level of information thought to be optimal. However, it is not easy to decide the optimal level of information: costs of information acquisition may be discernable but benefits may not.

2.4.6 Implicit Valuation

All decisions imply values. Thus, if project A is chosen over project B, and A has known net benefits of £100 and unknown benefits of £x, while B has known net benefit of £150, then X is implicitly valued at (150-100) > £50. There are two ways in which implicit valuation might be used:

a)   by inferring individuals' preferences (see Section 18.3 on negative time preference);
b)   by inferring politicians or 'decision makers' preferences

In both cases the problems are that individuals may be unaware of costs and benefits, and that they may have multiple objectives. However implicit values help to highlight the monetary valuation of non- efficiency benefits.

2.4.7 Small versus Big Change

Valuation studies often value 'big' (non-marginal) changes in quantity and quality. But a single power station is a small (marginal) addition to the power supply system. Non-marginal valuations should not, technically, be used to approximate marginal increments in environmental impacts.

2.4.8 Meta- Analysis

Where there is a significant sample of studies - e.g. hedonic property air pollution and noise studies - it may be possible to engage in meta- analysis. Meta- analysis pools the individual studies to see if they imply some consistent means values and/or explain the variance between means. The purpose is to see if a meta- valuation equation could be transferred to other contexts -with different local characteristics being substituted in the equation. Chapter 14 looks in more detail at the few meta-analysis so far carried out.

2.5 User Costs

The use of non-renewable energy resources today precludes the consumption of those resources at a future date. There is therefore an additional cost to be added to extraction processing and environmental costs of energy, namely user cost (also known as a depletion premium). Chapter 16 investigates the concept of user costs in more detail and evaluates whether it is already likely to be incorporated into market prices.

2.6 Discounting

2.6.1 The Problem

Energy production and use involves a number of potentially long-lived environmental problems - notably radioactive waste storage, nuclear power station decommissioning, and global warming. The costs are therefore likely to be borne by people alive in 50 years time and after that. Conventional benefit - cost approaches would regard £1 of future damage as being less important that £1 of damage now because of the phenomenon of <u>discounting</u>. The underlying value judgments of benefit-cost analysis are that 'people's preferences count' and that preferences are justifiably weighted according to the existing distribution of incomes. If the sovereignty of preferences is to be applied consistently, then the bias of the preferences of the current generation towards present as opposed to future benefits, and against present as opposed to future costs, needs to be accounted for. This is the essential rationale for discounting. It is an issue of <u>valuation</u> for the simple reason that the lower the discount rate, the greater will be the value of the future damage that is discounted; and vice versa.

Any benefit (B) (or cost) accruing in T years time is recorded as having a 'present value' of:

$$PV(B) = \frac{B^T}{(1 + r)^T}$$

where r is the rate at which future benefits are discounted, the discount rate.

The problem that arises with discounting is that it <u>discriminates against future generations</u>. In one sense this discrimination is not a problem - the discount rate is <u>meant</u> to discriminate in this way: this is its purpose. But such a discrimination presupposes an agreed objective to the effect that meeting current generation's wants is more important that meeting future generations' wants. The usual justification for this is that future generations will be better off anyway - their incomes will be higher because of economic growth. They will therefore attach less value to an extra £1 of income than a current generation (the 'diminishing marginal utility of income' argument) and will perhaps be better placed to counteract any ill effects of current generation activities that spill over to them. To see the kind of implied shifting of burdens, a cost accruing in 100 years time and amounting to £100 <u>billion</u> would, at a 10 per cent discount rate, have a present value of

$$\frac{£100 \text{ billion}}{(1.1)^{100}}$$

which comes to £7.26 <u>million</u>. That is, any benefit cost study of a project imposing such a future cost would record the damage done at only £7.25 million even though the actual damage done is nearly 14,000 times greater than this. If there is concern with intergenerational equity, then, discount rates of the order of 10 per cent would be inconsistent with that concern.

2.6.2 UK Practice

What discount rate should be used in estimating the social costs of energy? In the UK the Treasury guidelines (HM Treasury [1991]) recommend:

6% real discount rates generally: this is the 'true' discount rate that would be relevant to public investments in energy and environmental measures;

8% as the required rate of return for nationalised industries and central government bodies selling commercially: this is an average rate of return on assets and therefore tends to imply a discount rate of 8% or above
6% for forestry, but 3% as an overall target rate of return, the difference reflecting the subsidy to forestry;

a possible relaxation of the 6% rule for 'very long term' effects (HM Treasury [1991], para 12ix of Annex G), but with a presumption that 6% 'for time preference into the indefinite future should normally be taken as the central assumption'.

The Treasury's rationale for the main rate of 6% is set out in considerable detail in a separate document (Spackman [1991]). The central thrust of this paper is that the rate of 6% emerges whether one takes the recommended discount rate to be based on marginal real returns in the private sector (the 'opportunity cost' argument) or individuals' apparent preferences for the present over the future (their 'time preference'). The Treasury analysis makes due allowance for before and after-tax rates of return.

One concern is the effect of using a 6% discount rate for investments with significant environmental effects. Arguments for rates of discount lower than 6% might be twofold.

The first argument would simply be that discounting per se is unethical in contexts where there are potential long term risks and costs. Certainly, the philosophical literature tends to point towards either zero discount rates or very low discount rates in such contexts (Broome [1991]).

The second argument proposes modifications to conventional discount rates to allow for (a) the ethical irrelevance of 'pure time preference discounting' (sometimes known as 'utility discounting'), and (b) certain assumptions about the discounting of future consumption. Time preference discounting is usually taken as the sum of (a) and (b), i.e. the discounting of future wellbeing, of 'utility', simply because it occurs in the future, and the discounting of future consumption on the grounds that future generations will be richer than present generations (and hence £1 to them will mean less than £1 to us). If utility discounting is rejected, then it can be shown that, under certain circumstances, the resulting discount rate is equal to the projected rate of growth of real consumption per head. If this is, say, 1% then the discount rate would be 1%. Applying this approach to the UK post-war period: real aggregate consumers' expenditure increased at some 2.1% p.a., and population at 0.3% p.a, so that the effective discount rate would be only 1.8%.

Chapter 18 investigates the issue of discounting in more detail.

2.7 Non-Environmental Externalities

2.7.1 Introduction

Energy systems impose externalities other than those associated with the environment. Until recently, comparatively little research has been undertaken into these non-environmental externalities (NEEs). The potential importance of NEEs is illustrated by Hohmeyer's [1988] findings that fossil fuel electricity in Germany has associated externalities as follows:

	fossil fuel DM/kWh	nuclear
Environmental	0.06	0.21
User cost	0.02	0.06
NEEs	0.04	0.02
NEES/total	33%	7%

How far Hohmeyer's estimates are acceptable is discussed elsewhere in this report. For the moment we note that NEEs could be important.

The most rigorous discussion of NEEs is contained in Bohi, Burtraw and Krupnick (BBK) [1991] on which this section draws. BBK distinguish the following categories of NEES:
market failures
energy security
government failures (our term) or 'regulatory externalities' (BBKs term).

Since the discussion can be very involved it is important to note at the outset that interest will be confined to those externalities where there is a prima facie case for supposing that externality costs will differ across fuel cycles. Where there is an externality but it is not differentiated by fuel cycle, the effect on social cost pricing will simply be to add the same increment to each private cost. Such externality adjustments would not therefore influence choice between new generation technologies.

2.7.2 Market Failures

Market failures include:

(a) the costs of occupational health damage due to fuel cycles. This is discussed fully in Chapter 4. As BBK note, there is ample evidence that compensating wage differentials exist, but no real way of telling whether those differentials fully compensate for the externality. It seems correct to follow BBK in regarding occupational health as a NEE rather than an environmental externality. Public health risks are however typically regarded as EEs (environmental externalities);

(b) <u>multiplier and employment effects</u>. Some fuel cycles are more labour intensive than others, so one would expect employment impacts to vary by generating technology. How far such effects constitute externalities is dependent upon a view of how labour markets function. Technically, if unemployment differs from the 'natural rate' then the difference is an attributable cost (benefit) to energy technologies if employment impacts vary by fuel cycle. BBK regard this externality as potentially relevant. An alternative way to look at it is to argue that employment impacts should be shadow priced according to the nature of the impact - e.g. employment in sparsely populated regions (affecting perhaps wind and wave energy) or in declining coal mining regions might be shadow priced;

(c) <u>public infrastructure costs</u>. Some fuel cycles involve the movement of heavy vehicles which may damage infrastructure such as roads, generate congestion etc. Strictly, such costs should be attributed to the fuel cycle if road user charges are not differentiated by vehicle or are not thought to be high enough to capture the externality. Given the substantial literature of road user charging it may be possible to derive further evidence on this issue.

2.7.3 <u>Energy Security</u>

Fuel cycles differ according to the degree of security they give against interruptions of supply, where this term is construed broadly to include not just quantity restrictions but price hikes - e.g. those induced by OPEC. The kinds of considerations involved include:

- the idea that the social cost of oil is higher than the market price because of the military expenditures and loss of life involved in defending sources of supply (e.g the 'Gulf War argument');

- the idea that the social cost of imports of oil is high because of the potential for forced interruptions of supply, as with OPEC in the 1970s. In this respect the social cost of oil would be higher than the market price by some premium reflecting lost GNP due to oil price induced recession in oil importing countries. As BBK note, however, there is limited agreement on the role which past price hikes actually played in inducing recession. For oil exporters, price hikes are, of course, likely to be associated with increased GNP;

- variations in 'outage' cost due to transmission failure. However, it is unlikely to be the case that such costs will vary by fuel cycle if the comparison is always with base load supplies. Care has also to be taken, to include back-up systems where supply is variable (e.g. wind energy);

- prices may deviate from competitive market prices due to monopsonistic power on the part of the consuming country (e.g. USA and oil). This confers a benefit on the importing nation, even though from a world point of view it is a 'pecuniary externality' (a transfer from one part of the world to another). Such benefits should therefore be deducted in a social cost pricing equation;

- potential effects of the variability in import prices on the exchange rate. Quite how this is translated into a social cost indicator is not clear however.

Overall some of these arguments justify a premium on creating a <u>diversity of supply</u>. If so, then, an increment in supply brought about by a technology supply which involve low impact content should attach a premium. Chapter 17 looks at this issue in more detail.

2.7.4   Government Failure

BBK discuss many potential forms of regulatory externality. We report only those for which some form of further consideration needs to be given. BBK correctly state that the 'benchmark' against which to measure regulatory externality has to be some form of second-best policy given that first best is unattainable (e.g. marginal cost pricing everywhere). A particular feature of regulation of electric utilities is some form of cost plus pricing control. This is unlikely to foster cost minimising behaviour on the part of the utilities. As a result, under regulation, costs might be higher than otherwise would be the case. Arguably, the Non Fossil Fuel Obligation (NFFO) in the UK could induce such inefficiency by not allowing utilities to capture the true economies of scale they might obtain if the NFFO did not exist. On the other hand, the NFFO is, of course, directly relevant to the energy security argument above.

Regulatory approaches also tend to under-emphasise <u>energy conservation</u> by not providing utilities with sufficient incentive to see conservation as another fuel cycle. A second best regulatory policy would give adequate incentive to foster investment in energy conservation if the rate of return to conservation exceeds that of additional supply, then a second-best policy would introduce conservation measures before supply increments. As a result, actual regulatory policy may result in higher system generation costs than would be the case under efficient policy due to operation of an inefficient mix of technologies.

R&D expenditures are a favourite issue among those who debate subsidies to fuel cycles. <u>Past</u> R&D is not relevant, however, to the choice of new generating capacity - it is a sunk cost. <u>Current</u> R&D is relevant. R&D is subsidised due to its public good nature (sharing of information) and the subsidies are therefore costs which would be reflected in fuel cycle prices. Allocating such subsidies to new generating capacity is however problematic, e.g. how much of current nuclear power R&D should be allocated to one nuclear power station?

Liability limits represent another potential subsidy. Governments tend to set limits on the liability of nuclear facilities for accident costs, and for major oil spill accidents. The difference between the actual premia paid by the industry and those that would obtain if the industry was not safeguarded in this way would represent a subsidy, and hence the subsidy should be added to the private cost of generation. BBK do not discuss the situation if liability is regarded as being uninsurable. Technically, this makes the fuel cycle in question extremely costly.

Table 2.2 summarises the situation on NEEs.

TABLE 2.2
Non- Environmental Externalities

Subject Involved?	Externality	Vary by Fuel Cycle?
(1) Energy Security	Yes	Yes, possible premium for low import content technologies
(2) Liability Limits	Yes,	Yes especially relevant to nuclear power
(3) R&D Subsidies - Historical - Current Period	No Yes, when taxpayer financed	 Yes
(4) Administration Cost of Energy Regulation	Yes	No
(5) Income and Employment Effects	Depends on view of how labour made to work	Probably
(6) Deviation from Best Feasible Policy eg. energy conservation	Yes	Suggests energy conservation must be included in fuel cycle analysis
(7) Taxes and Subsidies	May be	Favourable tax treatment may capture energy security benefits
(8) Occupational Health Safety Benefits	Yes, unless Industry financed	Yes
(9) Infrastructure Costs	May be	Probably not

2.8 Energy Conservation

Instead of evaluating the net social costs of <u>adding</u> to generating capacity, it is possible to evaluate the net social costs of energy conservation as:

a)   any external <u>costs</u> from energy conservation, e.g. health hazards from heavily insulated houses (indoor air pollution);

b)   the <u>avoided external costs</u> of the supply technology that is displaced by the conservation, ie, the <u>external benefits</u> of conservation.

With respect to the marginal conservation decision, the displaced supply technology should be the least social cost technology, <u>not</u> the average social cost of the existing mix of supply technologies (this error is committed for example in Herz [1991]). Problems in making the comparison include:

i)   what kind of electricity is displaced: base load or others;

ii)   whereas supply measures are, by comparison 'yes-no' decisions, conservation needs <u>incentives</u> (e. g. higher energy prices, information) which themselves create changes in consumer welfare.

Chapter 13 looks more closely at conservation

2.9 Externality and Damage: a Note on Terminology

Typically, the valuation literature does not distinguish between <u>damage and externality</u>. An <u>impact</u> refers to the physical effects e.g. corrosion, health impairment. <u>Damage</u> refers to the monetary value of its impact. An <u>externality</u> is then <u>either</u> formally equivalent to damage, <u>or</u>, in some of the recent literature, is defined as <u>non-optimal damage</u>, i.e. that damage which should be internalised. The next section illustrates why the externality/damage distinction is thought by some to be more than semantic.

2.9.1 Externality Adders in the Face of Regulation

The relevant surcharge on an energy source should always be the marginal damage done at the optimum. In terms of Figure 2 this would be 'S'. However, there may be over or under-regulation and, arguably, this will affect valuation. At A_u, for example, there is under-regulation. If a new power plant is added, it will impose damage equal to the shaded area at A_u. But this area is greater than S. Which is the correct measure of the externality adder?. The situation is reversed at A_o where there is <u>over</u>- regulation. Is the adder the area at A_o or S? One way of analyzing this issue is to consider what would happen if the adder appeared as an actual surcharge on the price of electricity. At A_u the effect would be to shift MNPB leftwards, but if the tax was applied uniformly <u>across all power stations</u>, the effect would be to reduce power station activity below A^*, which is inefficient. If the tax is applied to the marginal power plant <u>only</u>, then the result would be perfectly discriminated taxes according to the marginal damage of each power plant.

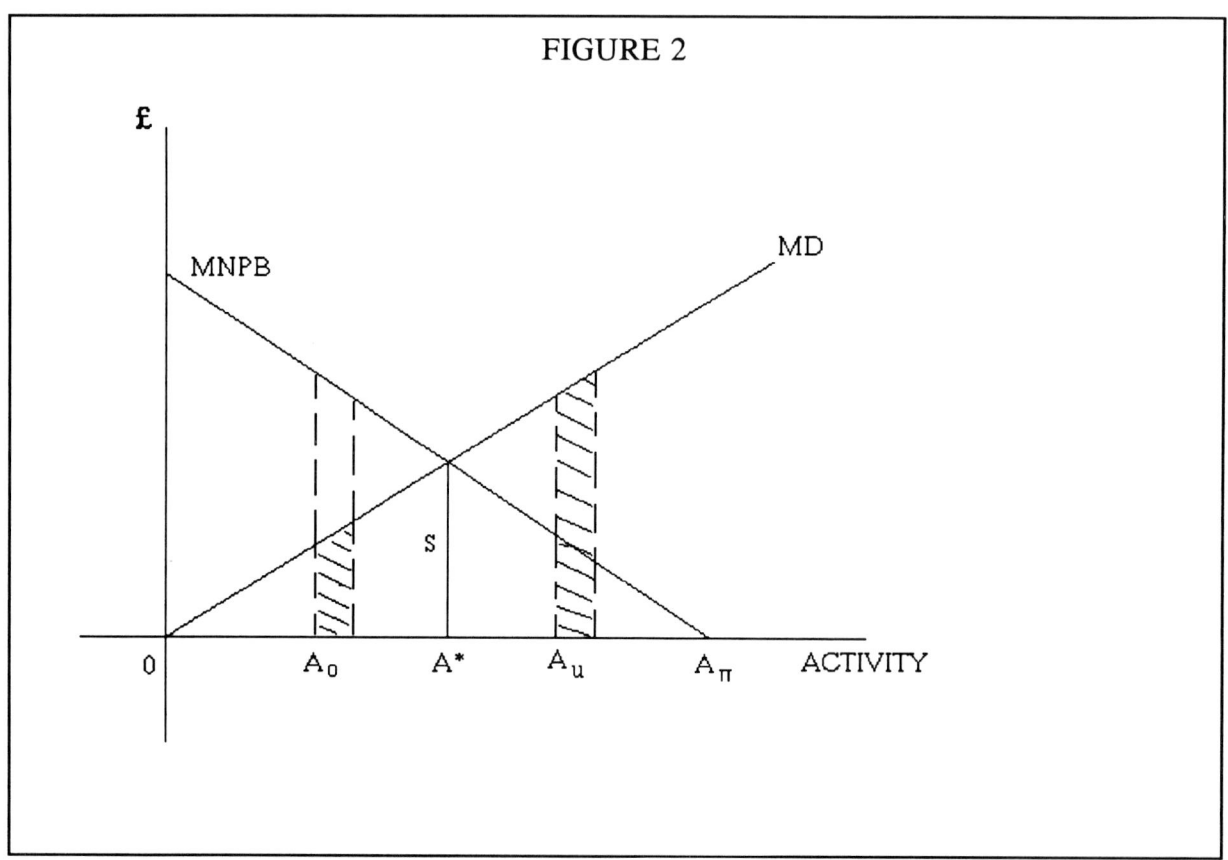

FIGURE 2

It would appear that the relevant adder should be that which is relevant when the overall activity level is optimal i.e. 'S' is the adder at all times. This issue is not resolved in the literature, however.

2.10 The Transboundary Issue

Some energy-related emissions are transported across national boundaries. This raises a potential complication for applying externality adders, but not for their estimation. Damage arises from a given concentration of pollutants. But this concentration will reflect domestic emissions, some of which will be deposited within national boundaries, and 'imported' emissions. In turn, the 'exported' emissions will cause damage in some other country. Chapter 1 showed the way in which externality adders are derived. Imagine that a domestic power station emits 100 units of pollutant, and that 60 land in the domestic area and 40 are 'exported'. Assume 15 units are 'imported' and deposited in the affected area. Then damage is due to 60 + 15 = 75 units. If damage is £X, then the 'adder' is £X/75 per unit of pollutant, and some transformation of this per kWh. The source of the pollution does not matter as far as estimating the adder is concerned. But the issue arising is whether the adder is then applied to all domestic emissions, or just those emissions which are deposited. A tax of X/75 on the 100 emissions would be too high if there was concern only with domestic damage. A tax of X/75 on emissions of 60 will not secure an optimal reduction in damage, however, because it will not affect the imported emissions. One solution is to tax 75 units of domestic emissions at X/75 to secure (marginal) damage reductions of X. But then the domestic emitter is 'unfairly' treated by being over-taxed. Of course, the 40 units exported may be doing damage elsewhere. If all 40 cause damage of Y then a tax of Y/40 could be applied. The issue becomes one of determining the appropriate boundary for the tax. This underlines again the need to look at the purpose of the adder (see Chapter 1).

FIGURE 2.1
OPTIMAL EXTERNALITY

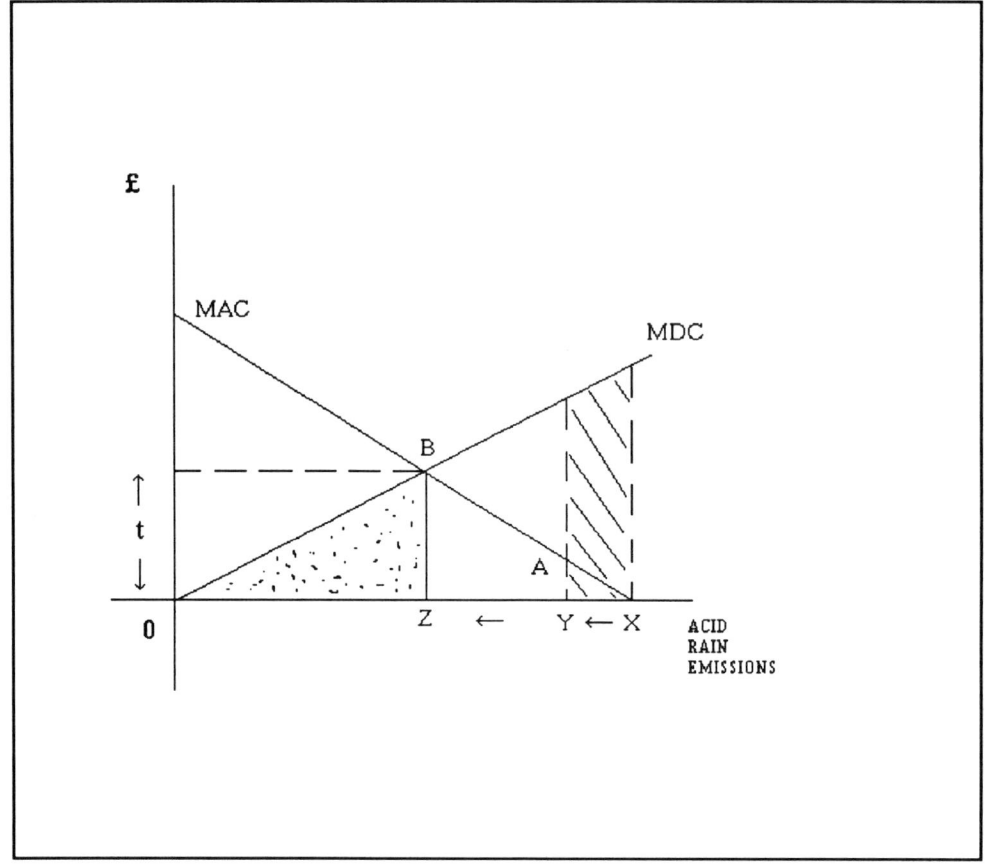

External cost is measured by the area under MDC. A move from X to Y incurs a gain (reduces damage) equal to the shaded area, for a cost of AXY. It pays to internalise external costs up to Z. The dotted area is the optimal externality - i.e. that level of externality which should not be internalised because the costs of so doing exceed the benefits.

FIGURE 2.2
WILLINGNESS TO PAY AND ACCEPT

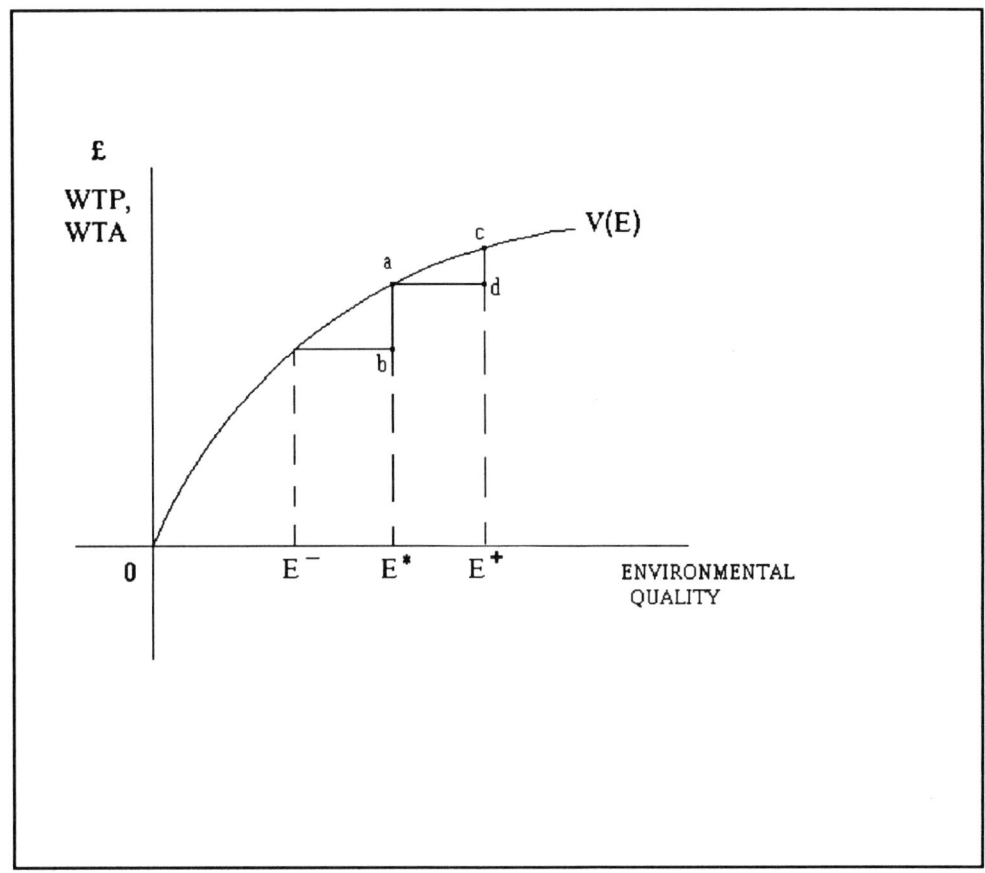

Suppose the <u>status quo</u> is at E*. V(E) is society's valuation function for environmental quality, E. Society's WTP to secure improvement in environment quality to E$^+$ is cd. Society's willingness to pay to <u>avoid</u> a reduction in quality, to E$^-$, is ab. Conversely, society's WTA compensation to forgo the move to E$^+$ should be cd (since that is how much better off they would have been), and WTA compensation to tolerate the move to E$^-$ should be ab. In practice, WTA and WTP appear to diverge markedly (see text).

FIGURE 2.3

FROM FUEL CYCLE TO EXTERNALITY: THE DAMAGE APPROACH

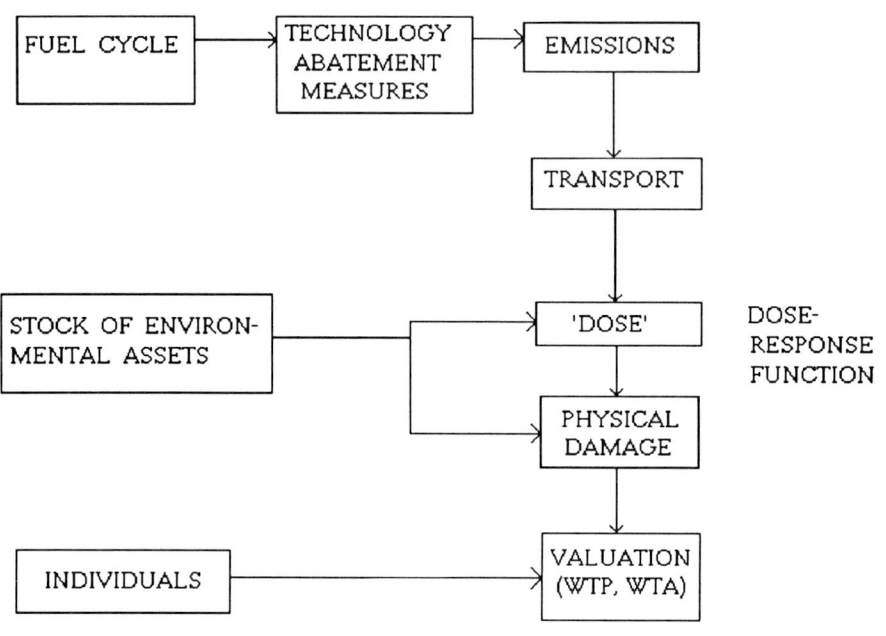

Source: adapted from Cantor et al. [1991]

FIGURE 2.4

DAMAGE CONTROL COSTS AS MEASURES OF EXTERNALITY

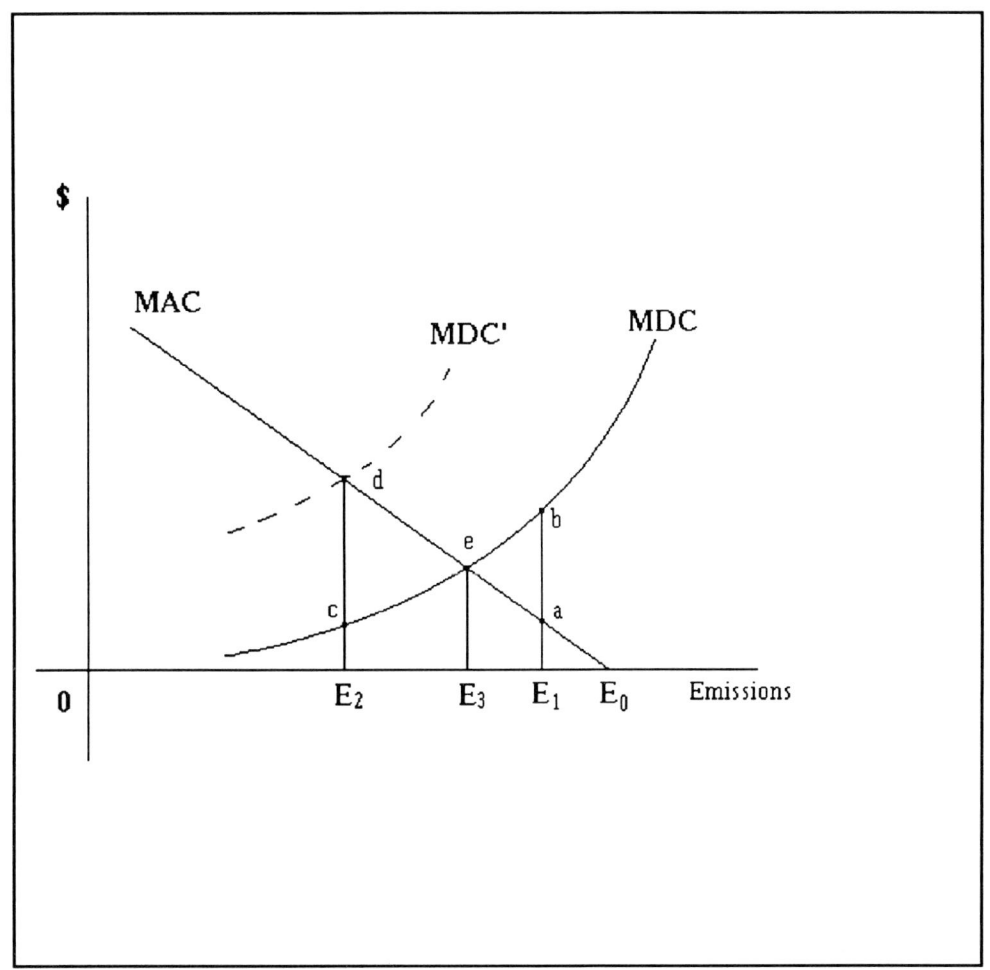

The diagram shows the marginal abatement (control) costs MAC and marginal damage costs MDC from electricity related emissions, E. Suppose it is decided to abate at level E_1. The correct valuation of the damage done by the last unit of emission is E_1b. Using control costs as a surrogate for damage costs results in E_1a being used to measure damage costs. Clearly, E_1a <u>understates</u> the true damage costs. At E_2, control costs will <u>overstate</u> the damage. Only if we know we are at the optimum E_3 will control costs correctly measure damage costs.

FIGURE 2.5

TRANSFERRING DAMAGE FUNCTIONS

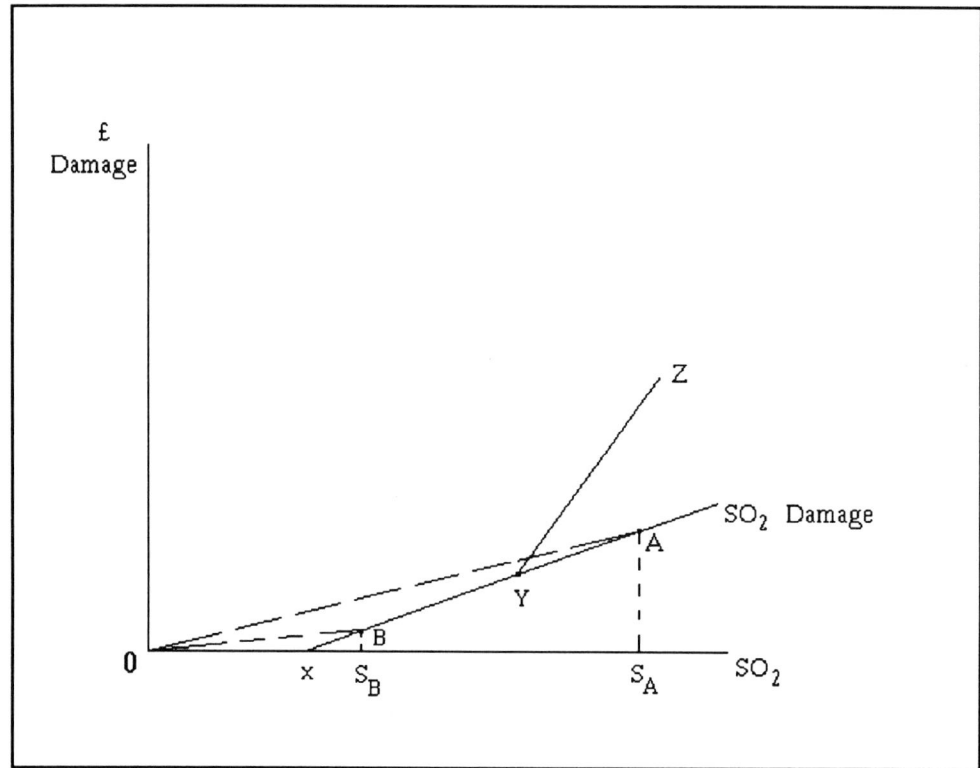

A damage function may be 'transferred' by assuming that it holds at A as well as at B, even though it may have been estimated for A only. But at B the emissions (or concentration) level lower than at A. The <u>average</u> damage at B is given by the slope of OB, whereas the <u>average</u> damage at A is given by the slope of AO.

FIGURE 2.6

TRANSFERABILITY BY NATURE OF DAMAGE

Type of Damage Endpoint	Degree of Transferability	Comment
Health	High	Region and site probably do not affect these values. Individual characteristics (eg.income) probably do.
Crops, forests, fisheries	Medium	Damages are location specific, but underlying dose-response functions may be generalised so that local prices and industrial conditions can be used to modify source values.
Buildings	Low	Damages depend critically upon stock of assets.
Recreation	High	Some evidence that functions can be transferred and suitably modified.
Visibility	Medium	Likely to vary with individuals' characteristics
Non Use Values	?	Some convergence of per capita/ household valuations for species loss
Global Damage	High	Greenhouse gas damage is a global externality unaffected by the source of the gas

FIGURE 2.7

AVERAGE AND MARGINAL DAMAGE

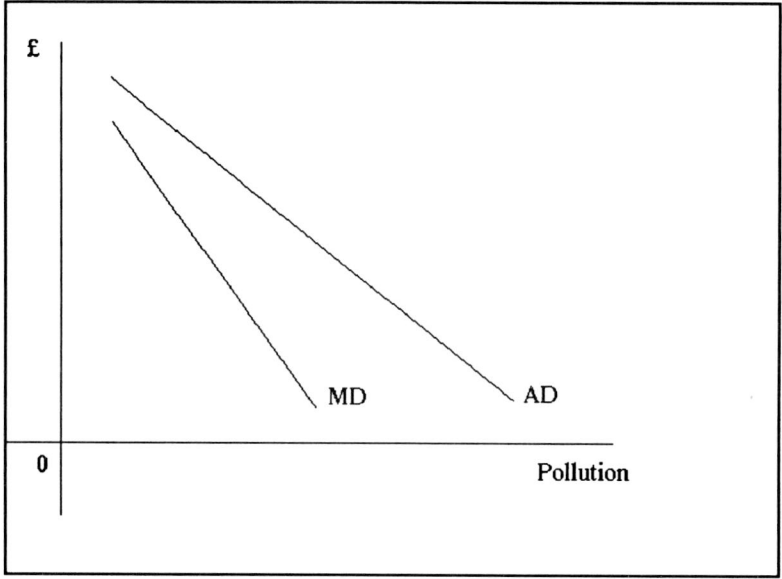

If marginal damage is declining, observation of average damage will overstate marginal damage.

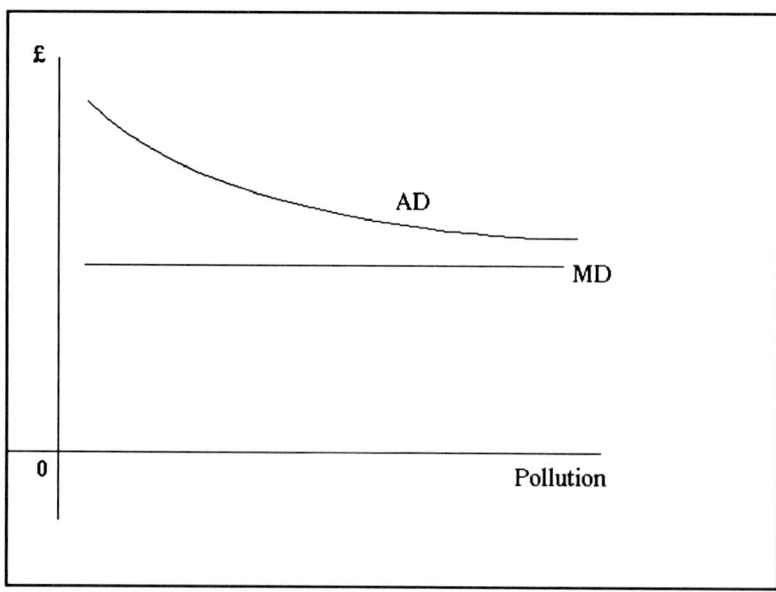

If marginal damage is constant, average damage will overstate marginal damage but, generally, only modestly.

Notes to Chapter 2

1. We do not pursue this point here. Essentially, in a competitive economy without externality, producers will operate where price equal marginal costs (P=MC), and, subject to a number of other qualifications, resources will be allocated optimally. When externalities are present, P=MC fails to 'internalise' the externality and the correct pricing rule becomes P=MC+MEC=MSC where MEC is marginal external cost and MSC is the marginal social costs.

2. That is, we would expect variations in WTP as we move along a Marshallian demand curve since real income changes. Income effects can be allowed for by operating with income- compensated demand curves.

3. The expected utility hypothesis suggests that faced with alternatives each of which is subject to some probability (Pi), the individual will seek to maximise.

    $$EV = \Sigma\ U_i(X_i) \cdot Pi$$

    where U is utility. But experimental evidence is not consistent with this assumption of linearity in the probabilities for many reasons. Thus, 'at the individual level EU maximisation is more the exception than the rule...' (Shoemaker [1987]).

4. Cantor et al [1991] distinguish between damage functions and the 'consequence' approach. An illustration of the latter is the hedonic property price method which could be applied to perceived air quality. They prefer the damage function approach because the values derived in the consequence approach "cannot be disaggregated into their components. Thus, transferability of values to other settings is virtually impossible". The seriousness of this reservation may well be exaggerated, however. Thus air pollution does have multiple impacts (e.g. soiling, health, visibility loss etc.), so that we cannot say what the value of any individual impact is if we use the hedonic pricing approach. But (a) we may not always need to disaggregate i.e. a 'composite' value may be sufficient and could be transferable, and (b) other impacts are best treated as composites - noise nuisance for example.

5. Jointness means that symptoms are produced jointly - e.g. a cough and sore eyes. Separability refers to values: separability exists if the sum of values for each symptom is the same as the value of all symptom together.

CHAPTER 3 FUEL CYCLES AND THEIR IMPACT

3.1   The Fuel Cycles

The fuel cycles under consideration are:

1. a) Conventional coal-fired systems with and without flue gas desulphurisation [FGD] and low NOx burners.

   b) Advanced coal burning techniques: fluidised bed combustion [FBC] and integrated gasification combined cycle [IGCC].

2. Conventional oil fired systems with /without flue gas desulphurisation and low NOx burners.

3. The combined cycle gas turbine.

4. Nuclear energy with pressurized water reactors [PWR].

5. Wind energy.

6. Generators using landfill gas.

7. Geothermal energy.

8. Tidal energy.

9. Hydroelectric power.

10. Wave energy.

11. Solar energy.

12. Industrial and district combined heat and power (CHP).

In practice evidence was not available at the time of writing on FBC/IGCC systems, geothermal, wind and tidal energy.

3.2 Fuel Cycle Impact Matrices

Figures 3.1 to 3.12 show for each of the selected fuel cycles the potential externalities of energy production and consumption. Each individual fuel cycle account follows the sequence of mapping each stage of the fuel cycle to its associated emissions and burdens which are then mapped to a list of impacts which can, in principle, be valued: i.e:

Fuel cycle stages	-----	emissions/burdens
Emissions/burdens	-----	impact
Impact	-----	valuations

Fuel cycle stages are all the various operations involved in the production of electricity. For example, the stages of the coal fuel cycle are - mining, benefication, storage, transportation to the power station, generation of electricity at the power station and transmission. Each stage of the fuel cycle is defined in terms of its associated emissions and burdens. Emissions are the discharges of polluting substances to air and water, burdens are stresses or afflictions imposed on the environment by each operation. For example, coal mining (the first stage of the fuel cycle) results in the emissions of dust and methane, and the burdens of subsidence and noise.

Impacts refer to the changes in the functioning or quality of an environment caused by the fuel cycle. Emissions and burdens impact receiving environments in different ways, e. g. air emissions will have impacts on human health, crops and forests, buildings and visibility.

The various damages that emissions and burdens may impart are categorised under human health, ecological, social and economic, non-environmental and global. For example the ecological impact category includes crops, forests, commercial fishing, recreational fishing, recreational forests and parks and biodiversity. When a receiving environment is impacted in such a way that there is a cost imposed on it, and it is not accounted for in the price of production of consumption, there is an external cost. It is these external costs that we seek to value in monetary terms through techniques such as hedonic pricing, travel cost, avertive expenditure, contingent valuation or the dose-response approach.

Annex 1 shows the detailed European Commission/US Department of Energy matrix approach to the valuation of energy externalities.

As Chapter 1 notes, most information relates to emissions/burdens from existing power stations, not from new capacities. This can be allowed for to some extent by seeking emission factors for new stations and applying standardised damage per unit emission figures.

3.3 Emission Factors

Tables 3.1 show the emission factors used for the relevant fuel cycles. They are based on ETSU data (Eyre [1991]).

Table 3.1
Emissions Factors for UK Fuel Cycles

(Aggregate of All Stages)

grms/kWh (rounded)
(Unoxidised weight C,N,S)

Fuel Cycle	CO2	CH4	N2O	SO2	NOX	CO	NMVOC	PART
Coal: Av.UK	294	4.1	.04	7.0	1.6	.07	.025	-
Coal Modern PF +FGD	255	3.6	0.3	.61	.83	.61	.022	0.160
Oil	269	.05	.13	8.2	.76	.10	.163	-
Gas	122	2.0	.005	.24	.27	.19	.025	-
CHP	125	1.8	0.1	0.30	0.41	0.30	0.11	-
Nuclear	11	0.2	.005	.24	-	.06	-	-

(Oxidised weight CO2,NO,SO2)

g/kWh

Fuel Cycle	CO2	CH4	N2O	SO2	NOx	CO	NMVOC	PART
Coal: Av.UK	1079	4.1	.08	14	5.3	.3	.025	-
Coal: modern PF +FGD	936	3.6	.06	1.2	2.7	2.2	.022	0.160
Oil	987	0.5	.26	16.4	2.5	.4	.163	-
Gas	448	2.0	0.1	.48	0.9	.7	.025	-
CHP	450	1.8	0.03	0.6	1.3	1.1	0.11	-
Nuclear	40	0.2	.01	=	0.2	-	-	-

Source: Adapted from Eyre [1990]. Data in original are in g/GJ.1kWh = 0.0036 GJ. Conversions from unoxidised to oxidised weights are given at beginning of this report. Estimates for the nuclear fuel cycle are adapted from Table 8 of Eyre [1990] on greenhouse gas emissions. CO_2 emissions from the nuclear fuel cycle are disputed - see Mortimer [1991] and Donaldson and Betteridge [1990]. This controversy relates mainly to the pollution impacts from the <u>construction</u> of the generating station. No account is taken here of the relative emissions from plant construction other than through human health effects.

3.4 Electricity Transmission Systems

All centralised generation requires <u>transmission</u> of the electricity to end users. Transmission systems themselves have environmental impacts which include:
- visual amenity of transmission towers
- possible electro-magnetic radiation hazards
- disruption to natural and managed eco-systems
- possible disruption of communications.

The aesthetic impact of high voltage transmission lines has been criticised. In response, considerable attention is given to the siting of transmission lines and efforts have been made to design more attractive towers (such as lower height towers and folded plate poles), and to select cables permitting longer free distances between towers.

Invisible electric and magnetic fields surround any wire conducting electricity. The two fields are often referred to collectively as EMF (electric and magnetic fields). There have been a number of studies which suggest, but do not establish, links between exposure to these fields and the incidence of cancer (particularly in children) and other health effects.

Reports twenty years ago from the Soviet Union first suggested that exposure to high electric fields caused various non-specific symptoms, such as headaches and fatigue, amongst staff working in high voltage substations. The first important epidemiological study - Wertheimer and Leoper [1979] - demonstrated a risk in Denver for childhood leukaemias, linked to surrogate measures of EMF exposure from overhead lines and household wiring. Following this, some studies have suggested an association between deaths from leukaemia and brain cancer and jobs which are classified under the broad heading of 'electrical', eg radio operators, electricians, cinema projectionists. The studies remain inconclusive in that little is known about this group's actual exposure either to mains frequency electrical or magnetic fields or other environmental factors. To date no study has been able to give an unequivocal answer on the issue (US OTA [1989], Morgan [1989] Savitz et. al.[1989]. Generally, anyone living 200 yards or more from the line is likely to receive more EMF exposure from domestic sources (Decicco et. al. [1992]).

The International Radiation Protection Association (IRPA), acting in conjunction with the World Health Organization (WHO), reviewed the studies in 1989 and concluded that the association was not proven. The UK National Radiological Protection Board (NRPB) agreed with this conclusion and consequently does not advocate any special precautions for people living close to high voltage power lines. However, both IRPA and NRPB recommend that there is a need for further basic research and epidemiological studies. Electric fields from overhead lines are readily screened by buildings, trees and bushes or, much less frequently, by underground, ie installing high voltage underground cables. There is, however, no practical way of screening magnetic fields.

In some instances the installation of power lines could have positive effects on wildlife habitat. The shear clearing through heavily forested areas creates long linear forest openings that are indefinitely maintained to prevent power outages. Sunlight penetrating the forest via the powerline right of way stimulates understorey growth beneficial to the wildlife habitat. Transmission lines can also have adverse impacts on wildlife. For wetland areas there is some evidence to indicate that behaviourial modifications may occur for waterfowl, which could result in absence of birds covering an area within one kilometer of the transmission lines. Direct current transmission could also have effects on migratory birds using magnetic homing.

High tension lines may cause some interference with nearby radio and television reception and may introduce fluctuation on signal strength on windy days or under icy conditions. Tall towers and multiple lines may pose a hazard to air traffic, particularly under conditions of poor visibility, and air traffic terminals need to be suitably located.

It is widely assumed that these environmental impacts can be avoided by underground, ie placing oil-filled cable systems underground. But undergrounding itself has environmental impact. Undergrounding has high heat loss and hence requires wide spacing of cables or heat removal systems. This may require access systems, with consequent environmental problems. Outages are also more serious with undergrounding cables due to problems of access, ie the system is less reliable. Clearly, undergrounding also involves disruption when lines are sunk. In the UK there exist only some 120 km of underground cable, against 9500 km of overhead line.

No valuation studies of the aesthetics of transmission lines appear to exist. In principle, however, visual intrusion should be capable of valuation through contingent valuation. Table 3.2 below sets out some provisional data on the costs of alternative transmission systems in the UK. It is against these costs that any damage reduction should be compared. As yet, then, no reliable information exists by which to estimate a 'transmission adder'. In any event, much of the adder would be common to all fuel cycles, although variations will occur if certain energy sources need specific locations (e.g. wave power).

Table 3.2
Costs of Transmission Systems in the UK

	Per km of line 1991 £ (capital costs only) (3800 mw)	Ratio against lattice system
Lattice tower systems[1]	£ 500,000	1
Folded plate systems[2]	£1,000,000	2
Undergrounding[3]	£8,500,000	17[4]

Source: National Grid Co.

Notes to Table 3.2

1.   400 Kv lattice tower systems are the conventional tower system in the UK, with 7 metre square base, and 360 metres between towers.

2.   400 Kv folded plate systems involve a single solid steel pole with 'arms', with pole diameter of 1.75 metres.   Span between poles is 250 metres - ie there are more towers per km than lattice systems.

3.   Underground cable requires substantial insulation around the current-carrying conductor.   Heat loss across the insulation material may be as much as 40% of the voltage.   Methods have therefore to be found to remove the heat either through wide spacing of cables or water cooling pipes.   The latter option involves a further cost increment of 15.20% on the £8.5 million, ie costs closer to £10 million per km would be appropriate.   Installation of 'reactive compensation' would add a <u>further</u> £800,000 per km.

4.   Ranges from 5-17 depending on voltage and power carried.   The higher end of the range would be relevant for a new major power station in the UK.

3.1. THE COAL FUEL CYCLE

EMISSION/BURDEN/RESIDUAL

IMPACTS

Human Health
- Mortality
- Morbidity

Ecological
- Crops
- Forests
- Commercial fishing
- Recreational fishing
- Recreational forest and parks
- Biodiversity

Social + Economic
- Building materials
- Land
- Water
- Visibility and visual insults
- Noise nuisance
- Public services
- Other quality of life effects

Non-enviromental
- Energy security
- Liability limits
- R + D subsidies
- Administrative cost of energy regulation
- Income and employment effects
- Non-fossil fuel obligation
- Occupational health and safety benefits
- Infrastructure costs

Global
- Global warming

MINING

DEEP MINING
- Acid mine drainage
- Dust
- Noise/vibration blast
- Methane emissions
- Subsidence

SURFACE MINING
- Erosion
- Water consumption
- Dust
- Noise/vibration blast
- Methane emissions

- Siting
- Sedimentation
- Chemical pollutants
- Trace metals
- Duissolved and suspended solids
- Risk of accidents
- Mine spoil

BENEFICATION

COAL WASHING
- Liquid waste/solid waste

COAL DRYING
- Air emissions: SOx, NOx, PM
- Dust

WASTE DISPOSAL
- Leachates

STORAGE
- Siting
- Risk of spontaneous combustion
- Visual impact
- Surface water run off
- Leachates

TRANSPORTATION

RAIL
- Noise
- Risk of accidents

ROAD
- Road wear
- Fugitive coal dust

POWER STATION
- Water disturbance
- Siting
- Thermal pollution
- Solid waste:
  - Fly ash

NO FGD HIGH SULPHUR COAL
- SOx Particles, NOx, CO_2

NO FGD LOW NOx BURNERS
- SOx Particles, NOx, CO_2

NO FGD LOW SULPHUR COAL
- SOx Particles, NOx, CO_2

FGD LOW NOx BURNERS
- SOx Particles, NOx, CO_2
- FGD sludge, Gypsum

FLUIDISED BED COMBUSTION
- SOx Particles, NOx, CO_2

INTEGRATED GASIFICATION COMBINED CYCLE
- SOx Particles, NOx, CO_2

Liquid Effluents:
- Suspended solids
- (H_2SO_4) sulphuric acid
- chlorides
- phosphates, boron
- chromates, organic compounds

TRANSMISSION
- Electromagnetic effects
- Visual intrusion
- Siting

3.2. THE OIL FUEL CYCLE

EMISSION/BURDEN/RESIDUAL

IMPACTS

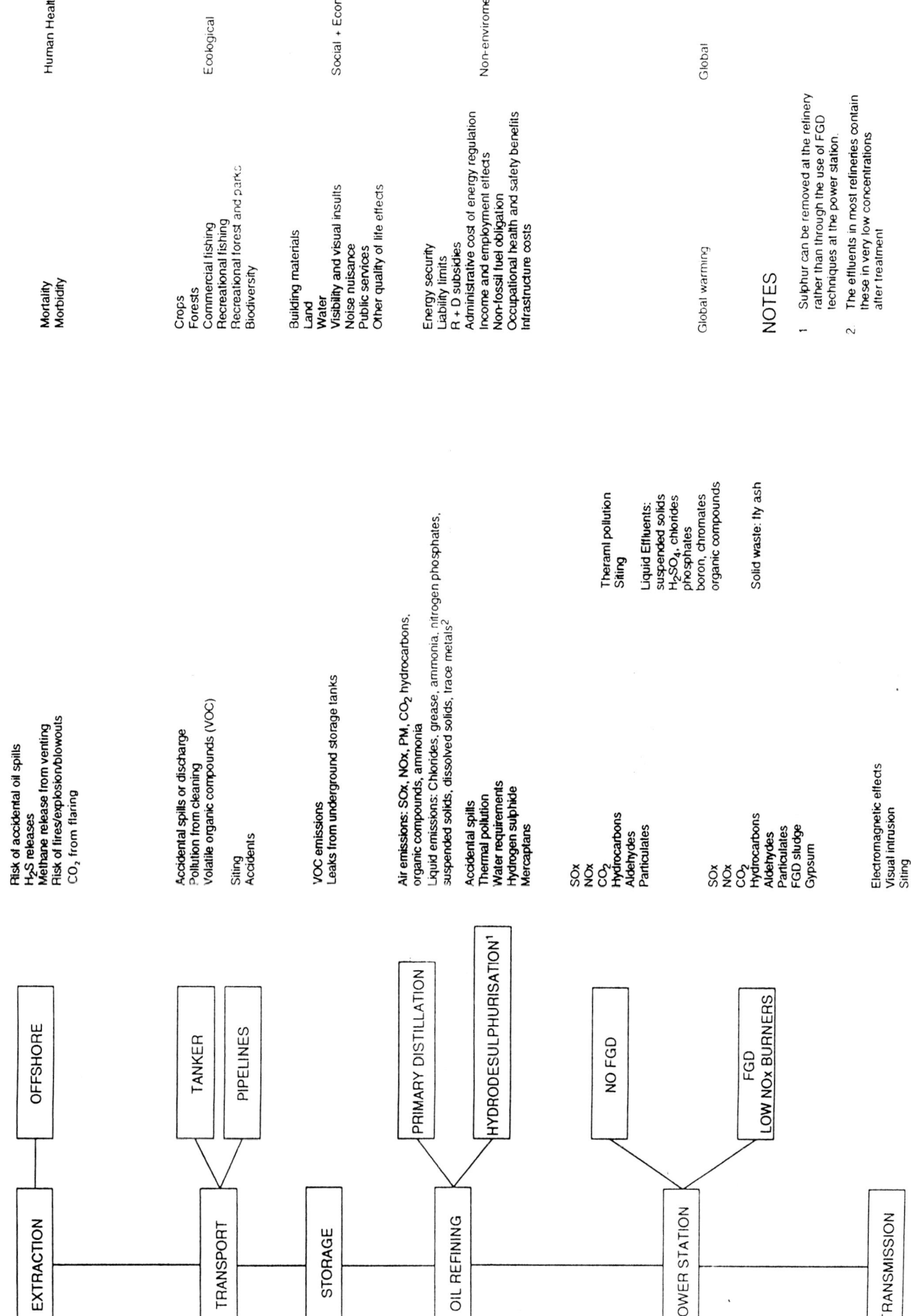

EXTRACTION

OFFSHORE

Risk of accidental oil spills
H₂S releases
Methane release from venting
Risk of fires/explosion/blowouts
CO₂ from flaring

Mortality
Morbidity

Human Health

TRANSPORT

TANKER

PIPELINES

Accidental spills or discharge
Pollution from cleaning
Volatile organic compounds (VOC)

Siting
Accidents

Crops
Forests
Commercial fishing
Recreational fishing
Recreational forest and parks
Biodiversity

Ecological

STORAGE

VOC emissions
Leaks from underground storage tanks

Building materials
Land
Water
Visibility and visual insults
Noise nuisance
Public services
Other quality of life effects

Social + Economic

OIL REFINING

PRIMARY DISTILLATION

HYDRODESULPHURISATION[1]

Air emissions: SOx, NOx, PM, CO₂ hydrocarbons,
organic compounds, ammonia
Liquid emissions: Chlorides, grease, ammonia, nitrogen phosphates,
suspended solids, dissolved solids, trace metals[2]

Accidental spills
Thermal pollution
Water requirements
Hydrogen sulphide
Mercaptans

Energy security
Liability limits
R + D subsidies
Administrative cost of energy regulation
Income and employment effects
Non-fossil fuel obligation
Occupational health and safety benefits
Infrastructure costs

Non-enviromental

POWER STATION

NO FGD

FGD
LOW NOx BURNERS

SOx
NOx
CO₂
Hydrocarbons
Aldehydes
Particulates

SOx
NOx
CO₂
Hydrocarbons
Aldehydes
Particulates
FGD sludge
Gypsum

Theraml pollution
Siting

Liquid Effluents:
suspended solids
H₂SO₄, chlorides
phosphates
boron, chromates
organic compounds

Solid waste: fly ash

Global warming

Global

TRANSMISSION

Electromagnetic effects
Visual intrusion
Siting

NOTES

1   Sulphur can be removed at the refinery
    rather than through the use of FGD
    techniques at the power station.

2   The effluents in most refineries contain
    these in very low concentrations
    after treatment

3.3. THE GAS FUEL CYCLE

EMISSION/BURDEN/RESIDUAL

IMPACTS

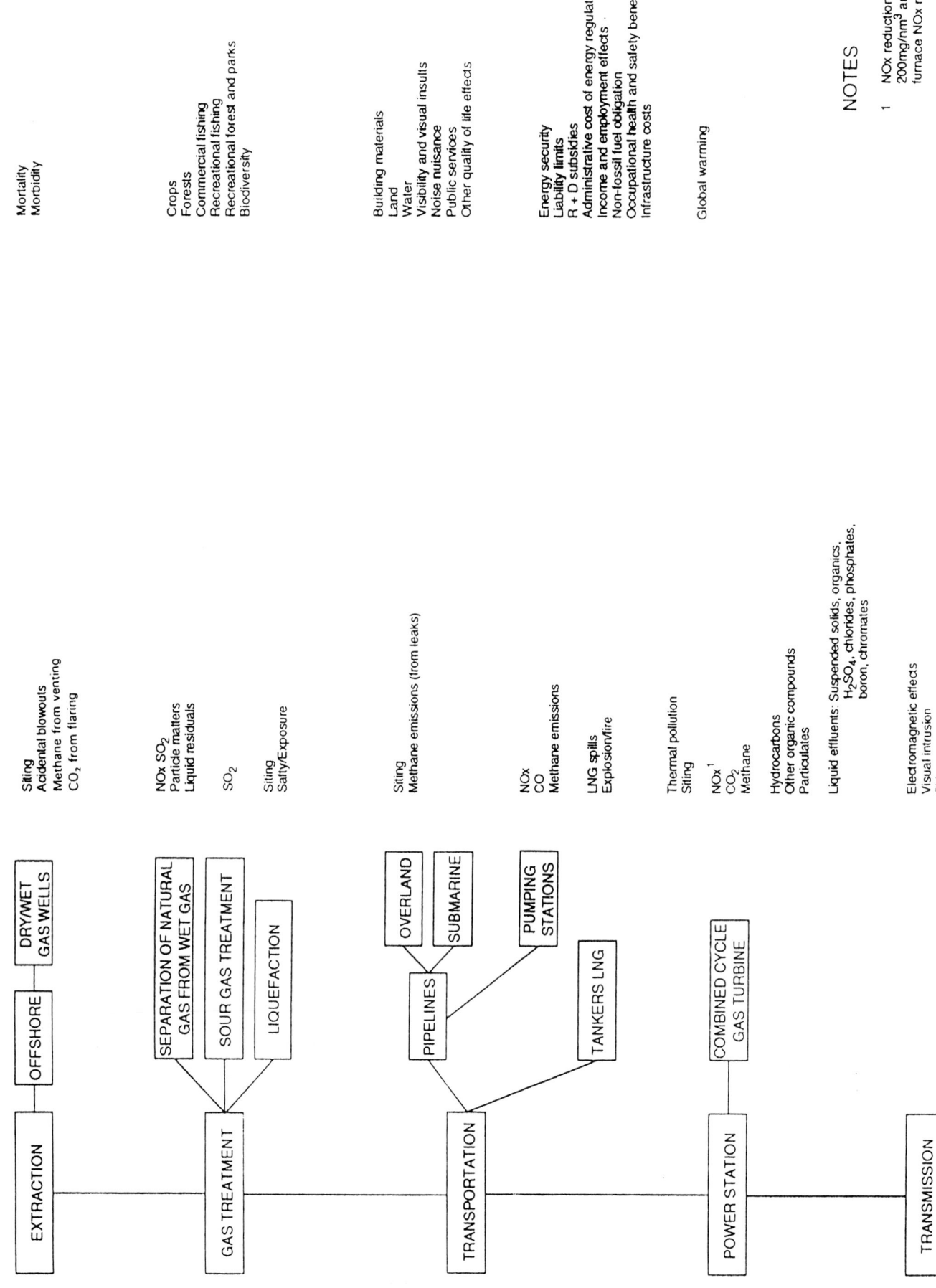

Human Health

Mortality
Morbidity

Ecological

Crops
Forests
Commercial fishing
Recreational fishing
Recreational forest and parks
Biodiversity

Social + Economic

Building materials
Land
Water
Visibility and visual insults
Noise nuisance
Public services
Other quality of life effects

Non-environmental

Energy security
Liability limits
R + D subsidies
Administrative cost of energy regulation
Income and employment effects
Non-fossil fuel obligation
Occupational health and safety benefits
Infrastructure costs

Global

Global warming

NOTES

1 NOx reduction considerably below 200mg/nm^3 are possible using in furnace NOx reduction

EXTRACTION

OFFSHORE
DRY/WET GAS WELLS

Siting
Acidental blowouts
Methane from venting
CO_2 from flaring

GAS TREATMENT

SEPARATION OF NATURAL GAS FROM WET GAS
SOUR GAS TREATMENT
LIQUEFACTION

NOx SO_2
Particle matters
Liquid residuals

SO_2

Siting
Safety/Exposure

TRANSPORTATION

PIPELINES
OVERLAND
SUBMARINE
PUMPING STATIONS
TANKERS LNG

Siting
Methane emissions (from leaks)

NOx
CO
Methane emissions

LNG spills
Explosion/fire

Thermal pollution
Siting

POWER STATION

COMBINED CYCLE GAS TURBINE

NOx^1
CO_2
Methane

Hydrocarbons
Other organic compounds
Particulates

Liquid effluents: Suspended solids, organics, H_2SO_4, chlorides, phosphates, boron, chromates

TRANSMISSION

Electromagnetic effects
Visual intrusion
Siting

3.4. THE NUCLEAR FUEL CYCLE

THE NUCLEAR FUEL CYCLE	EMISSION/BURDEN/RESIDUAL	IMPACTS
MINING — SURFACE, UNDERGROUND, PLACE LEACHING METHODS	Siting Dust Radon emissions Land subsidence Solid wastes Liquid wastes	**Human Health**: Mortality, Morbidity
MILLING — Yellow cake production U_3O_8	Siting Liquid waste SOx, NOx, particles Radioactive airborne particulates + gases Thorium-230, radium-226, natural uranium, radon, radon-222	**Ecological**: Crops, Forests, Commercial fishing, Recreational fishing, Recreational forest and parks, Biodiversity
URANIUM HEXAFLUORIDE PRODUCTION — WET PROCESS, DRY PROCESS	Siting Water effluents: dissolved solids, radium-226, thorium-280, uranium HF Solid waste HF	**Social + Economic**: Building materials, Land, Water, Visibility and visual insults, Noise nuisance, Public services, Other quality of life effects
URANIUM ENRICHMENT — GAS DIFFUSION, CENTRIFUGATION	Particulates NOx SOx CO_2 HF	
FUEL FABRICATION	Particulates NOx SOx CO_2 Hydrogen fluride (air emisson) Nitrogen compounds (liquid effluent) Radioactive waste (mainly low level)	**Non-enviromental**: Energy security, Liability limits, R + D subsidies, Administrative cost of energy regulation, Income and employment effects, Non-fossil fuel obligation, Occupational health and safety benefits, Infrastructure costs
TRANSPORT — ROAD, RAIL, WATER, AIR — Transport of fuel to power station	Accidents	
POWER STATION — MAGNOX REACTORS, ADVANCED GAS COOLED REACTORS, PRESSURISED WATER REACTORS, FAST BREEDER REACTORS	Siting Thermal discharge Risk off reactor accidents Radiological airborne emissions: fission Nobel gases (Kryton, xenon) tritium, carbon-14, iodine 131, 129, particulates Radiological solid waste (in the case of no-recyle option spent fuel elements which contain large quantities of fission products)	**Global**: Global warming
TRANSMISSION	Electromagnetic effects Visual intrusion Siting	

THE NUCLEAR FUEL CYCLE cont,d

EMISSION/BURDEN/RESIDUAL

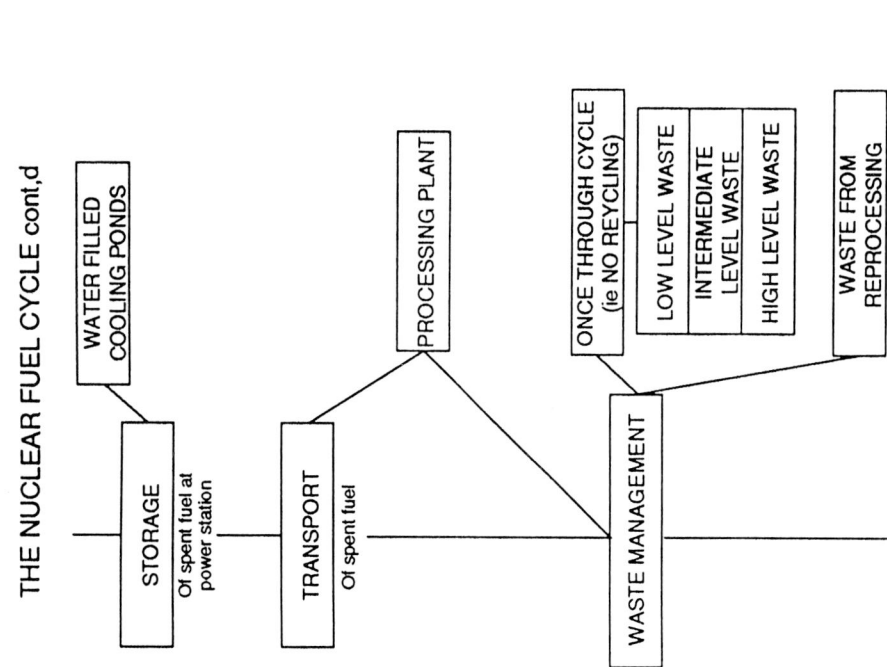

Atmospheric discharges: H-3, C-H, KT-85, 1-129, tritium

Liquid discharges (to sea): CS-134/137 , ST-90, tritium, 1-129
Risk of weapon proliferation
Risk of accident
Thermal pollution

Siting
Water emissions
Effluents from electricity generation:
SOx, NOx, ,hydrocarbons, CO, particulates

Radioactive effluents:
Airborne: Rn-222, Th-230, U, Tritium, Kr-85, 1-129, C-14

Liquid: Uranium daughters, fission + activation productions

Low level miscellaneous waste
Spent fuel
Fission products: TRU, βTRU

Non-radioactive solids
Calcined high level wastes
Fission products: TRU, βTRU
Miscellaneous transuranic solids

Activated material
Contaminated material
Radioactive wastes
Spent fuel

TRU material
Non-TRU material

STORAGE — Of spent fuel at power station

WATER FILLED COOLING PONDS

TRANSPORT — Of spent fuel

PROCESSING PLANT

ONCE THROUGH CYCLE (ie NO REYCLING)
- LOW LEVEL WASTE
- INTERMEDIATE LEVEL WASTE
- HIGH LEVEL WASTE

WASTE FROM REPROCESSING
- LOW LEVEL WASTE
- INTERMEDIATE LEVEL WASTE
- HIGH LEVEL WASTE

WASTE MANAGEMENT

POWER STATION

DECOMMISSIONING

REPROCESSING PLANT

3.5. THE WIND FUEL CYCLE

EMISSION/BURDEN/RESIDUAL

IMPACTS

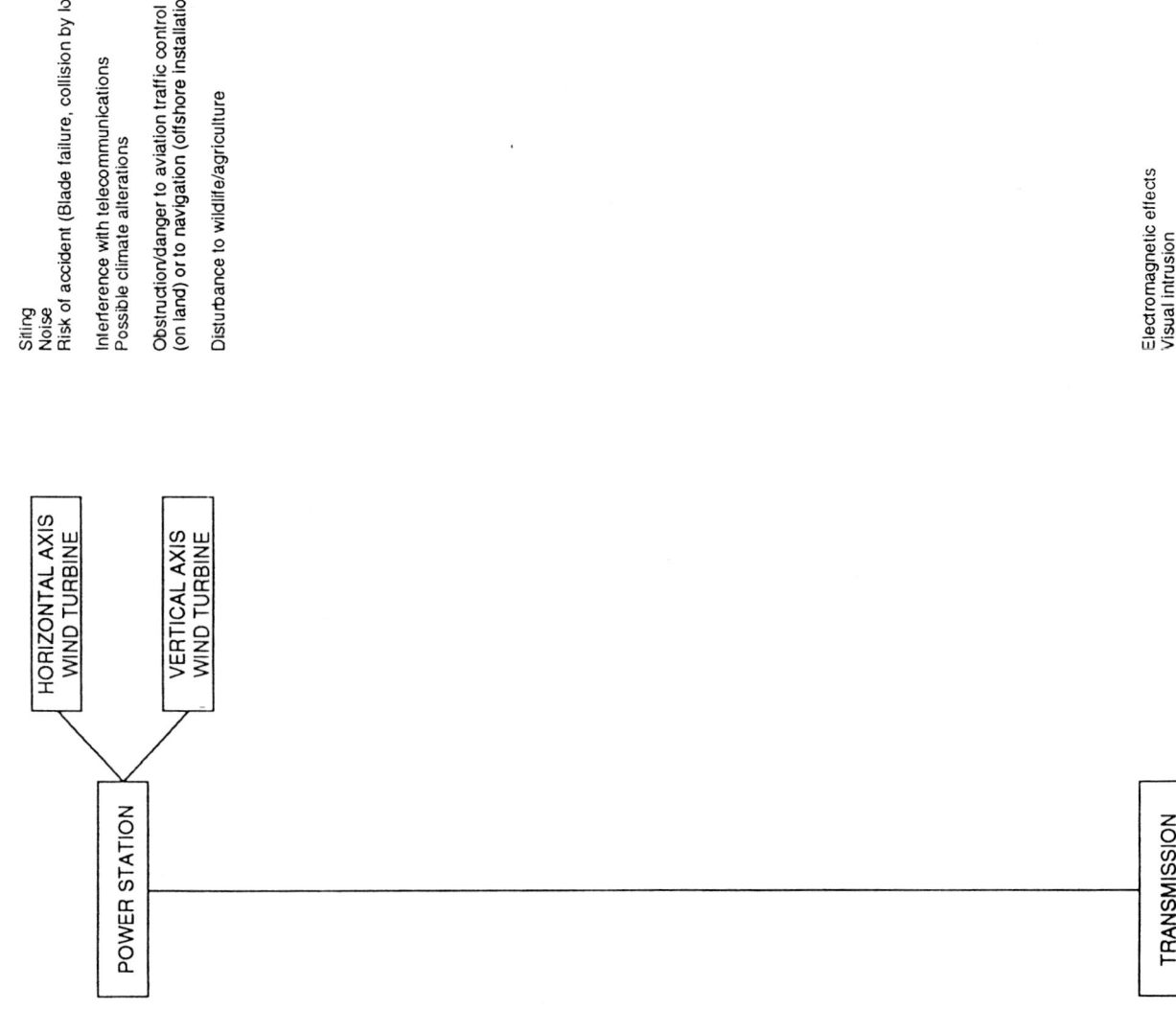

HORIZONTAL AXIS WIND TURBINE

VERTICAL AXIS WIND TURBINE

POWER STATION

TRANSMISSION

Siting
Noise
Risk of accident (Blade failure, collision by low-flying aircraft)

Interference with telecommunications
Possible climate alterations

Obstruction/danger to aviation traffic control
(on land) or to navigation (offshore installations)

Disturbance to wildlife/agriculture

Electromagnetic effects
Visual intrusion
Siting

Human Health

Mortality
Morbidity

Social + Economic

Land
Water
Visual insults
Noise nuisance
Impact on wildlife/agriculture

Non-enviromental

Energy security (+)
Income and employment (+?)
NFFO

3.6. LANDFILL GAS FUEL CYCLE

EMISSION/BURDEN/RESIDUAL

IMPACTS

LANDFILL SITE

Siting
Storage and handling of waste
Slurry
Risk of gas leaks/explosion/fires

Mortality
Morbidity

Human Health

LANDFILL GAS EXTRACTION

Hydrogen sulphide
Noise

Land
Water
Odour

Social + Economic

Energy security
Income and employment

Non-enviromental

ELECTRICITY GENERATION

Mercaptons
Hydrocarbons
NOx, SO$_2$

TRANSMISSION

Electromagnetic effects
Visual intrusion
Siting

NOTES

1. Studies indicate that waste to energy plants have externality values similar to or greater than coal-fired plants meeting NSPS standards.

2. The use of landfill gases in electricity generation reduces methane emissions from landfill sites, this is a positive externality.

3.7. GEOTHERMAL ENERGY

EMISSION/BURDEN/RESIDUAL

IMPACTS

EXTRACTION		Human Health
		Mortality
		Morbidity

EXTRACTION

- DRY STEAM FIELDS
- HYDROTHERMAL AQUIFERS
- WET STEAM (HOT BRINE) FIELDS
- HOT DRY ROCK
- GEOPRESSURISED

Brine disposal
Land subsidence
Noise pollution

Water use

Possible ecological impacts from air pollution and water pollution — Ecological

POWER STATION

- FLASHED STEAM GEOTHERMAL POWER CYCLE
  - GEOTHERMAL FLUIDS
  - SEPARATOR
  - SPENT FLUIDS
  - TURBINE
  - CONDENSER
  - NON-CONDENSING GASES
  - COOLING TOWER
- BINARY-FLUID POWER-CYCLE

Noise pollution

Liquid effluents

Dissolved solids (sodium chloride, sodium sulphate, potassium chloride, calcium carbonate) heavy metals, mercury, arsenic

Gas emissions:
CO2, methane, hydrogen sulphide, ammonia, nitrogen, hydrogen
(Minor emissions: benzene, mercury, radon, boron)

Siting

Visual insults
Noise nuisance — Social + Economic

Energy security (+)
Income and employment effects (+) — Non-environmental

TRANSMISSION

Electromagnetic effects
Visual intrusion
Siting

3.8. TIDAL ENERGY

EMISSION/BURDEN/RESIDUAL

IMPACTS

BARRAGE

TIDAL RESERVOIR

Siting

Disruption of spawning areas/pathways crucial for fish migration

Disruption of breeding zones for aquatic organisms (crustacea, shellfish)

Disruption of habitats + nesting places of water birds

Impairment of navigation/recreation

Build up of particulates/nutrients from upstream behind dam

Human Health

Mortality
Morbidity

POWER STATION

EBB GENERATION

EBB GEBERATION WITH PUMPING

Substantial modifications in flow patterns altering rates of erosion/sedimentation in bay

Loss of inter-tidal areas

Reduced inundation of saltmarsh

Disruption of mudflats/wetlands

Problems of land drainage + sewage

A tidal station at the mouth of a river can block the flow of polluted water into the sea

Ecological

Commercial fishing
Recreational fishing
Biodiversity loss (especially migratory birds)
Water-based recreation (+/-)
(Loss of recreation from water pollution and from water relocation)

Social and Economic

Tourism (+/-)
Infrastructure
(free river crossing)

TRANSMISSION

Electromagnetic effects
Visual intrusion
Siting

NOTE

1. The impact of any tidal energy sceheme is extremely site dependent.

EMISSION/BURDEN/RESIDUAL

IMPACTS

Human Health

Mortality
Morbidity

Ecological

Biodiversity (+/-)
Crops
Forests
Commercial fishing
Recreational fishing (+/-)
Recreational forests and parks (+/-)

Social and Economic

Land
Water
Visibility and visual insults
(Public services)
Other quality of life effects

DAM

RESERVOIR

Land irreversibly flooded

Siltation of catchment area of reservoir

Thermal stratification

Microclimate changes

Deleterious effects on migratory species: both anadromous/catadromous

Natural vegetation of shorelines (both reservoir and river) destroyed/radically changed

Proliferation of aquatic weeds/eutrophication

Risk of dam rupture

Seismic activities

Landslides

Visual

Free water flowing downstream of dam

PENSTOCK PIPE

TURBINE

GENERATOR

POWER STATION

TRANSMISSION

Electromagnetic effects
Visual intrusion
Siting

NOTES

1. The effects of large and small hydro dams are very different eg small schemes may not require a reservoir and the flooding of land. No further large scale hydro dams are planned for the UK.

2. It is not always easy or possible to ascribe the different environment implications to specific purposes of water development ie to flow regulation or power generation

3. A number of positive externalities may accompany a hydroelectric power scheme, eg the reservoir created by damming rivers can act as effective flood barriers. Further, reservoirs can become tourist and sporting attractions and provide habitat for different species of wildlife.

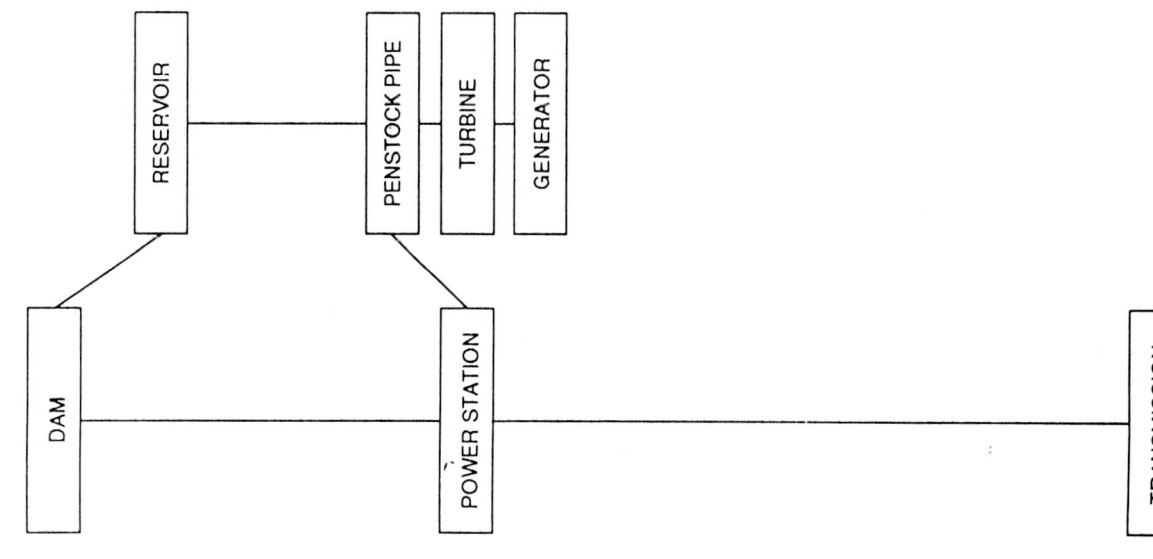

3.10. WAVE ENERGY

EMISSION/BURDEN/RESIDUAL

IMPACTS

WAVE ENERGY CONVERSION
- MOVEABLE BODY
- OSCILLATING WATER COLUMN
- DIAPHRAGM

POWER GENERATION

Impairment of reproductive environment of fish and aquatic life

Effects on the sedimentation rate on shores and beaches

Hazards for navigation

Visual (onshore)

Anti-fouling paint

Destruction of habitat amenity (on shore)

TRANSMISSION

Electromagnetic effects
Visual intrusion
Siting

IMPACTS

Human Health
- **Mortality**
- **Morbidity**

Ecological
- Biodiversity

Social and Economic
- Visual insults (-)
- Navigation (-)

NOTES

1. The effects of onshore/offshore schemes are very different

2. Although in general the environmental impacts of wave energy schemes seem relatively benign, further experience is necessary to have a full appreciation of these impacts. The practical difficulties of maintaining large scale wave devices in an extremely hostile and corrosive environment are enormous.

3. Secondary useful applications of wave energy conversion systems could also be found such as camping down the waves in harbour areas or in zones where wave erosion is a problem.

4. It has been argued that a wave scheme would be useful in the west Isles as beaches are disappearing and increased sedimentation would help

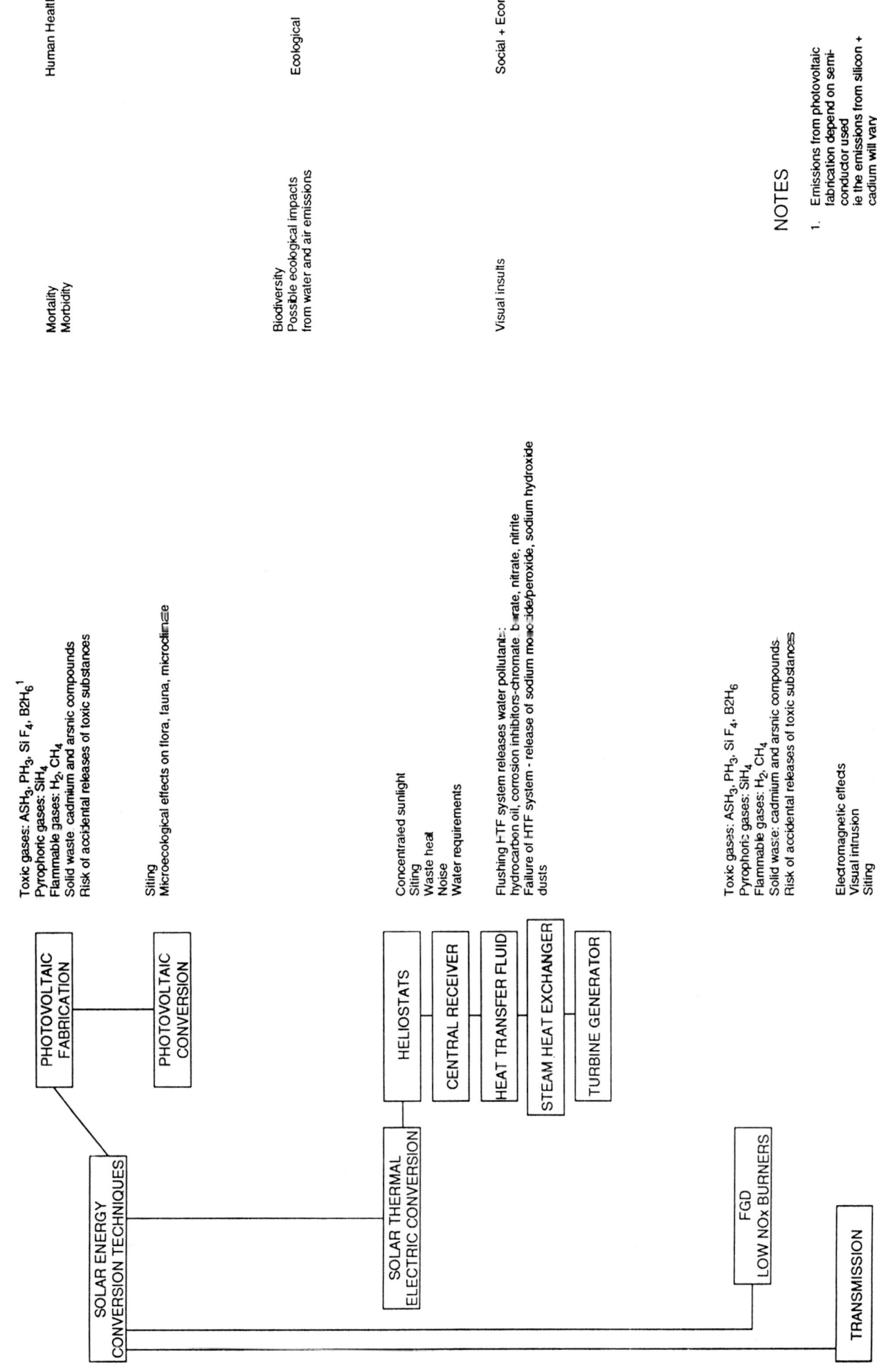

3.11. SOLAR ENERGY

EMISSION/BURDEN/RESIDUAL

IMPACTS

PHOTOVOLTAIC FABRICATION

Toxic gases: ASH_3, PH_3, $Si F_4$, $B2H_6$[1]
Pyrophoric gases: SiH_4
Flammable gases: H_2, CH_4
Solid waste cadmium and arsnic compounds
Risk of accidental releases of toxic substances

PHOTOVOLTAIC CONVERSION

Siting
Microecological effects on flora, fauna, microclimate

HELIOSTATS

Concentrated sunlight
Siting
Waste heat
Noise
Water requirements

CENTRAL RECEIVER

HEAT TRANSFER FLUID

Flushing HTF system releases water pollutants:
hydrocarbon oil, corrosion inhibitors-chromate borate, nitrate, nitrite
Failure of HTF system - release of sodium monoxide/peroxide, sodium hydroxide
dusts

STEAM HEAT EXCHANGER

TURBINE GENERATOR

FGD
LOW NOx BURNERS

Toxic gases: ASH_3, PH_3, $Si F_4$, $B2H_6$
Pyrophoric gases: SiH_4
Flammable gases: H_2, CH_4
Solid waste: cadmium and arsnic compounds
Risk of accidental releases of toxic substances

TRANSMISSION

Electromagnetic effects
Visual intrusion
Siting

SOLAR ENERGY CONVERSION TECHNIQUES

SOLAR THERMAL ELECTRIC CONVERSION

Human Health

Mortality
Morbidity

Ecological

Biodiversity
Possible ecological impacts
from water and air emissions

Social + Economic

Visual insults

NOTES

1. Emissions from photovoltaic
   fabrication depend on semi-
   conductor used
   ie the emissions from silicon +
   cadium will vary

3.12. COMBINED HEAT AND POWER
(CHP)

EMISSION/BURDEN/RESIDUAL

IMPACTS

Extraction →

Transport to
Power Station

```
┌──────────────┐
│ COAL         │
│ OIL          │
│ GAS          │
│ LANDFILL     │
└──────────────┘
```

As reported for Coal, Oil, Gas, and Landfill fuel cycles (see 3.1, 3.2, 3.3, 3.6)

As for alternative energy source,
(see 3.1, 3.2, 3.3, 3.6)
but reduced by approximately
one half.

```
┌──────────────┐
│ POWERSTATION │
└──────────────┘
```

Primary energy saving with CHP 30-40%.
Because of this change in the efficiency of
electricity produced, emissions at the power station
stage of production are scaled down
(see 3.1, 3.2, 3.3, 3.6)

```
┌──────────────┐
│ TRANSMISSION │
└──────────────┘
```

Electromagnetic effects
Visual intrusion
Siting

CHAPTER 4 HUMAN HEALTH

4.1 Voluntary and Involuntary Risk

Energy production and transport and electricity transmission have health impacts ranging from minor morbidity, through accidents to mortality. The issue of valuation of these impacts is complicated by a number of factors. One such issue is that health damage may be the result of a <u>voluntarily</u> assumed risks <u>involuntary</u> risk.

Observing the presence of <u>damage</u> does not necessarily imply that an <u>externality</u> exists. The most notable and relevant example of this concerns health and mortality risks in energy extraction and production. Consider, for example, the case of accidents.

Table 4.1 shows the number of reported fatalities and other accidents by main industrial sector in 1988/9 in the UK. The energy sector accounts for some 33% of all occupational fatalities, 6% of major accidents, and 8% of accidents involving incapacity beyond 3 days. The occupational fatality figure in 1988/9 is unusually large due to the Piper Alpha disaster: the previous year's figure would make energy account for only 7% of all occupational fatalities.

Table 4.1
Accidents at Work 1988/9

	Fatalities	Major Accidents	Over 3 days work absence
Agriculture	46	583	1615
Energy	203	1210	12456
of which:			
Extraction			
coal mining	(21)	(769)	(6427)
oil/gas	(172)	(64)	(692)
nuclear fuels	(0)	(12)	(313)
Electricity Dist	(8)	(324)	(4721)
Manufacturing	102	7514	56269
Construction	137	3660	17566
Transport, Services and other	122	8129	76716
Total	610	21096	164622

Source: <u>Annual Abstract of Statistics 1991</u>, Table 3.35.

Taking the figures for 1988/9, the 203 fatalities would, if the Department of Transport 'values of life' of £0.5 million are used (see section 4.3) indicate a social cost of £101 million on this count alone, and $406 million at a 'value of life' of £2 million.

How far are occupational and actual risks truly internalised by the wage-setting process?

The answer to this question has to be determined by inspecting the literature on hedonic wages. If risks are internalised we would expect wage equations of the form:

$$W = a + \Sigma_i\, b_i x_i + cF + dN + \mu$$

where a,b,c,d = constants

> x^i = job and person characteristics (age, education, nature of occupation, degree of unionisation etc)
> F = risk of mortality
> N = risk of non fatal injury
> μ = error term)

to reveal a statistically significant coefficient for c and d. Note that the resulting values for c are not 'values of life' but risk-money trade-off values, although the coefficient c is widely referred to as the implicit 'value of a life'. The evidence on the values of c and d is reviewed below.

Even where there are meaningful coefficients relating risk to earnings it may not be possible to use those values in energy related contexts where the risk is borne by the <u>population at large</u>. This is because wage-risk coefficients value <u>voluntary risk</u> whereas the population at large can generally be thought of as being exposed to <u>imposed risks</u>, i.e. risks over which they generally have little or no control. Even here the issue is fuzzy. Individuals choosing to locate their homes near a nuclear power station or near a transmission line could be argued to have internalised perceived risks and disamenity in the prices of property. A hedonic property price analysis of risks may therefore pick up these valuations, i.e. the property price differential may 'embody' many types of externality. This is not an argument against using property price studies to evaluate energy social costs, but it is a caution against oversimplified use of such valuations without analyzing what they reflect.

More seriously, however, if individuals value imposed and voluntary risk differently, then the use of wage-risk coefficients in imposed risk contexts could be seriously misleading. The available evidence suggests that involuntary risks are valued very much higher than voluntary risks. Figure 4.1 repeats a well known diagram introduced by Starr [1976] in which available evidence is used judgementally to define risk and benefit trade-offs. For current purposes the relevant magnitude is the horizontal distance between the 'voluntary' trade-off function and the 'involuntary' one. By reading from left to right it can be seen that risk valuations differ by a factor of around 10, i.e. involuntary risks might be valued 10 times more than voluntary risks. Litai [1980] has suggested that the difference might be up to 100 times more.

The final issue in this context concerns <u>levels</u> of risk.

Pollution exposure is usually related to low probabilities of death, although these probabilities may affect large number of people. Thus, typical exposure to radiation is at very low levels and the consequent probability of death is very low. This exposure may be very limited- say to small groups of workers in nuclear power plants, or local populations in the neighbourhood of such plants. Sulphur oxide pollution, however can have similar low probabilities of death associated with it, but can relate to very large populations, whole cities for example. This suggests that the relevant values of life are those relating to low probabilities of death. The empirical literature suggests that low probabilities may be associated with high values of life - see Figure 4.2. If this is correct, it places a high value on policies which set out to prevent pollution damage rather than remedial policies which deal with the consequences of the event through the health care of the sick. Not only is the policy implication important, but this result contradicts the expectations literature. The theory would suggests that higher values of life are associated with higher risks of death (Rosen [1981]).

Once again, therefore, there are problems of taking valuations in one context and applying them to another one.

4.2 Estimating Health Adders

The human health impacts of fuel cycles are significant components of the available aggregate assessments of environmental damage[1]. As such it is important to understand how the various impacts are derived. The procedure required is as follows:

a) estimate mortality/morbidity due to given pollution concentration (dose-response function - M/C)

b) estimate emission - concentration function C/E, to derive mortality/morbidity per unit of emission - M/C. C/E = M/E.

c) value mortality/morbidity by a value of statistical life and value of morbidity V to obtain health damage per unit of emission V. M/E = D/E

d) relate emissions to electricity technology to get total health damage due to that technology D/E.E/Ti = D/Ti.

In practice, steps a) and b) are often fused in studies of average damage cost owing to the difficulty of integrating diffusion models into the estimates. For any <u>new</u> capacity, however, this step should be undertaken, using a 'representative site'.

The major uncertainties surrounding the health impacts of fuel cycles relate not to the economics, although there is uncertainty in the valuation procedures, but in estimating dose-response functions. Ricci [1990] surveys the health effects of air pollution literature and finds substantial variation in estimates. Unfortunately, inspection of Ricci's literature base suggests that it is mainly related to the statistical studies carried out in the 1970s. Despite the variation found, Ricci concludes that dose-response functions can be used with some degree of confidence.

4.3 Health Risks from Fuel Cycles

Fritzsche [1989] has provided a very useful survey of health risks from fuel cycles. He surveys the literature, assesses its reliability and provides 'consensus' values for mortality risks from 'routine' emissions and accidents. While he surveys the major accident literature as well, it is not possible to derive similar summary statistics per gigawatt year. Hence we treat major accidents separately later in the chapter. Fritzsche's results are presented in diagrammatic form. Table 4.2 summarises the 'best estimates', but there is room for interpretation of Fritzsce's approach. Note that Fritzsche's estimates <u>include power station construction impacts</u>.

Table 4.2
<u>Fritzsche's Estimate of Mortality Risks</u>
<u>From Electricity Fuel Cycles</u>
(deaths per GW year (e))
(Risks relate to new power units)

Fuel Cycle	Occupational Risk		Public Risk		Total
	Acute	Delayed	Acute	Delayed	
Coal	1	0.1	0.5	8	9.600
Oil	0.8	0	0.01	8	8.810
Gas	0.5	0	0.10	0.05	0.650
Solar-th	1	0	0.10	1	2.100
Solar-PV	1	0	1.0	1	3.000
Wind	1	0	0.1	0.1	1.200
PWR	0.2	0.1	0.005	0.05	0.355
Hydro	1	0	0.005	0.01	1.015

Source: Fritzsche [1989]. The original estimates are in diagrammatic form and show ranges.

4.4 The Value of a Statistical Life

Often misleadingly called the 'value of life', the value of a statistical life measures society's WTP to reduce risks of death or its WTA compensation to tolerate risks. This value has nothing to do with the value of avoiding <u>certain</u> death. The valuations in question are for small changes in risk. For example, a value of £10 to reduce a 1/100,000 chance of death translates to £10 x 100,000 = £1 million if the lives of 100,000 people are affected by this risk. For 100,000 people, a risk of 1/100,000 means that, statistically, one person will die. The £1 million tends therefore to be expressed in terms of the one statistical death - the 'value of human life' - which gives rise to much of the misunderstanding about economic procedures for dealing with fatality risks.

Various reviews of statistical life valuations exist (Miller [1990], Fisher et al [1989]). Ives et al.[1991] have reviewed 46 studies of statistical life valuation (SLVs)[1]. Table 4.4 repeats

---

[1]   Their draft paper states that their review covers 78 studies but 46 separate estimates are recorded, plus three references to surveys.

their 46 findings with the valuations re-expressed in £1991 but rounded, and with the addition of 8 studies they did not detect (two of the Ives cited studies are conflated here) to give 53 separate studies. Table 4.4 also classifies the studies by the type of methodology used.

The resulting averages are of considerable interest and are set out in Table 4.3

Table 4.3

<u>Summary Value for Statistical Lives</u>

	'UK'	USA
	£m1991	
Wage-Risk	2.0-2.5	2.5-3.9
CVM	2.9-4.5	1.0-1.8
Market	0.5-2.4	0.7-0.8
Average	1.8-3.1	1.4-2.0

Several observations can be made. First, the range is fairly narrow, with values of £1.8-3.1 million overall average for the UK and £1.4-2.0 million in the USA. Second, the US values appear to lie <u>below</u> the UK values, which might appear counter-intuitive given the income differences. However, a full meta-analysis (see chapter 14) would be needed to establish the explanation for the variance. For example, it is known that valuations vary with the level of risk and this is not shown separately in Table 4.4. Third, there is not a major difference between estimates derived by different techniques. The possible exception is the market approach (based on implicit valuations shown through purchase of risky or safe products -e.g. seat belts), but the UK studies all relate to the 1970s, so that recent work incorporating more modern research approaches is not represented here. Fourth, the valuations can be compared to the UK Department of Transport 'value of statistical life' of £0.5 million. Only the (outdated) UK market valuations support this estimate: all others are well above this value. A valuation of £1.5 million would seem fairly conservative. Fifth, the PACE [1990] fuel cycle study uses a valuation of $4million (1989 prices) for a statistical life, i.e. around £2.3 million. This seems to be well supported by the estimates in Table 4.3.

Table 4.4

Empirical Estimates of Statistical Life Valuation

Wage-Risk		Year	£1991million
UK	Melinek	74	0.5
UK	Veljanovski	78	5.0-7.0
UK	Needleman	80	0.2
UK	Marin et al.	82	2.2-2.5
			_____
average UK wage-risk			2.0-2.5
			_____
US	Smith (R)	74	7.4-14.0
US	Thaler/Rosen	76	0.6
US	Smith (R)	76	3.5
US	Viscusi	78	1.2-3.6
US	Dillingham	79	0.4-1.3
US	Brown	80	1.7
US	Viscusi	80	2.5-6.9
US	Viscusi	81	3.4-6.0
US	Olson	81	7.2
US	Arnould et al.	83	0.6
US	Low/McPheters	83	0.6
US	Dorsey/Walzer	83	5.5
US	Smith (V)	83	1.6-4.9
US	Dickens	84	1.6-1.9
US	Smith(V) et al	84	4.2-5.0
US	Leigh/Folsom	84	4.6-6.0
US	Dillingham	85	1.4-4.0
US*	Gegax	85	1.1-1.4
US	Leigh	87	3.7-7.0
US	Viscusi/Moore	88	0.9-1.1
US	Garen	88	3.5
US	Cousineau	88	0.7-2.2
US	Viscusi/Moore	89	1.0-4.8
US	Blomquist	90	1.3
			_____
average US wage-risk			2.5-3.9
			_____

CVM Studies**

UK	Melinek	73	0.3
UK	Jones-Lee	76	9.2-11.4
UK	Maclean	79	3.1
UK	Frankel	79	3.1-12.5
UK	Jones-Lee	85	0.8-3.4
SWE*	Persson	89	1.6-1.9
AU+*	Maier	89	1.9

average 'UK' CVM   2.9-4.5

US	Acton	73	0.08
US	Landefeld	79	1.7
US*	Mitchell/Carson	86	0.1-1.8
US*	Smith et al.	87	neg-1.4
US*	Gerking et al.	88	1.8-4.5
US	Viscusi/Magat	89	1.6
US*	Magat et al.	90	1.5

average US CVM   1.0-1.8

Consumer Market Studies

UK	Melinek	74	0.2-0.5
UK	Ghosh	75	0.5
UK	Jones-Lee	77	0.6-6.6
UK	Blomquist	79	0.6-2.1

average UK Market   0.5-2.4

US	Dardis	80	0.3-0.5
US	Portney	81	0.2
US	Landefeld etal.	82	0.6
US	Jondrow	83	0.5
US	Ippolitos	84	0.2-0.5
US	Winston et al.	84	1.0
US*	Garbacz	89	1.9

average US market   0.7-0.8

* not surveyed in Ives et al.
** includes contingent ranking methods
+ Austria

4.5 Morbidity and Non-Fatal Injury

Unfortunately, morbidity valuation has been the subject of a smaller literature than the so-called 'value of life'. Moreover, what literature there is cannot be readily summarised in a form that permits the use of transferable values of injuries of differing gradations of seriousness, or of lost days of normal activity. Cropper and Freeman [1991] have brought together various estimates of (median) WTP to avoid a 'symptom day'. These are shown in Table 4.5. The WTPs are fairly similar across the different symptoms, but vary significantly by study. As yet then the possibility of transferability to other forms of illness does not look feasible.

Table 4.5

Value of a Symptom Day
(1984 US$)
Study

		Tolley	Loehman	Dickie
Symptom:	cough	11	4.4	1
	sinusitis	14	6	3.5
	short breath	-	8	0

Source: Cropper and Freeman [1991]

Pearce and Knight [1989] have surveyed the available non-fatal injury literature. They suggest that a full non-fatal injury valuation requires an estimate of:

NFIV = Private Value + Altruistic Value + Incidental Costs

or   NFIV = WTPi + WTPo + COI

where:
   private value is the individual's own WTP to avoid the illness or injury, and would be estimated by contingent valuation or avertive behaviour models;

   altruistic value is the value placed by others on the individual's wellbeing -i.e. their valuation of avoiding injury or illness in others. This could be estimated by contingent valuation;

   incidental costs refer to the costs borne by society because of the individual's illness or injury. This is the traditional 'cost of illness' approach.

Cropper and Krupnick [1989] show that, as in the equation above, cost of illness should be added to WTPi provided WTPi is not partially internalised in private medical and accident insurance payments. Pearce and Night's review of the literature suggests strongly that WTPi > COI. See also Berger [1987]. Some authorities have suggested doubling COI estimates to obtain the non-altruism element of the NFIV.

There is very little work on altruistic valuations (WTPo) but Viscusi, Margat and Forrest [1988] show that WTPo tends to decline with distance from the individual affected - as one would expect -but that total altruistic value could be 5-6 times WTPi. If borne out by other studies, this result would have dramatic effects on morbidity and mortality valuations. UK work by Needleman [1976] and Jones-Lee et al. [1985] suggests, however, that altruistic value is around 40-50% of WTPi. Jones-Lee [1989] has shown that it is right to include altruistic value if and only if the altruism is directed at individual i's survival prospects.

Pearce and Knight [1989] also suggest speculatively that the literature can be construed as showing the following relationship:

$$NFIVi = 0.01 \text{ FIV to } 0.08 \text{ FIV}$$

where FIV is the value of a statistical life. Section 4.4 lent support for FIV values of some £2 million, so that the NFIV/FIV ratio above would support values of £20,000-160,000 for NFIV. This range may be compared with the UK Department of Transport's use of just over £15,000 for a serious injury, most of which is 'pain' -i.e. should relate to WTPi rather than COI. Slight injuries are valued at some £300, £200 of which is due to pain. Using Krupnick's suggested values per symptom-day, this would amount to, say, 20 days of suffering.

Overall, the valuation of morbidity and injury remains an unsatisfactory area of research in terms of externality adders. PACE [1990] uses a value of statistical life of $4 million and an arbitrary 10% of this, $400,000 for morbidity and non-fatal accidents. On the basis of the previous discussion the latter figure may well be too high.

4.6   Risk Factors: Dose-Response Functions for Emissions

As noted in Section 4.2 the first step in estimating health damage is to derive the risk factor linking exposure to pollution and health effects. There are many studies of risk factors but few that bring different estimates together. Table 4.6 shows one set of estimates by Mendelsohn [1980], but these are already dated given the additional research done in the 1980s. The PACE [1990] study has been criticised for reliance upon these early dose-response functions. Thus, the response to SO_2 and sulphates is unlikely to be so high relative to particulates. Ozone is also not represented and is now thought to be a significant factor in some health damage. The data are shown here to illustrate the methodology rather than to offer the estimates as being reliable.

Table 4.6

Mendelsohn's Dose-Response Functions

Mortality in 10^{-4} deaths per $\mu g/m^3$

Morbidity in 10^{-6} cases per $\mu g/m^3$

	SO2	SO4	NO2	Nitrate	Partic.
Mortality					
M 18-44	0.5	20	3	-20	1.5
M 45-64	20	500	-30	-150	-1
F 18-44	1	11	0	5	0.3
F 45-64	20	320	-25	170	1
Morbidity					
Bronchitis	-9	4470	0	0	360
Lower resp.	75	792	0	0	0
Croup	750	792	0	0	0
Pneumonia	13	500	0	0	0
Acute	4	45	0	0	7

Source: Mendelsohn [1980] M = male, f = female

PACE (1990) review various dose-response functions for the USA, including some for a hypothetical new plant in western Washington. Clearly, however, the resulting risk factors cannot be transferred to other sites without knowing population density, population age-structure, and airshed factors that are likely to affect the relationship between emissions and ambient concentrations. Put another way, we cannot answer the question of the 'value' of damage from a hypothetical new generating plant somewhere in the UK without knowing these factors. What PACE [1990] sets out to do it to take risk factors from various studies, each of which relates to a different location and hence each of which has a different implicit emissions-concentration relationship, and select the 'best' starting point estimate on a judgmental basis. In practice, their chosen estimates are heavily influenced by a set of studies by ECO consultants since those studies relate to the hypothetical new plant that PACE are interested in. With some exceptions, PACE's 'starting point' risk factors are the ECO estimates for a fossil fuel plant. Table 4.7 illustrates their procedure for SO2. The Table shows results in terms of costs per 1lb of SO2. For example, the $1.72 /1lb mortality figure and the $0.05/1lb morbidity figure are derived by taking the ECO study estimate of 20.7

deaths and 5.9 'morbidity units'[2] for the ambient concentration of SO2. Each death is valued at $4m and each morbidity unit at $0.4m. So mortality damage is $82.8 m and morbidity damage is $2.36m. The ECO study estimated annual emissions giving rise to the resulting concentrations at 24,040 US tons or 48.08 million lbs. This gives $1.72 and $0.05 per lb of SO2 emitted.

4.7   Risk Factors: Nuclear Power

A virtual 'industry' has grown up around the risk factors associated with routine and non-routine radiation hazards from the nuclear power industry (see, for example, Inhaber [1978], Holdren et al [1979]. PACE [1990] review a number of estimates relating to:

Routine Radiation Releases
> occupational immediate mortality
> occupational latent mortality
> occupational morbidity
> public mortality
> public morbidity
> genetic disorders

Non-Routine Releases (i.e. accidents).

---

[2]. A morbidity unit is defined as 200 x 3 day short illnesses, i.e. 5.9 units is 1180 x 3 day illnesses or 3540 illness-days. Each unit is 600 days of illness and each unit is valued at $400,000, suggesting a 'symptom day' value of $666 which, as noted earlier, is rather high.

Table 4.7
PACE (1990): Illustrative Results for SO2

COST PER LB SO2

EFFECT	ECO (1987)	ECO (1984)	MENDELSOHN (1979)	KRAWIEC (1980)	HOHMEYER (1988)	STARTING POINT
	(1)	(2)	(3)	(4)	(5)	(6)
HEALTH						
Mortality	1.72		1.24		NA	1.72
Morbidity	0.05		3.16		NA	0.05
Total						
MATERIALS						
Corrosion	0.017		0.01	0.12	NA	0.12
				0.22		
				0.34		
VEGETATION						
Crops	0	0	0.005	0.00	NA	0
VISIBILITY		0.14	0.02		NA	0.14
OTHER						
Ecosystems	NA	NA	NA	NA	NA	NA
Historic						
Monuments	NA	NA	NA	NA	NA	NA
TOTAL	$1.79	$0.14	$4.54	$0.34	$0.23-1.24	$2.03

Which impacts to select for relevance to externality adders is not a resolved issue. If wages in the nuclear industry, for example, already contain compensating rewards for risk, it would be improper to include occupational immediate mortality, and, arguably, occupational latent mortality. Table 4.8 shows the PACE [1990] risk factors and some additional ones taken from Rostron et al [1991]. Rostron et al. also estimate risk factors for waste storage and occupational disease and accidents from decommissioning, but these are so small that they have no effect on the eventual size of any externality adder. The effect of including plant construction is seen to be important since it produces the same estimate of fatalities per GW-yr as arises with occupational exposure.

The procedure for going from risk factors to monetary cost per kWh can be illustrated as follows. A risk of 0.15 mortalities per GW/yr can be translated as a risk per kWh by:

$0.15/(8760 \times 10^6)$

where 8760 = hours per year
and 10^6 converts kW to GW

This needs to be multiplied by the value of a statistical life. In PACE (1990) this is $\$4 \times 10^6$, so the risk factor has the following externality adder value:

$(0.15 \times 4 \times 10^6 \times 10^2)/(8760 \times 10^6) = 0.068$ c/kWh.

Table 4.8

Risk Factors for the Nuclear Fuel Cycle

(Mortality in deaths per GW/yr)
(Morbidity in injuries per GW/yr)

	PACE[1990] 1.	Rostron[1991] 2.
Uranium Mining		
Enrichment		
Fuel Fabrication		
Plant Operation		
(a) occup.mortality immed.	0.15	
(b) occup.mortality latent	0.15-1.95	
(c) occup.morbidity		0.51-8.10
(d) publ.mortality		0.02-.025
(e) publ.morbidity		
(f) genetic		
Waste Reprocessing		
Waste Disposal		
surface		neg
deep		neg
Plant Construction		
mortality		.150
injury		
Plant Decommisioning		
occup. mortality		
pub mortality		.002
pub injury		.010
Accident	$407-579b	
Fuel Transport		
mort		.006
injury		.270

Sources and Notes for Table 4.5: PACE [1990], Ostron et al [1991]

Note: 1. PACE [1990] relies on early assessments of risk, notably the WASH-1224 report of 1974; the UK review by Cohen and Pritchard in 1980; an article by Spangler in 1979 and a paper by Shuman and Cavanagh in 1982.

Note: 2. The paper by Rostron et al. relates to French PWR reactors.

4.8   Risk Factors: Nuclear Power Accidents

Table 4.8 contains an entry for the cost of a nuclear power accident. This was obtained as follows.

Step 1: estimate the probability of a nuclear accident on the scale of a severe core meltdown. PACE (1990) adopt a figure of 1 in 3333 reactor years, but acknowledge that it is controversial (p.379).

Step 2: estimate the degree of radiation hazard and the dose-response function. PACE [1990] actually use the Chernobyl accident to illustrate what would happen with core meltdown. Using BEIR dose-response relationships they estimate 140,000 additional fatal cancers due to Chernobyl, at \$4million per life, to give \$560 billion. Non-fatal cancers, mental retardation and genetic disorders bring the total to \$579billion.

Step 3: convert to money per kWh by the equation:

$$D.p.100/5690.10^6$$

where D is damage
p is accident probability $= 1/3333$
100 converts \$ to cents
5690 is reactor hours in a year (PACE assume an approximate 65% capacity factor)
10^6 converts a 1GW plant to kW.

which gives 3.1 c/kWh. PACE (1990) reviews one other study and settles for 2 c/kWh as a starting point.

Clearly, this procedure is important because of the resulting very high penalty that accident costs impose on nuclear generation. The weakest part of the PACE procedure is clearly the accident probability. For investment purposes what matters is the probability of an accident in a new power station, not the probability of accident in existing reactors.[3] Design criteria

---

[3]   The complication here is obvious. Public fear and concern will be motivated by actual accidents, not by the probability of accidents in yet-to-be-built power stations. That is, they may perceive the risk in a new station to be the same as the risk of accidents in existing reactors. The issue then becomes the familiar one of the extent to which perceived and 'actual' risk should influence investment decisions.

for new PWR reactors in the UK require the total frequency of an accident leading to uncontrolled radiation releases to be less than 10^{-6} per reactor year. Applying this risk factor to the procedure above results in an externality adder of only 0.01 cents. Clearly, the treatment of accident costs is very important.

A study by Haywood et al [1991] estimates the health impacts of a hypothetical PWR accident in the South West of England. However, the simulated accident does not result in core meltdown. 'It is larger than a design basis accident but does not lead to degradation of the reactor core' (p.42). Damage costs are estimated in various ways. The relevant health costs are those that the authors describe as being based on the 'subjective' approach, by which they mean WTP. The value of a statistical life used is £1 million which, as we have seen, may well be too low. The health costs are shown in Table 4.9. In undiscounted form they amount to £310 million. Applying a 2% discount rate (the maximum rate used by the National Radiological Protection Board) produces a present value of £190 million. An additional (undiscounted) cost of £1.4 billion is estimated as countermeasure costs, so that around £1.7 billion makes up the total cost. If we hypothesise the maximum design 10^{-6} risk factor used in the electricity sector as applying to any new reactor, then an accident of this kind would result in an externality adder of:

$(1.7 \times 10^9 \times 100)/(5690 \times 10^6 \times {}^106) = 0.00003$ p/kWh.

This figure cannot be compared to the PACE estimate because the accidents are very different in nature.

Table 4.9

Costs of a PWR Accident in the UK

Time since accident (years)	Treatment costs					Subjective costs					Total cost (£)
	Fatal cancers	Non-fatal cancers	Early fatal	Early non-fatal	Hereditary effects[1]	Fatal cancers	Non-fatal cancers	Early fatal	Early non-fatal	Hereditary effects	
0–20	$6.1\ 10^5$	$8.1\ 10^4$	0	0	$2.2\ 10^7$	$4.1\ 10^7$	$2.0\ 10^6$	0	0	$1.1\ 10^8$	$1.7\ 10^8$
20–40	$7.9\ 10^5$	$1.0\ 10^5$	–	–	–	$5.3\ 10^7$	$2.6\ 10^6$	–	–	–	$5.6\ 10^7$
40–60	$7.4\ 10^5$	$9.7\ 10^4$	–	–	–	$4.9\ 10^7$	$2.4\ 10^6$	–	–	–	$5.2\ 10^7$
60–80	$3.8\ 10^5$	$5.0\ 10^4$	–	–	–	$2.5\ 10^7$	$1.2\ 10^6$	–	–	–	$2.7\ 10^6$
80–100	$3.5\ 10^4$	$4.6\ 10^4$	–	–	–	$2.4\ 10^6$	$1.2\ 10^5$	–	–	–	$2.5\ 10^6$
TOTALS	$2.6\ 10^6$	$3.8\ 10^5$	0	0	$2.2\ 10^7$	$1.7\ 10^8$	$8.4\ 10^6$	0	0	$1.1\ 10^8$	$3.1\ 10^8$

Note

(1) Total costs of hereditary effects occurring in the first two generations.

Source: Haywood et al. [1991]

Western [1988] estimates the probability of fatalities from nuclear power accidents in the UK as follows:

Frequency of Accidents Resulting
in Deaths of 100+ and 1000+ in the UK

	100+	1000+
Design Basis	0	0
Containment Bypass	7.5×10^7yr	4.6×10^{-8} yr
Degraded Core	5.7×10^{-8}yr	3.7×10^{-8}yr

For a 1 GW plant and the highest risk factor then, deaths per kWh would be 7.5×10^{-7} x 10^{-6} x 6000 hours per year. Further multiplying by 2×10^6 x 10^2 for the £2 million 'value of life' converted to pence, we get, for, say 500 deaths:

$$\frac{500 \times 7.5 \times 2 \times 10^6 \times 10_2}{10^6 \times 10^7 \times 6 \times 10^3} = 0.0000125 \text{ p/kWh}$$

On the analysis provided here, nuclear accident costs are so small, when expressed as p/kWh, that they have no effect on the size of the nuclear externality adder.

However there is evidence to suggest that people do not value risks of 'group' accidents in the same way they value individual deaths. Indeed, casual empiricism suggests this is so since of the many road deaths each year those that are reported by the media tend to involve only multiple deaths. This suggests that there should be some multiplication factor for 'group accidents' reflecting 'disaster aversion'. But just what the factor is open to debate and there appears to be no consensus in the literature.

The number of exceeded fatal cancers per reactor year for a degraded core accident are taken from NRPB as reported in Ferguson [1991[. These give the second row in Table 4.10 below (f for frequency, N for number).

Table 4.10

The Effect of Disaster Aversion in Accidental Costs

1	$f =$	10^{-8}	10^{-9}	10^{-10}	10^{-11}
2	$N =$	11000- 35000	46000- 150000	110000- 250000	180000- 580000
3	fN^2	1-12	7-22	4-12	1-3
4	$300fN$	0.03 to 0.11	0.01 to 0.05	0.003 to 0.01	0.0005 to 0.002
5	$f.N^{3/2}$	0.01 to 0.07	0.01 to 0.06	0.004 to 0.02	neg to 0.004

The last three rows show how various 'disaster aversion' functions might be used to reflect the fact that society tends to weight group losses more heavily than single deaths. The 'square rule' (row 3) is suggested by Ferguson [1991] but he notes that it is not based on empirical studies, Ferguson states that the relevant UK risk perception studies do not exist to enable selection of empirically based functional forms for 'disaster aversion'.

Ferguson concludes that ' the risk of low probability, high consequence PWR accidents may be valued comparably with as much as about twenty individual deaths per reactor year' At £2 million per statistical life, this could produce an adder of £40 million, or 0.67p/kWh across 6000 million kWh p a. Closer inspection of the table above shows that 20 is an upper estimate. An average of 8 might be preferred. 8 deaths x £2m = £16. across 6000m kWh per GWyr would give 0.27p/kWh.

Row 4 in the table above uses a disaster aversion function suggested by Rocard and Smets (R-S) [1991]. Self-evidently, the R-S rule gives higher values for 'damage' up to value of n = 300. After that, the R-S rule gives lower damage values compared to the square function rule. if one reworks the above table with f. 300N instead of the square rule, then the lives lost are very few, the highest value would be £0.21 million and the lowest a thousand £ or so. At£0.2m the adder would be negligible at 0.003p/kWh and at £1m it would be 0.016p/kWh. Record-Smets claim that their function is derived from work by Bohneblust in Switzerland and Germany and Hubert in France. But they also caution that the factor of 300 could be a factor of 1000 which would the upper estimate of the adder to, say, 0.01 to 0.05 p/kWh. Whereas R-S has some empirical foundation, Ferguson's proposal square rule has none. On the other hand, R-S is linear in n and this seems to offend the general institution in the risk aversion literature. Looking at non-linear functions, we illustrate a further possible function of n to the power3/2. This produces similar small adders to the R-S rule.

Overall, then, a 'disaster aversion' adder remains very uncertain, Use of a square function could make the adder as high as 0.27p/kWh, but the square function has no apparent empirical basis. Use of a Rocard-Smets function which is linear in the number of people in the group accident, produces adders of 0.02p/kWh and perhaps as high as 0.05p/kWh. the issue is unresolved in the absence of fully fledged risk perception studies for the UK.

As far as nuclear accident costs are concerned, the health damage costs noted here do not take into account any property and output losses, nor any other economic costs of land sterilisation. It is also important to note that 'major accidents' occur in other fuel cycles, notable with coal (mining accidents, oil and gas (offshore disasters, gas terminal explosions) and hydropower (dam bursts). Owing to the absence of a suitable literature, these impacts have not been estimated in the current exercise.

4.9 Radiation and Human Health

4.9.1 Valuing Radiation Detriment

The basis unit of radiation dose is the g ray(Gy) and is a measure of the energy transferred by radiation to a given mass of tissue. One Gy gives rise to different levels of cell damage according to the type of radiation e.g. alpha, beta radiation. Hence a weighted measure of dose is required and the common unit used is the sievert (sv). One Sv is equal to 1 Gy of X-rays, for example, but is equal to only 10^{-1} Gy of neutron radiation. The Sv is a measure of 'dose-equivalent'. In turn one Sv of radiation has different levels of harm according to which part of the body receives the dose. To allow for this, 'whole body effective dose equivalents' are calculated.

Statistical detection of excess cancer risks from low levels of radiation is extremely difficult. Dose- response functions therefore tend to be extrapolated from higher exposure - response data. The UN committee on the effects of Atomic Radiation (UNSCEAR), the International Commission on Radiological Protection (ICRP), and the UK National Radiological Protection Board (NRPB), recommend the assumption that the risk of fatal cancers is proportional to dose at all doses, without thresholds. The overall risk factor is set at 2×10^{-2} per sievert for fatal cancers and genetic defects in all future generation. Hence the expected number of any irradiated population is:

$$\Sigma_i \chi_i . f(\chi_i) \times 2 \times 10^{-2}$$

Where $f(\chi_i)$ is the number of people receiving a dose level of χ_i Sv. $\Sigma_i \chi_i.f(\chi_i)$ is the collective effective dose equivalent and is measured in 'man-sieverts. 1 man Sv could involve 10 people each receiving 10^{-1} Sv, or 5 people receiving 0.05 Sv and five others receiving 0.15 Sv. etc. The proportionality assumption means that the expected number of health effects is always equal to the product of collective dose and the risk factor.

A significant literature exists on the cost of a man sievert. In the UK the NRPB has made several assessments of the cost of a man Sv. A baseline value is used for every low individual doses and general values are obtained by using multipliers to reflect the individual's increasing risk aversion to increasing levels of individual dose. Table 4.11 shows the changes in these values as NRPB has made revisions to the methodology over time.

Table 4.11

Valuation of a Unit Collect Dose of Radiation (£ per man Sv)

	Before 1988 NRPB [1986] (1)	1988-1992 Robb and Wrixon [1988][2] (2)	1992+ Robb and Croft [1992][3] (3)
	1988 prices		1990 prices
Base line	3,000	5,000	40,000
General			
- Workers	15,000	30,000	?
- Public	5,000	10,000	?
BNFL[4]	-	-	100,000

Notes:

1 based on the human capital approach i.e. forgone earnings. This understates WTP.

2 Revised due to changes in estimated risk factors.

3 Unofficial. Revision due to review of the WTP literature on statistical mortality risk, plus potential revision of recommendation on discounting. Zero discount rates may be preferred due to

(a) evidence that ill health is less preferred in later life when less family and fewer friends are available to support the individual at risk;

(b) new evidence on hereditary links between parents and children with respect to leukaemia (the Gardner Report). Parents may value risk to children and grandchildren more than risk to themselves.

4 BNFL use such a figure to reflect both statistical risk and corporate profile - see Robb [1991].

The 1992 revised baseline estimate (to be confirmed) reflects a fresh look at the 'value of life' literature in Ives et al [1991]. Dividing the value of statistical life figures by the average age of respondents produced a 'value of life year' figure of £ 40,000. Robb (1991) estimates that 1 man Sv at low dose and dose rate generates a loss of 1 year statistical life lost, so that the baseline man SV figure would be £40,000.

4.9.2 Radiological Impacts of the Fuel Cycle

Table 4.12 shows estimates of the radiation impacts of the nuclear fuel cycle in terms of man Sv.

Table 4.12
Fuel Cycle Routine Radiation Exposure
(a) UNEP Estimate by Fuel Cycle Stage

	(man Sv per GW year)		
	Workers	Public	Total
Mining and milling	0.7	0.44	
Fuel fabrication	0.5	0.003	
Reactor operations	10.0	2.50	
Reprocessing	0.25	1.30	
Transport	0.20	0.10	
Waste	neg	neg	
Total	11.65	4.34	16.00

(b) UK fuel Cycle 1986 (man Sv)
Total Installed Capacity

	Routine Releases		Occupational
	Liquid	Atmos	
Sellafield	35.3	1.5	37.9
Other BNFL	0.1	0.8	14.5
UKAEA	3.8	0.4	24.6
Power Stations	0.4	5.3	18.3
	40	8	95
Approx: Total			
		48	95

Sources: (a) UNEP [1991]
            (b) Cooper [1991]

As an approximate check, Table 4.12(b) suggests exposure of around 145 man Sv for about 19 GW installed nuclear capacity, assuming all AEA sites are part of the fuel cycle. Hence man Sv/ Gw = 14.5 which is in agreement with the UNEP overall estimate of 15 man Sv, allowing for the inclusion of mining and milling in the UNEP figure.

The analysis suggests valuations for the nuclear fuel cycle as shown in Table 4.13

Table 4.13
Health Damage Costs from Routine Radiation

	Excluding Mining and Milling	Including Mining and Milling
Exposure per Gw/yr	15.0 Man Sv	16.0 Man Sv
Value of Man Sv	£40-100,000	£40-100,000
Total per Gw/yr £m	0.6 - 1.5	0.64 - 1.6
x10^8 /8760 x 10^6 *		
=p/kWh	0.007-0.020	0.007-0.020

* 10^8 to go from £m to pence, 8760 x 10^6 to go to kWh.

We therefore suggest a best estimate for routine radiation damage of 0.01 -0.02 p/kWh.

Ferguson [1992b] concludes that a UK PWR fuel cycle would be associated with routine radiation occupational and public health costs of 0.01 to 0.3 p/kWh. The major item in his study is a high public impact from reprocessing, but, in turn, the 0.3 p/kWh figure relates to a 'value of life' of £10 million. Reducing this to £2m to be consistent with the rest of this report, the range becomes 0.0002 to 0.06 p/kWh.

4.10 Conclusions: Health Adders by Fuel Cycle

The health impacts of fuel cycles turn out to be potentially important in externality adder exercises. Accordingly, they deserve careful scrutiny. The major issues that need to be resolved are:

(a) the dose-response functions between routine fossil-fuel pollutants and mortality/morbidity;

(b) the valuation of early death and morbidity;

(c) the probability to be used in estimating nuclear accidents;

(d) the response function to be used for routine and non-routine radiation releases.

Of these issues the most unsatisfactory is (a), whilst the most controversial and important is (c). In the existing studies, fossil fuel dose-response function data appears to be very dated.

Revisions to these data are likely to be more important than changing the 'values of life' which, as we have shown, appear to be fairly consistently estimated by the literature (although well above those currently used in the UK). The nuclear accident probability is critical to the health 'adder' that should apply to nuclear power. The PACE (1990) study applies a 1 in 3333 chance that an <u>existing</u> reactor will experience meltdown in any year. <u>If</u> such an accident had geographically dispersed effects on the scale of Chernobyl (although PACE's treatment of these is also controversial) then the adder could be very significant. If, however, the probability is the design risk of 10^{-6}, then the adder is insignificant for a 'modest' accident, and significant but small for a major accident. The issue of how to value a 'disaster' in which many people are killed or injured remains the subject of debate.

We can bring together the various estimates to obtain 'health adders' as follows:

Table 4.14

<u>Health Adders</u> (p/kWh)

Fuel Cycle	Deaths per GW/yr (1)	p/kWh Mortality (2)	+ Major + Accidents (3)	Morbidity (4)	= Total
Coal(5)	9.60	0.32	neg	0.12	0.44
Oil(5)	8.81	0.29	neg	0.12	0.41
Gas	0.65	0.02	neg	0.04	0.06
Solar-Th	2.10	0.07	neg	0	0.07
Solar-PV	3.00	0.10	neg	0	0.10
Wind	1.20	0.04	neg	0	0.04
PWR	0.36	0.01	neg(6)	0.02-0.07	0.03-0.08
Hydro	1.02	0.03	neg	0	0.03

Notes

(1)   From Fritzsche [1989]

(2)   At 6000 hrs/p.a operation

(3)   Whilst surprising at first sight, this item excludes 'routine' accidents which are in the mortality adder.

(4)   Taken from PACE [1990]. The high morbidity for the PWR arises from PACE's treatment of the Chernobyl accident, which is suspect.

(5)   <u>Without</u> FGD and PF.

(6)   Subject to the treatment of 'disaster aversion'.

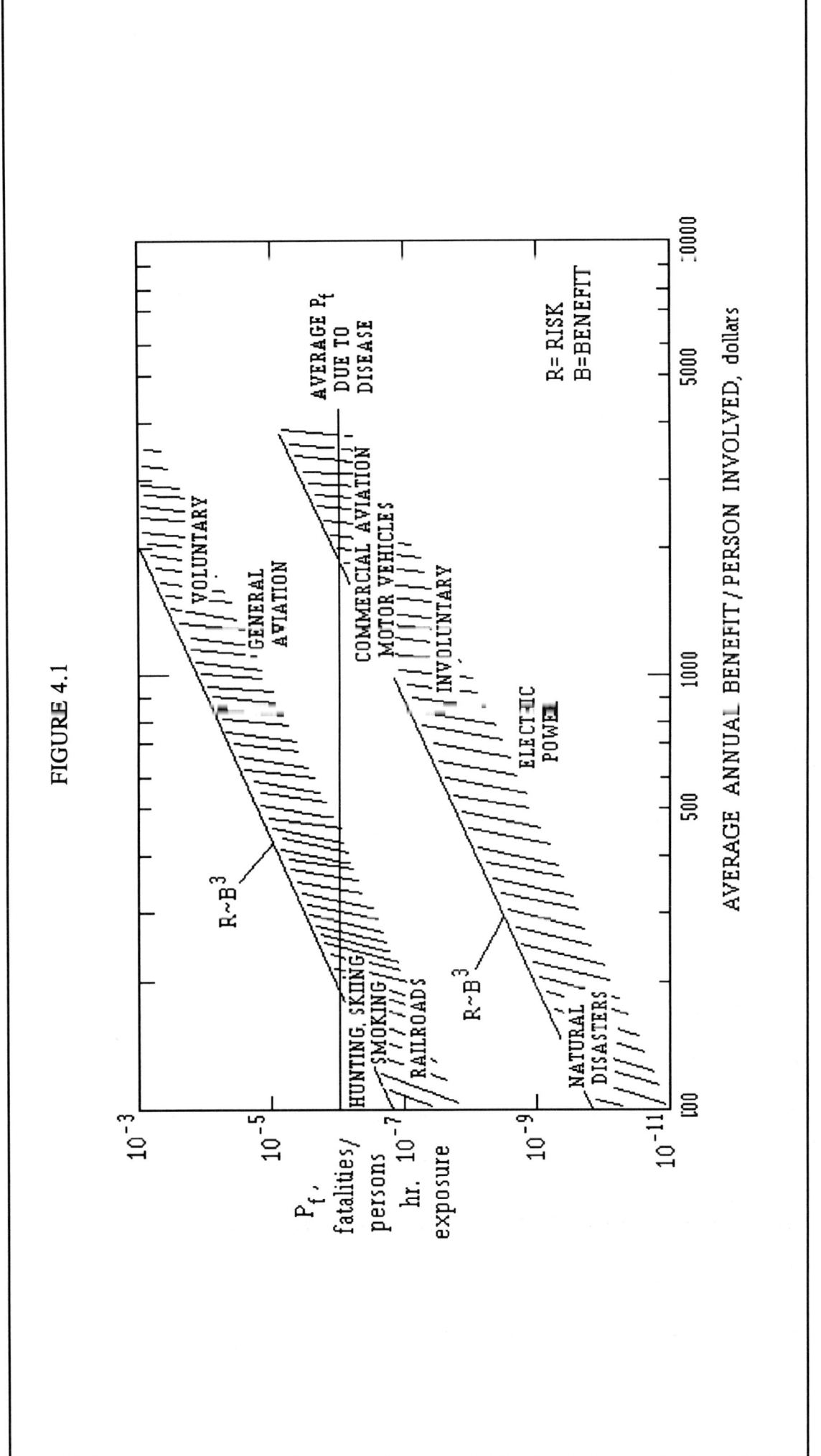

FIGURE 4.1

4-2

FIGURE 4.2

VALUATION OF RISK OF DEATH AGAINST RISK

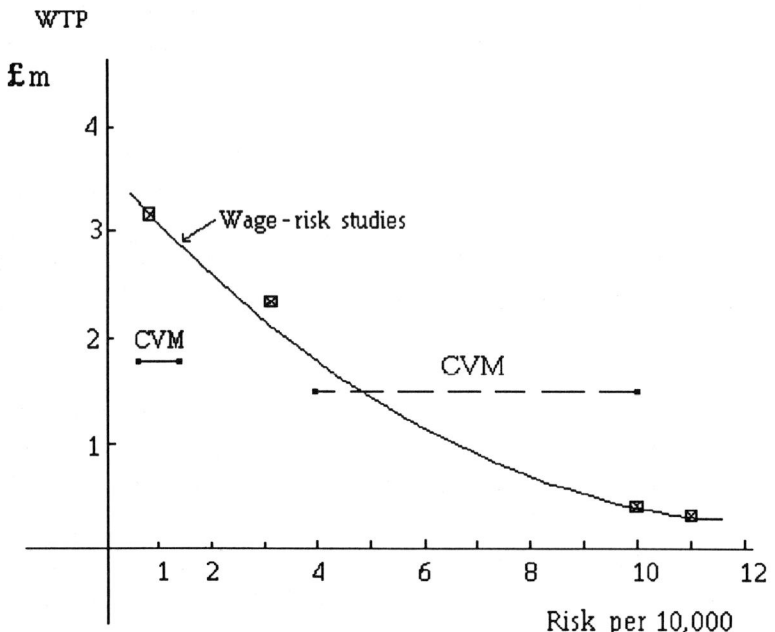

CHAPTER 5 CROP DAMAGE.

5.1 Introduction: Scientific Assessment of Crop Damage.

If the production of energy affects the growth and productivity of crops it is likely to be through the negative impact of acid deposition from SO2 and NOx emissions of fossil fuel combustion, and the indirect effects of ozone (O3).   Recent work suggests that ozone - produced by sunlight - is of considerable significance.

Crop damage from acid deposition and other pollutants may include acidification of soils, reductions in plant growth and vigour, reductions in plant yield, and increased susceptibility to biotic and abiotic stresses.   Factors such as light, plant variety, and the amount of rain may increase the levels of pollutants absorbed by the plant and therefore affect the amount of damage. These factors must be considered when assessing the amount of pollutant-induced damage from crops.

The mechanism by which air pollutants affect crop yields have been extensively studied over the last 25 years.   Recently a cohesive picture has begun to emerge as a result of research programs initiated by the US National Acid Precipitation Assessment Program (NAPAP), the Canadian Long Range Transboundary Air Pollution Program (LRTAP), the Norwegian Acidic Precipitation - Effects on Forests and Fish Program (SNSF), the OECD LRTAP program, the Electric Power Research Institute, and major efforts in the U.K. and Germany. (ETSU/ITE [1992] have carried out a detailed dose-response study for SO2 crop damage from a coal fired station at West Burton, Nottinghamshire. Using a dose-response function from Roberts [1984] they estimate losses of around $2.7 * 01^{-5}$ ecu/kWh), suggesting an insignificant effect from SO2.

The U.S. National Acid Precipitation Assessment Program (NAPAP) Report [1991] represents a detailed scientific synthesis of the information on the causes, effects and controls of acid deposition and associated pollutants.   The NAPAP report relies heavily on the extensive investigations under the U.S. National Crop Loss Assessment Network (NCLAN). The study concludes that there are four pollutants capable of impacting the growth, yield, or quality of sensitive crops in the U.S.; O3, SO2, acidic deposition and NO2. Ozone is shown to impose significant stress on agricultural production. Yield reductions greater than 2% and up to 56% were recorded for 26 out of 29 cultivars.   Commercial crops affected include alfalfa, corn, cotton, soybean, sorghum, forage, rice and spring and winter wheat (which together account for 755 of U.S. crop production) (NAPAP [1991], p. 55).   International evidence and other U.S. studies support this conclusion. However, NAPAP concludes that there is no evidence that acid precipitation is harming crops.

Acid deposition can cause both direct and indirect effects on crops. Indirect effects include a fertilizer effect from greater inputs of nitrogen inputs and acidification of the soil requiring additional lime to be added.   In terms of the indirect effects, NAPAP cites McFee who asserts that a change in liming as a result of a change in acid deposition is a small proportion of the liming required to counteract soil acidification (Fertilizers applied to crops increase acidity of the soil, and lime is commonly applied to fields to prevent acidification). If lime is not used, in the long term, acidic precipitation may leach soil nutrients or mobilize toxic metal.

5.2 Economic Valuation Methodologies in Crop Assessment.

Dose-response relationships are frequently used in crop damage assessments. The earliest crop damage estimate studies simply multiplied the reduction in output attributable to the pollutant according to the biological dose response relationship by the market price. This measure can be taken as a very rough estimate of cost of pollution damage since it ignores behavioral responses or price changes. In the context of higher pollution levels producers are likely to switch to crop varieties whose yields are resistant to a particular form of air pollution in the region, or they may alter the use of other inputs such as calcium carbonate which mitigates the pollution impact. In relation to price changes, a fall in yield as a result of pollution will generally mean less output at a higher market price. If market prices are at all sensitive to output, consumers lose when pollution increases, but producers either lose or gain, depending on whether the percentage reduction in quantity is greater or less than the percentage increase in the price. Adam, Crocker and Thanavibulchai [1982] found that this simple multiplication approach produced estimates 20% higher than those obtained when the behavioral and price responses were modelled.

A correct assessment of crop damage needs to link the physical manifestations of environmental change to the <u>behaviour</u> of affected producers and consumers. The changes in profits and utility that accompany these behavioral responses are indications of their effects on the welfare of producers and consumers.

The following components are typically employed to value crop damage:

1. Scientific studies are employed to specify the dose-response relationships i.e. the physical damage resulting to a crops as a function of specific pollutants. These studies also characterize the different permutations that environmental change presents in terms of production and consumption opportunities. Statistical relationships are used to estimate the physical relationship between inputs and outputs for the varying levels of environmental effects.

2. The response of input/output market prices to these relative changes in output is determined (demand).

3. The adaptations that affected agents can make so as to maximise gains or minimise losses from the changes in opportunities and prices are identified (supply)

4. Once the parameters of the market demand and supply equation have been estimated the system is simultaneously solved by a market clearing identity which equates quantity supplied with quantity demanded.

Mathematical programming has also been used in crop damage assessments (Adams, Crocker and Thanavibulchai 1982). This approach is able to account more completely for the

Van der Eerden et al [1987] value crop losses in the Netherlands for three air pollutants; ozone, SO2 and hydrogen fluoride. Dose response relationships were established for sensitive crops using domestic and foreign studies, and a model of supply and demand was developed to arrive at changes in producers' and consumers' surplus. In 1983 the loss in consumers' surplus was estimated at 642m Dfl, due to a 5% reduction in the yield of sensitive crops (compared to the situation with no air pollution). Converting to 1988 prices, total damages would be 680 Dfl. In 1988 dutch SO2 depositions were 86,300 tonnes = 7880 Dfl/tonne. At 1.98 Dfl = $1, this results in a crop adder of $1.8 per U.S lb of SO2.

AED [1991] estimate the value of reduced losses of wheat and corn in Spain due to reduced air pollution. Dose-response relationships between several air pollutants and the crops were estimated from a literature review. The increased consumer and producer surplus for the whole of Spain was estimated at 1.7 billion pesetas per year. Unfortunately, the data available do not permit an estimate of damage per tonne of pollutant.

Eyre and Holland [1992] estimate a crop loss of £300.000 per annum for a single power station, or around 0.003p/kWh, for enhanced SO_2 concentration. As noted above, however S02 is acknowledged not to be important as a source of crop damage.

Crop damage valuation studies have been much more prolific in the U.S. Table 5.2 summarises the recent American studies in this area.

Table 5.2
Recent American Studies of the Economic Effects of Air Pollutants on Agriculture.

Study	Type of valuation	Results	Comments
Adams, Crocker and Thanavibulchai [1982]	Benefit of reducing 1976 ambient oxidant exposures of 14 annual crops in Southern California	approx $46m	Use a price-endogenous programming model
Adams and McCarl [1985]	Benefit of imposing more stringent ozone regulations (NAAQS) in the Corn Belt Region of the U.S. from 0.12ppm to 0.08 hourly max. Corn, soybean, and wheat considered.	approx $0.7b. (Relaxation in present standard from 0.12 to 0.16 ppm may result in a loss of benefits in excess of $2.0b)	Estimates are based on NCLAN data through 1982. an analysis using response information prior to NCLAN estimated much lower benefits to ozone control. Models price changes and input and output changes.
Howitt, Gossard, and Adams [1984]	Estimate the benefits of a reduction in ozone to 40ppb for 18 crops in the Corn Belt Region of the U.S.	$45m (Consumer benefits: $17m, producer benefits $28m)	Model price changes and input and output substitutions.

Mjelde et al [1984] Garcia et al [1986]	Benefits from a 10% decrease in ozone from 46.5ppb for corn and soybean in Illinois.	$226m (all producer benefit)	Do not consider price changes but do include inputs and output substitution.
Adams and Crocker [1985]	Measure the effects of ozone reductions in the U.S. from 53ppb to 04ppb for corn, soybean and cotton.	$220m	Model price changes, and input and output substitutions.
Adams, Crocker and Katz [1984]	Estimate the benefits of ozone reductions in the U.S. from 48ppb to 40ppb for corn, soybean, cotton and wheat.	$2400m	Consider price changes but not substitution changes.
Adams, Hamilton and McCarl [1986]	25% ozone reductions in each state of the U.S. from 1980 level for corn, soybeans, cotton, wheat, sorghum, barley.	$1700 (consumer benefits $1160m, producer benefits $550m)	Consider price changes and input and output substitution.
Knopp et al [1985]	Ozone reductions in the U.S. from 53ppb to 40ppb for corn, soybeans, cotton, wheat and peanuts.	$1300m	Consider price changes and input and output substitutions.
Shortle, Dunn, and Phillips [1986]	Ozone reductions in the US. from 53ppb to 49ppb for soybeans.	$790m (consumer benefits $880m, producer benefits $-90m)	Consider price and quality changes but not input and output substitution.
Adams et al [1989]	Estimate the benefits of a 95% compliance rate with the seasonal standard of ozone of 50ppb in the U.S. for corn, soybean, wheat, sorghum, rice, hay and barley.	$167m (consumer benefits $905m, producer benefits $769m)	Consider price changes and input and output substitutions.
NAPAP [1991]	Estimate consumer and producer surplus change due to 10 and 25% reduction in ozone from 25ppb.	10% = $739 m 25% = $1,732 m	

It is interesting to note that the agricultural studies of annual crops exhibit several regularities in behavioral responses and sensitivities to imposed conditions and to data accuracy and precision (Adams and Crocker [1989]).

The regularities are:

1. Producers can gain from increases in air pollution. Shortle, Dunn and Philips [1986] and Adams and McCarl [1985], found that substantial increases in ozone increased the economic rents of corn belt growers. A condition for this is that the pollution reduced percentage reduction in output for a given crop is less than the associated increase in the market price.

2. Losses to consumers are a significant portion of the total agricultural losses due to air pollution. Of the studies that accounted for air pollution induced changes in the price of agricultural goods, the percentage of the total loss attributable to consumers ranged from 50% (Adams, Hamilton, and McCarl [1986]) to 100% (Adams and McCarl [1985]). Given that producers can sometimes gain from an increase in air pollution, not including consumer impacts can understate total losses and misrepresent the distribution of the welfare effects.

3. As the air becomes more polluted, the percentage changes in total economic surpluses are less than the percentage changes in the biological yields that triggered these losses. This is because substitutions allow producers and consumers to attenuate the losses they would otherwise suffer from declines in air quality.

4. Changes in air pollution affect both productivity and the aggregate demand for factors of production. ie specific inputs. Mjelde et al [1984] estimate that a 10% increase in ozone in Illinois will result in a 4% decline in the demand for variable inputs such as labour, water and fertilizer.

5. Changes in air pollution have differential effects on the comparative advantage of agricultural production regions. Several studies have concentrated on the effects of air pollution across large geographical areas. Adams, Hamilton, and McCarl [1986], and Knopp et al [1985] indicate that local producers benefit economically when air pollution was reduced in areas characterised by high ambient levels of pollution and pollution sensitive crops. In these areas, the percentage increase in yield was greater than the overall reduction in prices nationwide, thus increasing regional net income.) Therefore, while there might be a national net gain from a reduction in air pollution, some subregions are seen to gain at the expense of others.

5.4 Conclusions

Crops appears to be one area where a fair level of confidence can be placed on the dose-response functions employed. Valuation techniques have also become more precise due to the modelling of changes in producer and consumer surpluses. Where fuel cycle cost studies are looking at marginal changes in crop production there is, however, no reason to do this. The market price can be used and the valuation procedure is relatively straightforward. Adams, Crocker and Katz [1984], among others, maintain that the precision in existing estimates of crop damage is sufficient to distinguish between alternative regulatory policies options i.e. that the underlying crop responses-ozone pollution data are sufficient to answer economic policy questions.

The majority of the studies to date are American and the issue of transferability therefore arises. Damage functions cannot be transferred to other crops in the same region since other crops will have a different susceptibility to different pollutants. Nor can estimates be transferred to areas of much higher or lower concentrations of the air pollutants, or where other air pollutants are more critical, or where there are other climatic conditions, crops and land use patterns.

NAPAP [1991] conclude that 'significant benefits for agricultural production are projected to result from ozone reductions in the range of 10% to 25%' (NAPAP [1991] p.509). Benefits in the range of $0.7 - $1.7 billion could ensue. The problem of translating this into an externality adder is how to relate ozone to source pollutants. If related to NO_x, for example, the benefits would amount to about 0.02 pence/gram NO_x. While the procedure is open to question, it has been used in the literature surveyed. Such a valuation would produce adders as follows:

'old' coal	0.10 p/kWh
'new' coal	0.05
oil	0.05
gas	0.02
CHP	0.03
Nuclear	Zero

Again, it must be emphasised that this procedure is controversial.

CHAPTER 6 FOREST DAMAGE.

6.1 Introduction: Scientific Assessment of Forest Damage.

Acid depositions from SO2 and NOx emissions and the indirect effects of ozone caused by the reaction of nitrous oxides in the atmosphere are at the forefront of concern over forest damage. Valuation of the damage caused to forests by air pollutants is hampered by uncertainties over the relative contribution of air pollution compared to other factors.

In Europe acid rain has been implicated in the death and damage of forests, but scientists agree that no single cause can be blamed and that causation tends to be site specific. In the U.S. the net effect of acid rain on forest ecosystems is not well established. The NAPAP assessment (NAPAP [1991]) concluded that, with the exception of red spruce at high elevations, there is no evidence that acid rain has caused a general decline in American forests. As with crops, however, ozone is implicated in forest damage.

Forest decline is a process of high causal complexity, involving a variety of natural and human made factors. Forest health problems associated with weather changes and droughts, the age of the trees, fragility of the soils at high altitudes, insects and pathogens are natural features of the forest system. Human stresses include such things as emissions of air pollutants and inappropriate forest management. In many cases air pollution is accepted as playing a crucial role, but it is evident that the influence and effects of other factors affecting forests are subject to wide variation in space and time.

Quantification of forest damage is further complicated by the fact the forest damage does not have a standard meaning. Indicators of damage include abnormal growth reductions, loss and decolouration of foliage, decrease in canopy density, changes in the chemical content of the soil and stress effects in tree and plant cells.

The NAPAP [1991] report assesses the changes in forest health and productivity in the U.S. and Canada.

NAPAP classifies forest health problems as 'declines' if they are

1. not the result of normal maturation and senescence
2. not clearly attributable to a single predominant natural factor
3. sufficiently severe and extensive to be detected by routine forest monitoring or special field investigations.

The study concludes that the vast majority of forests in the U.S. and Canada are not affected by decline. With respect to possible regional scale impacts on North American forests, ozone is cited as the pollutant of greatest concern. Acid deposition appears to be a relatively minor factor, excepting the case of red spruce at high elevations in the Northern Appalachians whose decline may have been caused by acid deposition. Sugar maple declines are a significant problem in Quebec, and in some parts of Ontario, Vermont and

Massachusetts, and a regional decline in southern pines has been demonstrated. However, natural factors are considered to be significant cause of these effects and the contribution of air pollutants to these declines cannot be deduced on current information. NAPAP [1991] does estimate the economic benefit of a 2% reduction in ozone in the south-east USA. They estimate that $18 - 40m p.a. would be the gross benefit of such a change. Unfortunately, on the data provided it is not possible to estimate any relationship to precursors - NOx and HC.

While the NAPAP conclusions reflect the current state of science, not all investigators agree on all the findings. The computer models used are unable to produce precise quantitative projections because of uncertainty about the key growth processes and the lack of adequate data sets, while possible interactions among acidic deposition, ozone, and other natural and man-made stresses are poorly understood.

An important question remains about the long term effects of acid deposition. There is some indication that sulphur is accumulating in some forest soils which will increase leaching losses of nutrient cations from soils and over the long term may reduce the fertility of soils with low buffering capacity or low mineral weathering rate. Moreover, the possible existence of thresholds generated by synergies implies that simple projections will not be adequate to capture the long term effects of acid deposition. It is therefore not possible to hypothesise on current data what the long term effects might be.

In the light of these shortcomings NAPAP recommends a sustained programme of basic research and forest monitoring to evaluate more precisely and quantitatively the significance to forest health of the stresses imposed by acidic deposition and associated pollutants.

The Forest Study of the International Institute for Applied Systems Analysis (IIASA) [1991] presents an assessment of the effects of air pollutants on forests in Europe.

The study combines the IIASA Forest Study database, which is the most detailed database on forest resources in Europe, with the IIASA RAINS (Regional Acidification Information and Simulation) model, which generates information on future deposition patterns. RAINS models the entire sequence of air pollution events in all of Europe including the European USSR, from the generation and emission of pollutants, to their transport in the atmosphere, to their deposition and effect on the environment. The impacts on forests were estimated using the dose-response relationships of PEUM, an Eastern Germany model developed from data based on field observations since the 1960s at a series of test sites along emission gradients.

In contrast to NAPAP, IIASA's findings are extremely pessimistic. They estimate that about 75% of Europe's commercial forests endure damaging levels of sulphur deposition; about 60% suffer from deposition of nitrogen above critical loads.

Nilsson [1991] calculates that in 1980 about 75% or 17 billion cubic metres, of commercial wood in Europe suffered annual depositions of sulphur above the critical load. The projected reductions in emissions by the year 2000 would reduce that figure by just 9%. In the case of nitrogen, where fewer commitments to control have been made, current trends would result in a cut of only 2% of the timber subjected to damaging nitrogen depositions.

6.2 Commercial Forestry Studies.

As with commercial crops (see section 5.2), commercial timber is typically valued by combining information on the pollution-induced physical change in the resource, deduced from scientific dose-response studies, with market prices. On the whole, possible market reactions such as price changes and input and output substitutions are not modelled.

The IIASA Forest Study [1991] suggests that economic losses due to air pollution for all European countries amounts to $30b each year for forest damage alone.

The study incorporates two conservative assumptions considered by IIASA to be conservative.

1. Only the negative effects of sulphur emissions are calculated, assuming no ill effects from other pollutants.

2. That by the year 2000 SO2 emissions are reduced by 18% from the 1980 level (the likely reductions in SO2 calculated within the RAINS model based on current reduction commitments), after which the emissions are reduced to zero.

The study covers losses in timber, primary forest products and the costs of non-timber social benefits. The losses in timber/roundwood and primary forest products are calculated using current market prices i.e. no account is taken of possible supply changes. In a rigorous model the value of incremental forest loss would be calculated as changes in producer and consumer surplus.

The annual, potential European (including the European part of the USSR) losses in timber products were approximately $6.3 billion 1987 U.S.$. The value of the primary forest product industry was estimated at approximately 7.2 billion 1987-U.S.$. The estimate of the lost industrial process value took into account basic products such as softwood and hardwood lumber, pulp and wood for energy; values for lumber and pulp were based primarily on export price data from the UN Food and Agriculture Organisation.

Costs of non-timber social benefits (i.e reduced quantity and quality of forest related environmental goods) have been calculated by multiplying the timber value by a factor of 2.7. This factor was calculated from a survey of the few existing valuation studies of these environmental goods, and there is much uncertainty surrounding it. The annual potential European (including the European part of the USSR) non-timber losses were estimated at $16.9 billion 1989 U.S. $. In W.Germany, such benefits are valued at 4.0-4.5 times the country's industrialised timber production.

Nilsson [1991] estimated the final cost to Europe, including the European USSR, of sulphurous damage to forests to be $30.4 billion each year for the next 100 years. Table 6.1 shows the potential harvest losses for Europe and the value of this harvest reduction in 1987$.

The results of other studies estimating the costs to commercial timber as a result of forest damage are shown in Table 6.2. A number of the studies use dose response functions based on expert judgement. They should therefore be seen as approximations as they are not supported by any empirical evidence. The estimates cannot be compared directly because they build on different damage scenarios.

Table 6.1
IIASA's Estimated Losses Attributable to Air Pollution, by Volume and Value.

Region country	Potential harvests (million m³/yr) Losses attributable to air pollution	Value of harvest reduction[b] (million 1987$ US/yr) roundwood	industrial products	non-wood benefits	total
Finland	4.5	234.9	317.7	635.0	1187.6
Norway	0.8	42.0	54.9	113.5	210.4
Sweden	5.8	302.8	406.0	818.3	1527.1
NORDIC	11.1	579.7	778.6	1566.8	2925.1
Belg & Lux	0.7	52.0	60.1	140.5	252.6
Denmark	0.4	22.6	33.6	60.9	117.1
France	3.5	232.1	314.0	627.5	1173.6
Germany (W)	11.9	700.9	1018.6	1894.5	3614.0
Germany (E)	4.9	250.4	233.2	677.2	1160.8
Italy	3.1	333.5	595.1	901.9	1830.5
Netherlands	0.2	13.3	18.1	36.0	67.4
UK & Ireland	3.7	234.0	306.5	632.6	1173.1
EEC-9	28.6	1838.8	2579.2	4971.1	9389.1
Austria	3.4	191.8	206.1	515.5	913.4
Switzerland	2.4	140.4	140.2	379.6	660.2
CENTRAL	5.8	332.2	346.3	895.1	1573.6
Greece	0.1	4.1	8.1	11.2	23.4
Portugal	1.5	64.5	95.1	174.5	334.1
Spain[a]	n.a	n.a	n.a	n.a	n.a
Turkey	2.8	125.4	206.9	339.1	671.4
Yugoslavia	2.8	175.3	119.3	474.0	768.6
SOUTHERN	7.2	369.3	429.4	998.8	1797.5
Bulgaria	2.2	107.6	122.5	290.8	520.9
CSFR	9.5	540.6	369.5	1461.1	2371.2
Hungary	3.0	171.0	156.6	462.3	789.9
Poland	11.1	585.0	491.8	1581.7	2658.5
Romania	3.8	219.3	185.0	592.8	997.1
EASTERN	29.6	1623.5	1325.4	4388.7	7337.6
EUROPE	82.3	4743.5	5458.9	12820.5	23022.9

a   Spanish data insufficient to allow calculation of pollution effects.
b   Preliminary data.

Source: IIASA [1991].

Table 6.2
Recent Commercial Timber Studies.

Study	Type of valuation	Results	Comments
NNM [1988]	Calculates average timber loss in Norway	1b 1988-NOX per year, starting from 25-30 years from now.	Uses current market prices Expert judgement used about reduced tree growth. Assume that the current levels of ozone and acid deposition continue.
Ewers et al [1986]	Evaluates direct commercial losses incurred in Germany as a result of declining forests.	Total losses for forest decline estimated at 1.7 - 4.8b 1984-DM (depending on the discount rate used)	Commercial timber losses calculated using market prices. A simulation model for spruce and expert judgement for other tree species is used to link three different air pollution scenarios to forest loss.
Linden and Oosterhuis [1988]	Estimates the cost of forest loss in the Netherlands in 2010 as a result of a decline in forest quality from the present standard to the expected scenario if no additional measures against acid deposition are taken.	Timber losses were estimated at 13.1 m Dfl per year (probably 1988-prices).	
The Austrian Ministry for Environment [no date]	National economic evaluation of forest decline attributable to air pollution	Total forest loss estimated at AS 4.5b per year (1983)	Some forestry costs were discounted. 85% of forestry losses came from items other than commercial timber losses.

PACE [1990] reviews only two damage studies in this category concerned with the effects of acid deposition on forests (see Table 6.3). In their opinion because the US damage studies are so equivocal in this area, there are no credible estimates of acid deposition damage to forests. PACE therefore puts damage to forests at zero.

Table 6.3
Forest Damage Studies Reviewed by PACE [1990]

Study	Type of valuation	Results	Comments
Callaway, Darwin and Nesse [1986]	Hypothetical forest growth reductions of 10%. 15% and 20% in Eastern U.S for hardwoods and softwoods.	$2.7b to $5.6b present value to 2030	Use forest sector model accounting for price changes and limited input substitution.
Crocker and Regans [1985]	Benefits of 100% reduction in acid depositions in Eastern U.S.	$1.75b (1978)	Market value of timber used; method of valuing other uses unspecified.

The study by Callaway, Darwin and Nesse [1986] is discussed in the NAPAP state of science/technology assessment. The study estimates the economic effects of a hypothetical reduction in tree growth in the northeastern and southeastern US on stumpage and primary forest product markets. The economic effects of hypothetical reductions in tree growth caused by acid deposition were estimated using existing softwood and hardwood inventory and forest sector market models, together called The Timber Assessment Market Model (TAMM). The present value of damages (assuming a 10% discount rate) between 1985 and 2030 ranged from $3.4b to a little more than $5.0b depending on the severity of the hypothetical growth reductions. The NAPAP report does not specify the assumed growth reductions. This estimate represents less than 1% of the then roughly $70b total surplus estimate.

This study has been criticised on a number of grounds:

1. Economic surplus changes were short run estimates not adjusted to include investment costs in mill capacity.

2. The analysis did not explore the possibility of incorporating more intensive forest management practices so as to counteract slower tree growth through improved forest management.

3. Models did not take account of the dynamic aspects of stumpage markets e.g. the model did not reflect the likely effect of higher expected stumpage prices on current harvesting decisions.
As a result, simulated harvests were considerably higher than might reasonably be expected.

6.3 Forest Recreation.

Table 6.4 provides a summary of the studies valuing forest recreation. These studies employ the contingent valuation approach and the travel cost methodology.

Table 6.4
Forest Recreation Studies.

Study	Type of valuation	Results	Comments
Ewers et al [1986]	Recreational use values in Germany	Total forest recreational benefits in the base year 1984 are estimated at DM 24.1b. (use values DM 13.4b; option value DM 0.2b; tourist income DM 10.5b)	Uses a fixed value of a forest visit which is questionable. The WTP measure of option value is based on a CV survey which does not relate exclusively to option value but to total forest value (option and bequest). Argued that losses in tourism should be omitted as it represents a distributional shift not a real cost.
Van der Linden and Oosterhuis [1988]	Estimates WTP using CV for maintaining the existing good quality of the forest and heath.	Mean WTP estimated at Dfl 22.83 per household per month. This amounts to Dfl 1.5b per year for all Dutch households.	Uses state of the art CV techniques.
Navrud et al [1990]	Estimates the recreational value of mountainous forest area to hikers, car tourist and cottage tourists that has been subject to three different management practices; clear cutting, selection forest, and preservation.	Hikers had the highest WTP per visit to the area. Their median WTP per visit was 6ECU for selection forestry, and 8ECU for preservation virgin forest compared to clear cutting.	Uses carefully constructed CV survey.
Hoen and Winther [1991]	Estimates the total value of 'multiple use forestry' and the preservation of virgin coniferous forests in Norway.	The mean annual WTP per household for multiple forestry and preservation of virgin forests ranged from 16-46 ECU to 26-51 ECU respectively.	Uses CV survey. Commodity misspecification seems to be present, ie. people had difficulties in perceiving the changes in the environmental good to be valued.

Kristrom [1988]	WTP to preserve selected virgin forest areas in Sweden.	Damage estimates range from 3.0 - 8.2 b SEK	Uses CV survey.
T.D. Crocker [1984]	Valuation of stock-ozone damage to forests in S.California. Attempts to value non-harvest values.	Mean WTP to prevent 'slightly damaged' environment $2.09 (in addition to the $7 already paid by visitors.	CV questionnaire put to outdoor recreationists. Photographs used to illustrate various levels of ozone damage. Weak dose-response for ozone/tree material.
Grayson et al [1975]	Estimates the consumer surplus for recreation of all Forestry Commission forests aged 25+ in 1969 -1971 (U.K).	Consumer surplus per visitor: £0.33 per hectare: £30.50 (1987£).	Consumer surplus per hectare is calculated from consumer surplus per visitor * all forest visitors divided by the total area of FC land aged 25+ years.
Everett [1979]	Estimates the recreational value of forest in Dalby, U.K. 1975/1976.	Consumer surplus per visitor: £1.82 per hectare: £64.60. (1987£).	Different estimates of annual visitor numbers produce different estimates of consumer surplus per hectare.
Christensen [1983]	Estimates the recreational value of forest in Gwydyr, U.K. 1981	Consumer surplus per visitor: £0.53 (1987£).	
Willis and Benson [1989]	Estimates the consumer surplus associated with forest recreation for six different sites	Consumer surplus per visitor for all six sites: £1.90 per hectare: £31.78 and £100.51 (see comment) Consumer surplus per visitor for Dalby only £1.82, per hectare: £52.44. (1987£) (for Dalby, different estimates of annual visitor numbers produce different estimates of consumer surplus.	For the consumer surplus per hectare values: £31.78 represents consumer surplus per visitor * total visitors to the sites divided by the total area of the sites. £100.51 represents consumer surplus per visitor * all U.K. forest visitors divided by the total area of Forestry Commission land aged 27+ years.
Willis and Benson [1989]	Estimates the recreational value of eight sites in the U.K. 1988.	Average consumer surplus for the eight sites: per visitor - £1.97 per hectare - £18.55 (1988£)	

Benson and Willis [1990]	Estimates the recreational value of fifteen sites extrapolated to the whole Forestry Commission estate 1987-1988.	Consumer surplus for recreation: per visitor - £2.00 per hectare - £47 (1988£).	

The Nordic studies (Norway and Sweden) examine the social value of different management practices, rather than the valuation of air pollution, and it seems reasonable to conclude that changes in forest related goods due to the impacts of the fuel cycle are different from the changes induced by different management practices. Even if they are not we have no way of converting these values to energy related externality adders.

In the case of forest recreation damage, transferability to other countries and regions seems limited. The marginal damage of forests as a recreational asset is largely dependent upon local supply and demand conditions which may differ considerably between areas. Thus one Swedish study estimated a positive WTP to preserve agricultural land (open space) in a densely forested area in Sweden (Drake, [1987]). In this case the marginal value of forests was negative. In the Netherlands, such a result would be very unlikely since recreational values have been shown to be large.

In the case of CV surveys, when asking people for their WTP to preserve forests it is often not clear what exactly is being measured. Is it mainly use value (recreation, hunting) that is being measured or is a wider value concept involved (existence value , ethical considerations)? Commodity misspecification is also a recognised problem, (see Hoen and Winther [1991], Crocker [1983]) i.e. the interviewees were unable to clearly distinguish between different forest quality changes.

Where the effects of air pollution are being studied, it has been suggested that in some cases the stated WTP not only aims at the forest resource per se, but that respondents really express their concern over air pollution in general, of which forest decay is a powerful symbol. If this is the case, all impacts of air pollution will be included in the forest damage estimate and the adding up of damages of the different estimates of different impacts results in double counting. It points to the necessity of carefully designing the CV survey. There is also significant overlap between forest recreation and activities such as fishing, and calculating the values of each separately and adding them up will is unlikely the correct total value.

6.4   Forest Adder Estimates.

Considerable doubts surround the IIASA estimates of forest damage. They appear not to be consistent with the NAPAP study for example. However, taking the IIASA study, it is possible to derive estimates of externality adders for the different fuel technologies. Table 6.5 shows externality adders pence/per gram of SO2 for selected European countries using Nilsson's damage estimates. Note that these adders relate to commercial and non-timber values.

Table 6.5
Externality Adders (pence/per gram of SO2)

Country	Emissions 1989 ooootS	Deposition 1988 tSO2	Nilsson 1990 Forest damage 10^6 US$	Damage per ton SO2 deposited	Pence/per gram SO2 deposited[a]
CZECH	1387	1,316,000	2,371	$1800	010
FRA	636	1,028,200	1,174	$1141	0.07
E.GER	2621	1,572,800	1,161	$2088	0.12
FRG	530	1,077,000	3614	$3356	0.20
ITALY	1205	947,400	1830	$1932	0.11
NETH	127	172,600	67	$390	0.02
POL	1955	703,800	2658	$3778	0.22
SPAIN	1559	957,000	na	na	na
USSR	4659	7,141,600	(7400)	$(1036)	0.06
UK(incl. Ireland)	1776	1,099,400	1173	$1067	0.06
Norway	21	151,000	210	$1393	0.08
Sweden	77	260,000	1527	$5873	0.34

a = $ damage per ton/ $1.7 * 100 / 10^6$ = divide by 17000

If we take the UK figure of 0.06 p/g SO2 damage and apply this figure to the fuel cycle emission factors in Chapter 3 we derive the following externality adders.

Technology	g/kWh	*	0.06 p/g	=	p/kwh
Coal	14 0				0.84
Mod.Coal	1.2				0.07
Oil	16.4				0.98
Gas	0.5				0.03
CPH	-				-
Nuclear	0				0.00

Note that, if credible, these figures <u>understate</u> damage from UK <u>emissions</u> in so far some of these emissioms are exported. and <u>overstate</u> damage in so far as some of the SO2 concentrations are imported.

6.5 Conclusions

Most of the studies reviewed are relevant to energy in that they consider the affects of major air pollutants. However, deposition data are often not available to convert the findings of these studies into pence per kWh externality estimates.

The forestry studies demonstrate the problems inherent in comparing studies defined for different purposes and in different contexts. It seems unlikely that dose-response functions and results would be transferable as there may be differences in the physical damage to forests from the same level of ambient air pollution due to the differences in susceptibility of certain tree species to different pollutants.

There is still a fair amount of uncertainty over the scientific explanation of forest damage and more accurate dose response relationships seem necessary. The emphasis that should be put on refining the dose response functions is however debated, Nilsson [1991] states ' We know enough to be sure of the links between acid emissions and forest decline - if we wait any longer until we have a detailed understanding of the situation before taking action it will be too late.'

The basic value of reduced timber harvests is relatively easy to calculate; prices of timber are knowable. But there are no market prices for the forests other functions e.g. protection of soil and water; recreation; wildlife habitat; microclimate amelioration; and sequestration of atmospheric carbon, the major cause of increased global warming. There is some consensus that these non-wood benefits are of significant value, but only recently have researchers tried to assign those values.

Walsh et al [1990] attempts to measure total forest quality, i.e. option, existence and bequest values, using CV in the Colorado Rocky mountains. They consider a major outbreak of mountain pine beatles and spruce budworm the effects of which are too different to those caused by energy pollution to be used in our study. However the study revealed that public preservation values represented nearly 3/4ths of the total benefits, illustrating the importance of adding them to forestry evaluations.

The IIASA externality adders reported here are controversial since they assume the validity of acidic pollution dose-reponse functions which have been severely questioned by the US NAPAP study.

CHAPTER 7 BIOLOGICAL DIVERSITY

7.1 Valuing the Benefits of Biological Diversity

Probably the greatest challenge to economic valuers is to derive some values for people's preferences for biological diversity. 'Biodiversity' is frequently used as a shorthand for both the <u>quantity</u> of species and the <u>range</u> of species, and equally frequently as a catch-all phrase for <u>wildlife</u> and <u>habitat</u>.

7.2 The Total Economic Value Framework

The economic value of environmental assets can be broken down into a set of component parts. This can be illustrated in the context of decisions about alternative land uses for a given site. According to a benefit-cost rule, decisions to 'develop' a site would have to be justified by showing that the net benefits from development exceed the net benefits from 'conservation'. Development here is taken to mean some use of the land that would be inconsistent with its retention in its natural state. Conservation could have two dimensions: preservation, which would be formally equivalent to outright non-use of the resource, and conservation which would involve limited uses of the land consistent with retention of its natural state. The benefit - cost rule would be to develop only if the development benefits minus the development costs is greater than the benefits of conservation minus the costs of conservation. Put another way, the development benefits minus both the development costs and the net conservation benefits must be positive.

Typically, development benefits and costs can be fairly readily calculated because there are attendant cash flows. Conservation benefits, on the other hand, are a mix of associated cash flows and 'non-market' benefits. This fact imparts two biases. The first is that the components with associated cash flows are made to appear more 'real' than those without such cash flows. There is 'misplaced concreteness : decisions are likely to be biased in favour of the development option because conservation benefits are not readily calculable. The second bias follows from the first. Unless incentives are devised whereby the non-market benefits are 'internalised' into the land use choice mechanism, conservation benefits will automatically be downgraded.

Conservation benefits are measured by the <u>total economic value</u> of the land. TEV comprises <u>use</u> and <u>non-use values</u>. <u>Direct</u> use values are fairly straightforward in concept but are not necessarily easy to measure in economic terms. <u>Indirect</u> use values correspond to the ecologist's concept of 'ecological functions'. A tropical forest might help protect watersheds, for example, so that removing forest cover may result in water pollution and siltation, depending on the alternative use to which the forest land is put. Similarly, tropical forests 'store' carbon-dioxide. When they are burned for clearance much of the stored CO_2 is released into the atmosphere, contributing to greenhouse gas atmospheric warming. Tropical forests also store many species which in turn may have ecological functions - one of values of biological diversity.

Option values relate to the amount that individuals would be willing to pay to conserve a given environmental asset for future use. That is, no use is made of it now but use may be made of it in the future. Option value is thus like an insurance premium to ensure the supply of something the availability of which would otherwise be uncertain. While there can be no presumption that option value is positive it is likely to be so in the context where the resource is in demand for its environmental qualities and its supply is threatened by development.

Existence value relates to valuations of the environmental asset unrelated either to current or optional use. Its intuitive basis is easy to understand because a great many people reveal their willingness to pay for the existence of environmental assets through wildlife and other environmental charities but without taking part in the direct use of the wildlife through recreation. To some extent, this willingness to pay may represent 'vicarious' consumption, i.e. consumption of wildlife videos and TV programmes, but studies suggest that this is a weak explanation for existence value. Empirical measures of existence value, obtained through questionnaire approaches (the contingent valuation method), suggest that existence value can be a substantial component of total economic value. This finding is even more pronounced where the asset is unique.

Total economic value can be expressed as:

TEV = Direct Use Value + Indirect Use Value + Option Value + Existence Value

While the components of TEV are additive, care has to be taken in practice not to add competing values. There are trade-offs between different types of use value and between direct and indirect use values.

7.3   Birds

7.3.1 National Studies

Few studies exist of the economic significance of birds. One Canadian study looked at the direct benefits from recreational and other activities associated with birds (see bibliography: Jacquemot and Filion [1987]). Over 100,000 people were surveyed to see their actual participation in bird-related activities and to ask their willingness to pay to participate. Expenditures by participants amounted to $C 1.9 billion (1986 C$) and incremental benefits (the excess of WTP over actual costs) was some $C 350 million. For all wildlife (birds and mammals) the total net benefit was $780 million p.a. Birds thus accounted for around 45% of all wildlife related activity net benefits. Of the expenditures on bird-related activity - which results in direct income and employment to others - half was accounted for by non-consumptive activities (i.e. birdwatching). Bird-related expenditure accounted for some $2.4 billion of Canadian GDP, and for $C 870 million of government revenues. Protection of a single species often results in significant gains from recreational viewing. Canada's 'capistrano' (the Pembroke swallow) was protected in 1983. The mass flocking of these birds produces a spectacle much appreciated by recreationists. Estimated net benefits, based on the travel cost approach (Annexe 3) were some $C 0.5 million p.a.(see bibliography: Clark [1987]).

7.3.2. The Mersey Barrage

Travers Morgan [1991] carried out a CVM survey in Bristol and Sheffield to ascertain non-user values for wildlife and habitat in the Mersey Estuary. The estuary's wildlife would be affected by a proposal to construct a barrage to capture tidal energy in the estuary. Bristol and Sheffield were thought to be far enough away to be sure that the values being captured are non-user rather than user values. The sample size was 300. A hypothetical trust fund was the hypothetical payment instrument suggested. The sample is very small and sample bias may therefore be significant. An equation of the form:

$$WTP = aY + bV$$

was estimated, where WTP is willingness to pay, Y is income and V is number of visits. The mean income level of £164 per month and the mean proportion of people who paid outdoor visits, 0.72, were substituted in the equation

$$WTP = 0.0169Y + 2.709$$

to give a mean WTP of £4.7 p.a. This was then extrapolated to twenty-two million Great Britain households to obtain a total non-user value of £104 million. This value will be an exaggeration since it cannot be assumed that all households will be WTP such sums for 'existence value'. Moreover, the sequence of questions asked are not in keeping with modern CVM questionnaires. The Travers Morgan study also sought user values, but with less success. User values will offset to some extent the likely upwards bias in the existence value figure obtained. If the result is meaningful, however, then it permits a 'biodiversity adder' to be estimated for the Mersey Barrage. The Barrage is expected to produce some 1.3 TWh of electricity p.a. Hence the biodiversity adder is:

1.3×10^9 kWh at 104×10^6 = 8p/kWh.

The Barrage is expected to have private costs of generation of some 9.2 p/kWh, so that the biodiversity adder suggests a doubling of costs. But the process of extrapolating from sample households to <u>all</u> households is misleading for a resource that does not have unique characteristics. Taking an arbitrary 10% of the value gives an adder of 0.8p kWh. The Barrage does, of course, have environmental benefits in the form of reduced carbon dioxide emissions. These would be allowed for in an externality adder analysis since they appear as debits to fossil fuel sources.

7.4 Ecosystem Valuation

It is possible that an energy development could threaten an entire ecosystem. If so, the TEV of an ecosystem would be the appropriate 'ecosystem adder' for that energy source.

7.4.1 Wetlands

The world's wetlands are under threat from agricultural, residential and industrial development, and from pollution. Wetlands comprise areas of marsh, fens, mangroves, and other wet areas usually, but not always, at the interface between aquatic and terrestrial environments. They account for some 6% of the global land area. They are especially fragile ecosystems because they are 'open' and are fed by river systems which are themselves subject to pollution and man-made changes in flow. Because their economic functions have been so poorly understood, they also tend to be regarded as being relatively unimportant. But there is now a wider appreciation that wetlands are <u>multifunctional</u> and that many of the unpriced functions are economically important.

Table 7.2 shows some estimates of the economic values of wetlands. By themselves they are of little interest, apart from showing that wetlands <u>do</u> have economic value and the value is not negligible. Of more relevance is the relationship between these economic values and the values of the alternative use of the wetlands. It is often assumed that water feeding a wetland is not serving a useful function when in fact, as Table 7.2 shows, natural wetlands serve a number of direct economic functions such as supporting agriculture and fisheries. A useful way of presenting such findings is in terms of the net economic value per cubic metre of water supplied to the wetland system.

Table 7.2

Economic Values for Wetlands Functions

Area	Source of Value	Valuation (1990 prices)	
Louisiana (1)	Commercial Fishery	$ 400 per acre	Present value at 8%
	Fur Trapping	$ 190	
	Recreation	$ 57	
	Storm Protection	$2400	
	Total	$3047	
Louisiana (2)	Recreation	$ 103 per acre	Present value at 8%
Charles River, Mass. (3)	Recreation	$3400 per acre	Present value at
	Water supply	$80,000	8%
Hadejia-Jama'are Floodplain, Nigeria (4)	Agriculture	$ 41 per acre	Present value at 8%
	Fishing	$ 15	
	Fuelwood	$ 7	
	Total	$ 63	
Mangrove: Trinidad (5)	Mainly fisheries	$15000 per acre	Present value at 8%
Fiji (5)		$11000	
Puerto Rico (5)		$13000	

Sources: (1)R.Costanza, S.Farber and J.Maxwell, 'Valuation and Management of Wetland Ecosystems', Ecological Economics, Vol.1, No.4, December 1989, 335-362; (2) J.Bergstrom, J.Stoll, J.Titre, V.Wright, 'Economic Value of Wetlands-Based Recreation', Ecological Economics, Vol.2, No.2, June 1990, 129-148. (3) F.Thibodeau and B.Ostro, 'An Economic Analysis of Wetland Protection', Journal of Environmental Management, 12 (1), January 1981; (4) E.Barbier, W.Adams, K.Kimmage, Economic valuation of Wetland Benefits: the Hadeja-Jama'are Floodplain, Nigeria, London Environmental Economics Centre, Paper 91-02, London, 1991; (5) Handbook for Mangrove Area Management, Section IV.

7.4.2 Valuing Preferences for Unique Habitat

The 'existence' value component of total economic value can be important, particularly where the object of valuation is unique (as with the Grand Canyon - see Chapter 11) or, if not unique, the subject of extensive familiarity to people some distance from the asset. The Kakadu Conservation Zone is in northern Australia. The zone is a 50km square zone surrounded by the 20,000 square kilometre Kakadu National Park. The Park is visited by over 200,000 people every year and has outstanding scenery, wildlife, wetlands and Aboriginal archaeological sites. Mining operations threatened to disrupt the Conservation Zone. Australia's Resource Assessment Commission therefore determined to elicit economic values for the Zone in order to compare them to the benefits of mining development. The approach used was <u>contingent valuation</u> (see Annex 3) whereby respondents are asked to respond to a questionnaire which includes questions about willingness to pay to conserve the area. The resulting 'market' is hypothetical and hence the problem with the CVM is to test for 'hypothetical bias' -i.e. the extent to which answers given to hypothetical questions would be borne out if there was a 'real' market in conservation. Part of this bias-minimisation process involves asking 'discrete choice' questions in which respondents answer yes/no to a specified question about willingness to pay, rather than answering questions about what their willingness to pay is.

The Kakadu CVM produced the following results:

Type of Mining	Valuation: $A p.yr per person for 10 years	
Impact	National sample	Northern Territory sample
Major	$A 124-143	$A 7-35
Minor	$A 53-80	$A 14-33

with the analysts showing a preference for the lower end of the range, so that valuations are some $A 50-120 per year for the national sample, according to whether the mining development would have a minor or major impact, and $7-14 for the minor impact. Extrapolated to the whole Australian population the total willingness to pay to conserve the area against mining ranges from $650 million to $1750 million, greatly in excess of the net benefits from mining (see Imber et al [1991]). CVM is controversial partly because of its use of 'hypothetical questions', but also because it is the only valuation technique capable of capturing the option and existence value components of total economic value. No attempt was made in the Kakadu study to separate out the component parts of value, but it is clear that much of the stated willingness to pay was made on behalf of people who were very unlikely to visit the area. How far the valuations recorded would be validated if there was a real market in conservation of the Kakadu Conservation zone is unknown. There are some reasons for supposing that so-called 'framing bias' arises in highly targeted valuation studies of this ind: individuals state a willingness to pay for a single purpose without reference to the many alternative uses of the money they say they are willing to pay. Some commentators feel that framing bias is particularly relevant when it comes to valuing endangered species.

The relevance of Kakadu to energy development is that it related to an open cast plus underground mine proposal for the area.

7.4.3 Valuing Preferences for the Conservation of Endangered Species

Contingent valuation techniques currently provide the only available technique for eliciting preference valuations for environmental assets that have no related market. Endangered species provide one such example. The problem with CVM is that because the market is created experimentally - through the use of interviews and questionnaires - there is no obvious way to validate the estimated willingness to pay (WTP) for conservation. A great deal of the CVM literature is therefore concerned with procedures for validation (see Annex 3). Broadly speaking, validation tests include (a) checking the CVM results against other valuation techniques (usually the travel cost method - see Annex 3), (b) checking for biases in responses to the questionnaire, and (c) checking, where possible, against actual market - revealed willingness to pay.

One virtue of the CVM approach is that it alone can capture 'existence' and 'option' values. All other valuation techniques focus on use values. Table 7.3 shows the results of CVM studies for endangered or rare species, and highly valued ecosystems. The various estimates have been converted to per person WTP in 1990 prices. The data are interesting because of their broad consistency. Valuations of preferences for species conservation, for example, cluster around £5 if the relatively high value for humpback whales is excluded, and £10 if they are included. The range is £1-11 excluding humpback whales and £1-30 including humpback whales. For prized habitat the range is £2-63 per person per year. While a great deal more work is needed in this area, the results are suggestive in that (a) they are not large proportions of respondent income, and (b) habitat appears more highly valued than species which, given the role that habitat conservation would play in species conservation, is the difference one would expect: a wider array of benefits is being secured through conservation of habitat than through targeting species. One problem area is clearly framing bias. The sum of the species valuations in the USA, for example, is much higher than average personal contributions to conservation societies, although the latter may reflect 'free rider' phenomena (many who value the environment do not pay because others pay). The international comparison of per capita values is also problematic. There are no particular reasons to suppose that 'unit values' of this kind would be the same between countries or even between different regions of the same country. But where there are reasons to suppose that environmental awareness is on approximately the same scale - which is testable through opinion polls - then, allowing for variations in income, one might expect similar valuations. As yet little work has been done to test this 'transferability' of values.

Table 7.3

Per Capita Preference Valuations

for Endangered Species and Prized Habitats

(US 1990 $ p.a per person)
(UK £ p a per person)

Species

		$	£	
Norway:	brown bear, wolf and wolverine	15.0	8.8	
USA:	bald eagle	12.4	7.3	
	emerald shiner	4.5	2.6	
	grizzly bear	18.5	10.9	
	bighorn sheep	8.6	5.0	
	whooping crane	1.2	0.7	
	blue whale	7.5	4.4	
	bottlenose dolphin	5.4	3.2	
	california sea otter	6.0	3.5	
	Northern elephant seal	8.1	4.8	
	humpback whales[1]	40-48	23.5 - 28.2	(without information)
		49-64	28.8 - 37.6	(with information)

Habitat

		$	£	
USA:	Grand Canyon (visibility)	27.0	15.9	
	Colorado wilderness	2.7-6.0	1.6- 3.5	
Australia:				
	Nadgee Nature Reserve NSW	28.1	16.5	
	Kakadu Conservation	40.0	23.5	(minor damage)
	Zone, NT[2]	93.0	54.7	(major damage)
UK:	nature reserves[3]	40.0	23.5	('experts' only)
	Flow country	28.6	16.8	
Norway:	conservation of rivers against hydroelectric development	59.0-107.0	34.7 - 62.9	

Notes: (1) respondents divided into two groups one of which was given video information; (2) two scenarios of mining development damage were given to respondents; (3) survey of informed individuals only.

Sources: <u>Norway</u> - L.Dahle et al., 'Attitudes Towards and Willingness to pay For Brown Bear, Wolverine and Wolf in Norway', Department of Forest Economics, Agricultural university of Norway, Report 5/1987, (in Norwegian); A.Hervik et al., 'Implicit Costs and Willingness to pay for Development of Water Resources', in A.Carlsen (ed), <u>Proceedings of UNESCO Symposium on Decision Making in Water Resources Planning</u>, May 1986, Oslo; <u>USA</u>: K.Boyle and R.Bishop, 'The Total value of Wildlife Resources: Conceptual and Empirical Issues', Paper presented to Association of Environmental and Resource Economists, Boulder, May 1985; D.Brookshire et al., 'Estimating Option Prices and Existence Values for Wildlife Resources', <u>Land Economics</u>, 59, 1983; R.Stoll and L.Johnson, 'Concepts of Value, Non-market Valuation, and the Case of the Whooping Crane', Department of Agricultural Economics, Texas A&M University, 1984; R.Hageman, 'Valuing Marine Mammal Populations: Benefit Valuations in a Multi-Species Ecosystem', National Marine Fisheries Service, Southwest Fisheries Center, Report LJ-85-22, La Jolla, California, 1985; K.Samples et al., 'Information Disclosure and Endangered Species Valuation', <u>Land Economics</u>, 62, No.3, 1986; W.Schulze et al., 'Economic benefits of Preserving Visibility in the National Parklands of the Southwest', <u>Natural Resources Journal</u>, 23 (1983); R.Walsh et al., 'Valuing Option, Existence and Bequest Demands for Wilderness', <u>Land Economics</u>, Vol.60, No.1, 1984; <u>Australia</u> - D.Imber et al., <u>A Contingent Valuation Survey of the Kakadu Conservation Zone</u>, Resource Assessment Commission, Research Paper No.3, Canberra, February 1991; J.Bennett, 'Using Direct Questioning to Value Existence Benefits of Preserved Natural Areas', School of Business Studies, Darling Downs Institute of Education, Toowoomba, 1982; <u>United Kingdom</u> - K.Willis and J.Benson, 'Valuation of Wildlife: A Case Study on the upper Teeside Site of Special Scientific Interest and Comparison of Methods in Environmental Economics', in R.K.Turner (ed), <u>Sustainable Environmental Management</u>, Belhaven Press, London, 1988. N.Hanley and S.Craig, 'Wilderness Development Decisions and the Krutilla-Fisher Model: the Case of Scotland's 'Flow Country'', <u>Ecological Economics</u>, 4, 1991, 145-164.

7.5 Conclusions

Biological diversity valuations may be important in selected energy production and use circumstances. Cases where pollution or siting affects natural habitats are likely to be the most important. However, biodiversity may be important in other contexts - e.g. if acidification of surface waters causes reductions in biodiversity, or if forest decline affects biodiversity. The transferability issue is of major importance here, however. It is very unlikely that values obtained from one site will apply to other sites as biodiversity will vary according to location, as will valuations, as will the impact of energy related damage. It is possible to conclude therefore that biodiversity changes would have to be evaluated separately for each energy investment. This chapter has shown that such values may be very significant, as with the possible surcharge of some 10% or more on the private costs of generating electricity from the Mersey Barrage.

CHAPTER 8   BUILDINGS and MATERIALS.

8.1 Introduction

The valuation studies relating to buildings and materials have been categorised as far as possible under the following headings;

1. materials
2. residential and commercial buildings
3. historic buildings and monuments
4. household soiling.

Acid deposition arising from the combustion products of fossil fuels, or the further reactions of these products, is the process most widely implicated in damages to materials and buildings. The main pollutants of concern are SO2, particulate matter, and chlorides. NOx may be involved either directly or indirectly but as yet evidence for this is inconclusive. These primary pollutants can also lead to the formation of equally damaging secondary pollutants such as sulphates and nitrates.

The types of damage include the corrosion of metals; decay of building stone; erosion and discolouration of paints and organic coatings; embrittlement and discolouration of paper; reduced strength and fading of textiles; and aging of rubbers and plastics. Damage to culturally significant materials is now widespread. Stone buildings and monuments have deteriorated, the artwork on many bronze monuments has been partially destroyed, and medieval stain glass windows in various parts of Europe are fading, but the links to pollution as opposed to ageing, are disputed.

It is useful to distinguish between materials and buildings which are "standard", i.e. residential property or the stock of commercial buildings and infrastructure , and "historic" i.e. historical buildings and monuments, as these two categories require different valuation approaches. For the "standard" stock of buildings and materials, damages are best estimated using dose-response functions. For the "historical" stock, the only approach capable of fully accounting for the damage is the contingent valuation approach.

Most of the quantitative work to date has used dose-response relationships to value the damage caused to buildings and materials by sulphur compounds and particulates.

The studies reviewed place a varying degree of confidence on the monetary estimates derived. Three main concerns emerge:

1. the problem of estimating damage functions
2. the problem of estimating the stock at risk
3. the problem of finding "aesthetic" values.

The fundamental problem of valuation lies not so much in determining economic parameters, but in estimating the dose-response relationship. The interaction between pollutants and materials/buildings is very complex and imprecisely understood. The deposition of pollutants on building surfaces depends not only on their atmospheric concentration, but also on climatic factors (such as the strength and direction of the wind, rain intensity and humidity). The natural structure and reactivity of different materials and the degree to which they are protected also influences the degree of damage done. A further complication is that natural factors produce the same types of damage as man-made pollutants, which makes it difficult to determine how much of the damage is due to natural causes such as weathering. Additionally, there is concern over threshold levels, synergistic effects and the 'memory' effect.

There is some evidence that the stock-at-risk can be estimated through probability density functions for modern buildings in which surfaces of buildings and materials are estimated by taking a detailed sample of a particular tract and then extrapolating the results to a larger area. Inventories and censuses are necessary for historic buildings.

"Aesthetic" values can be obtained from CVM studies. Such studies still require dose response functions, however, because of the need to relate various states of repair to pollution concentrations and hence to pollution control policy.

8.2 Materials Damage.

The materials considered in the literature reviewed range from electrical contacts and components, to paints, metals - especially zinc and steel - fibres, textiles, rubber and elastomers

Material damage is best estimated using the dose-response approach. The stages in a damage function exercise are typically:

1.   estimate a physical dose-response function of the form

     $$D = f(P, W, N)$$
     where
               D = damage e.g. in the form of corrosion.
               P = pollution concentration.
               W = a climate variable.
               N = any other factor thought to be relevant.

2.   estimate the physical stock of exposed materials.

3.   estimate one of (per unit of material):

  * costs of repair or extra maintenance.
  * material replacement cost
  * loss of the perceived consumer value of the material.
  * the cost of developing pollutant resistant materials, such as fade resistant dyes.

Costs per unit are multiplied by the stock at risk to find the cost for the total stock.

Clearly, materials damage from pollution will tend to show up in more frequent replacement, maintenance and repair of materials, and it is these extra costs which are most typically used to value damage. The issue arises as to whether this can be used as a basis for valuation ? Such an approach is relevant only if the preferences of the people for the repair/restoration exceed the costs of restoration. Many empirical studies assume that this relationship does exist. If it does, then the costs of restoration are a lower bound of the "true" value. If the relationship between preferences and costs cannot be assumed then the restoration cost approach is not legitimate as an estimator of damage.

8.2.1. USA Valuation Studies

Gillette [1975]

Gillette employs a dose-response function to value the effects of SO2 on materials. The costs examined are the increased expenditures for materials maintenance and from replacement and substitution resulting from sulphur damage. The damage function for zinc or galvanised coatings exposed to ambient SO2 incorporates coefficients for corrosion rates and for annual average relative humidity, explaining over 90% of the observed variation in the corrosion rate for zinc. Based on this model the annual replacement costs incurred due to sulphur dioxide for galvanised products is estimated at $6.85 per capita in 1972$. Based on a national population of approximately 210m (1972), the total cost of SO2 to galvanised products is $1.44b. Relating this figure to total emissions of SO2 in 1972 of approximately 30.3 million tons the national average materials damage done by SO2 is $47/ton, or $0.024/lb SO2 (1972$) which converts to $0.12/lb SO2 (1989$).

Fink et al [1971]

Fink et al , evaluate the damage costs caused by SO2 to galvanised steel by comparing the increased protection and maintenance costs incurred and the decrease in structure life due to acid rain corrosion in polluted and unpolluted areas. It is assumed that 80% of materials are located in polluted areas. Total national corrosion cost from all air pollutants is of the order of $1.45b (1971$) or $7.10 per person per year. It is asserted that 90% of the national economic burden imposed by air pollution corrosion is due to the accumulative corrosion of zinc by SO2. National emissions of SO2 in 1971 were estimated at 30m tons. If the damage caused by SO2 is approximately 90% of the total costs of $1.45b (4.10b,1989$) then this yields a national average estimate of $135/ton SO2 (1971$), i.e. 0.34/lb SO2 (1989$) for corrosion damage.

No attempt is made to relate materials damages to the severity or type of air pollution, and the rate of relative humidity is also not considered. The estimates are therefore probably understated for areas with high humidity and/or high ambient levels of pollution.

Salmon [1970]

This is a comprehensive study of pollution damage to materials in that it analyses all interactions of 53 economically important materials with pollutants and environmental parameters. The rate of economic loss ($/yr) was calculated as the product of the economic value of materials exposed to air pollution ($/unit of material) and an interaction value (units lost/yr). The interaction value is calculated by estimating the difference between the rate of material deterioration in a polluted environment and in a clean environment.

Salmon estimates that deterioration of materials causes yearly damage losses of approximately $4b ($19b 1989). Combining this damage estimate of $4b with national S02 emissions of 31m tons yields an average national S02 damage to materials of $0.004/lb S02 or $0.22/lb 1989$.

Gillette and Upham [1973]

Gillette and Upham used an assessment of economic damages to materials from S02 and relative humidity for 150 Standard Metropolitan Statistical Areas (SMSAs). The amount of metal work at risk in SMSAs was estimated from local data on: population distribution (it is assumed that materials are allocated according to human population distributions), ambient sulphur dioxide levels, and average annual relative humidity. Using damage functions for corrosion and paint deterioration, Gillette and Upham estimate that in 1970 S02 damages to metals and paints was approximately $0.4b.

ECO [1987]

ECO [1987] studied a generic coal plant located in several hypothetical locations around Washington state. ECO estimates emissions related material damage by assuming that materials exposure is proportionate to the exposure of the population as a whole, and by estimating an average national per capita materials damage effect per unit of pollutant. ECO estimates that S02 accounts for 80% of the total materials damage due to air pollution. For a generic plant located in a populated area, the damage due to S02 is estimated at $744,000 (87$) for emissions of 24,040 tons S02 per year. ECO's figures imply that the average materials damage due to S02 was $0.016/lb (87$) in this case, or $0.017/lb 1989$.

Charles River Association (CRA) [1984].

CRA use a value of zero for materials damages from S02 claiming that the relationship between acid precipitation and damages to materials is not known with enough certainty to include acid rain effects in the study. This is a simplification of the damages due to S02, since most other sources discussed indicated that S02 causes significant damages to materials.

The studies reviewed by PACE [1990] quantify materials damages from S02 emissions related costs at $0.017-$0.34/lb S02 (1989 $). PACE acknowledges that it is difficult and perhaps inappropriate to distinguish between the materials damage due to acid rain (caused by emissions of S02) and ambient S02 materials damage. However, some estimates have been developed for the damage caused by S02 in general but these are difficult to apply to specific cases or plants because:

1. Many are national averages that will understate the damage in highly populated regions, while overstating the damage in other regions.

2. Some of the estimates were made 10-20 years ago and have little relevance to current situations.

NOx and Ozone.

ECO [1987].

ECO [1987] assesses the annual materials damage due to "nitrogen compounds" as $184,471 [1987$] for its case study area with the highest population density . ECO admits that its material damage estimates are only rough as they are based on the national average per capita material damage estimates developed by Waddell [1974]. ECO assumes that materials damage due to NOx is approximately 20% of the total damage (with S02 and particulates making up the remainder). NOx-related damages are on the order of $19/ton NOx [1989$], or just under 1 cent/lb NOx.

ECO [1983].

ECO [1983] estimates almost negligible materials loss due to the pollutants NOx and ozone.

Midwest Research Institute Report (MRI) [1970].

After defining the value of the materials exposed to air pollution, the MRI study assess the damage costs as a product of the material value and the percentage reduction in the economic life per year of exposure. MRI used research prepared by Spence and Haynie [1972]. MRI concludes that the national damage costs to exterior paints such as automotive refinishing, household paints, coil coatings and industrial maintenance caused by air pollution, totalled $225m [1970$] in 1968. The materials value does not account for the value of exposed paint in rural areas and therefore understates total damages to paint caused by oxidant pollution. In 1968 national NOx and VOC emissions were approximately 19m tons and 30m tons (ie 49m tons of ozone precursors). Assuming NOx and VOC contribute equally to ozone formation and that ozone is the predominant pollution responsible for damage to paints, the average cost of ozone related damages is on the order of $4.60/ton of ozone precursor [1970$] or $23/ton ozone precursor [1989$] i.e. 1.15cents/lb. The marginal damages to paint materials in areas of high ambient levels of ozone and high population and materials density could be significantly higher.

The total damage cost figure understates the actual damage costs inflicted on exterior paint because it does not include damages suffered by the consumer. Spence and Haynie estimated that the loss at the consumer level ie. the cost of the paint applied to surfaces including labour, was three times the manufacturers' cost. Therefore the damage cost to exterior paint for manufacturers and consumers would be closer to $70/ton ozone precursor [1989$] i.e. about 3.5 cents/lb.

Mueller and Stickney [1970]

Mueller and Stickeny estimate the damage caused to elastomers (any rubber-like substance) by ozone. They conclude that the total retail cost of ozone damage to elastomers is $596m. This figure includes retail costs of $257m for special formulations and $339m for early replacements. Special formulation costs represent the cost to the manufacturer of avoiding ozone damage to rubber products by introducing ozone resistant chemicals such as polymers and antiozonants and changes in rubber production techniques such as paper wrapping, protective finishes, compound development and waxing. Mueller and Stickney predict future ozone damage to rubber products by approximating the percentage increase in rubber production over a fixed period of time and then multiplying that number by $596m or the total retail damage cost in 1969. Based on expected growth of rubber production of 25% over 1968 levels, the study concludes that in 1975 the cost of ozone damage to elastomers would be $750m [1969$]. Using 1968 national NOx and VOC combined emissions of 49m tons of ozone precursors, the ozone damage to rubber products is of the order of $15.30/ton of ozone precursor [1969$], or $77/ton [1989$]. In their review, PACE [1990] conclude that NOX and ozone damage to materials is 1 cent per lb NOx.

Particulates.

ECO [1983, 1984, 1985].

The studies by ECO estimate the materials damage due to particulates to be zero .

Acid Rain

Lipfert [1987].

Lipfert values S02 and acid rain damages to materials (paint, galvanised steel, mortar, and stone) in the New Haven, CT region. The unit cost factors, which are based on the costs of repainting or replacing, are as follows: $1/ft2 for repainting 15% of the total area, $3/ft3 for repainting mortar, $4/ft2 for replacing galvanised steel, $22/ft2 for replacing stone facing. Lipfert finds that the costs for hydrogen ions alone are $3.42m annually, or about $8.50 per capita, with total costs from S02 and hydrogen ions at about $6m, or $15 per capita. Repainting is responsible for the lions share of the costs. Assuming a linear damage function the benefits of a 50% reduction in acid rain are about $3.25 per capita.

This study is a reasonable example of an "engineering" approach to damage valuation, in that damage functions are linked to unit values for repainting and replacement, but these values have no behavioral content. These unit values do not reflect the frequency and type of response made by building owners to signs of materials damage or to the prospect that acid rain may damage materials in the future. Therefore these estimates may be a poor estimate of the benefits of a reduction in acid rain.

The results of the Lipfert study <u>could</u> be generalised to other areas, using population as a scaling factor, particularly to cities of the same average age and size as New Haven. It should be recognised however that these estimates will reflect the mix of materials and the ratio of population to affected materials found in New Haven. Further, since Lipfert does not link acid rain reductions back to SO2 emissions the results of this study need to be linked to an SO2 / acid deposition model for it to be applied to other areas.

Horst et al [1986].

Horst et al estimate materials damage from air pollution in four US cities - Cincinnati, New Haven, Pittsburg and Portland. First they estimate a dose-response function relating rates of materials damage to levels of SO2 and H+. This relationship is applied to an inventory of building materials, calculated by the probability distribution approach. From this the rates of loss of physical quantities of materials due to these forms of air pollution are obtained. To estimate economic damages the following assumptions are made:
a) That in the presence of air pollution maintenance rates will be such as to keep buildings in the condition they would have with no air pollution.
b) that the materials used for this purpose are the same as those that are always used and are to be valued at their current market price; and
c) That the labour used for maintenance is valued at the current market wage rate.

The figures obtained are taken to be an estimate of the damage done by the current levels of air pollution in these four cities. As an extension of the same study the methodology was also applied to 113 U.S. cities in the North East quadrant of the country. The basis of this extrapolation was an estimated inventory of buildings and materials in the wider area, based on the more detailed inventories of the four cities cited above.

A weakness in this study is that it is assumes that no mitigating behaviour is undertaken. Principally this involves the use of pollutant resistant materials in the areas of high pollution. Mitigating behaviour would only be employed if it was cheaper than using regular materials and undertaking regular maintenance, therefore, the latter will overestimate the costs of maintenance. However the use of pollutant resistant materials could lead to an underestimate of the materials costs e.g. vinyl coated gutters are more expensive than galvanised gutters and more frequently used in high acid deposition areas.

It is assumed that there is a fairly mechanical relationship between increases in air pollution and increases in the frequency of maintenance. In fact the behavioral response to pollution can be quite complex, e.g. pollution causes erosion to paint, but repainting decisions are likely to be based on factors such as peeling and cracking rather than erosion as such. Furthermore, victims in polluted areas can simply leave paintwork to deteriorate more than they would in a pristine environment. In that case the costs of pollution are overstated by assuming a constant level of maintenance. On the labour side, uncertainty arises because the overall cost of labour depends very much on the quality of the painting that is being done and who does it.

In the range of estimates obtained for each city, the top estimate was sometimes 12 times as large as the bottom estimate. The main uncertainty appears to be paint costs, the relative importance of which determines the range of valuation estimates for each city.

The EPA reviewed the Horst study and concluded that, although the study was well done, given the limitations of the data, the uncertainty inherent in the physical and economic relationship made the results unsuitable for the determination of policy in this area. The main source of this uncertainty was identified as the physical damage functions relating to paint and mortar erosion to the levels of SO2 and H+.

Horst et al [1990].

Probably the most detailed analysis of one aspect of materials damage is Horst et al [1990] which deals with acid deposition damage to painted wood surfaces in the south coast (California) air basin. The study involved detailed household surveys on maintenance expenditures together with physical dose-response functions. On the <u>physical damage function</u> approach (looking at corrosion rates and valuing the resulting accelerated maintenance at market prices), annual cost savings from a 10% reduction in NO_2 concentrations is $0.7 million [1988 $] with a range of $0 to $1 million. In the <u>economic approach</u> - based on direct questionnaire approaches concerning maintenance expenditures - the estimate is $3.6 million per annum. <u>Per household</u> savings range from $0.32 to $0.82 for the physical damage approach.

Unfortunately, the study does not report NO_2 emissions, so it is not possible to relate the damage cost (benefit of 10% NO_2 reduction) to emissions. Significantly, however, the study does implicate NOx in materials damage.

General Air Pollution: Haynie (1982)

Haynie estimates that the annual cost of corrosion damage due to air pollution on galvanised steel roofing, siding and guttering in the U.S. could range from $0.6 to $1.5 per person at an average existing SO2 level of 30 ug/m³. The best estimate at this level was $1.05, but at the primary ambient air quality standard of 80 ug/m³ the best estimate was $1.80. The total cost on a national scale at a level of 30 ug/m³ in 1980 was estimated to be $242 million, with $115 million of that going to replace prior damaged products. The per capita function derived for the premature loss of galvanised steel roofing, siding and guttering only was $1.5 +/- 0.5 per ug/m³ of SO2 plus $0.1 for substitution costs and $0.5 in 1980 for prior years of accumulated damage.

8.2.2 <u>Non - USA Studies</u>.

Fenger <u>et al</u>., [no date] (Denmark).

Fenger <u>et al</u>., in a study under the Danish "Acid Deposition Project" value annual damage to materials and related social costs due to acid deposition (mainly S02) at Dkr 500m. The main contribution comes from the degradation of paint and galvanised steel. The authors conclude that damage to historic buildings and monuments and to objects in museums and archives cannot be unambiguously valued, but that the total annual loss for this category may be of the same order of magnitude as for the "service-materials". In the late 1980s SO2 depositions in Denmark were some 121,800 tonnes of SOx per annum. This would suggest damages of some 4105 Dkr per tonne of SO2 or $586 tonne at 7 Dkr = $1, or $0.13 per US lb.

Jansen et al., [1974] (Netherlands).

Jansen's study was the first in the Netherlands with respect to air pollution damage to materials. Damage to materials (steel and steel coatings such as paint and zinc) was estimated at Dfl. 110m.

Jansen and Olsthoorn, [1982] (Netherlands).

Jansen and Olsthoorn estimated annual damages to be Dfl 40m (ECU 22m) in the Netherlands. A doubling of the emissions of S02 was estimated to result in annual damage of Dfl 151m (ECU 83m), i.e. the damage function was thought to be non-linear.

Both the 1974 and 1982 studies on materials damage are dated and are of little use for present research, suffering from a lack of data (physical and economic) and dose-response functions. SO2 emission figures were used instead of deposition figures.

National Environmental Programme of the Netherlands [1990]

The Environmental Programme of the Netherlands gives the following annual materials damage estimates.

steel and zinc sheet	Dfl 40 m
metals	Dfl 113 m
concrete damage	Dfl 175-350 m
facade cleaning	Dfl 12-25 m
total	Dfl 340-528 m

Depositions in the Netherlands are put at 172,600 tonnes of SO2 for 1988. Hence damage per tonne SO2 is DFL 1970 -3060 per tonne SO2. At 1.98 DFL = $1 in 1988 and 1 tonne = 2205 US lb, the cost per US lb is $0.45 - 0.70.

Lanting and Morree [1984] (Netherlands)

Lanting and Morree estimated that materials damage due to air pollution in the Netherlands from 1978-84 cost from 125 to 180 million Dutch guilders per year excluding cultural property.

Glomsrod and Rosland [1988] (Norway).

Glomsrod and Rosland [1988] use a dose-response function to estimate the direct costs of materials damage due to sulphur dioxide in Norway. They also employ a multi-sectoral macroeconomic growth model to estimate the indirect costs of S02 due to allocational effects.

The materials studied include galvanised steel, paint on steel, wood and stone, and stain on wood. Damages to other materials are not included due to lack of dose-response functions. Other air pollutants can also have corrosive effects e.g. nitrogen oxides, but Norwegian results so far have shown this effect to be small. However, N0x can increase the corrosion of the zinc cover on galvanised steel in S02-polluted air. This effect is difficult to quantify and has not been taken into account in this study.

The dose-response functions used are linear. The most researched function is that for galvanised steel based on five years of observation in southern Norway. The function describing the number of years (LG) needed to corrode 1um of the zinc cover of galvanised steel is given below.

$$(1) \quad LG = E/K = 7.1 / (0.45 * (SO2) + 0.7).$$

where E is the specific weight of zinc in g/cm^3 and K is the speed of corrosion given in $g/m^2/year$.

Based on data from the U.S.A. and Norway the Norwegian Institute for Air Research estimated the following dose-response function between S02-concentrations and the lifetime (LPS), measured in years, for paint and steel:

$$(2) \quad LPS = 11.7 - 0.0042 * (SO2).$$

Similar functions have not been estimated for paint on wood/stone or stain on wood, but based on expert judgements the following functions were used for the lifetime of paint on wood and stone (LPWS) and stain on wood (LSW):

$$(3) \quad LPWS = 12 - 0.042 * (SO2)$$

$$(4) \quad LSW = 6 - 0.042 * (SO2)$$

The SO2 concentrations are measured in um/m^3 in all functions.

These functions, and assumptions about behavioral responses to the perceived damage, are used to estimate the change in the maintenance interval for materials. The valuation is based on the difference in costs, calculated from market prices, associated with the changes in repair/replacement intervals.

The study concludes that local and long-range transported S02 emissions lead to an additional maintenance cost of approximately 420m 1990 Nkr in Norway annually. 27% of these costs is due to long-range sources. In addition, indirect costs were valued at 136m 1990 Nkr, making a total of 556m Nkr. Depositions of oxidised sulphur were 302,400 tonnes, so that damage would be 1389 Nkr/tonne, or $201/ tonne or $0.09 per U.S. lb.

The study is limited in that the estimates do not include the corrosive effects of all air pollutants on all materials, and the direct cost estimates are based on the crude assumptions that economic agents are limited in the ways in which they can adapt to this environmental effect and that the effect is small enough to have little or no effect on relative prices. However they do provide an order of magnitude of these effects in Norway.

8.3 Residential and Commercial Buildings.

Buildings Effects Review Group, BERG, [1989]. (UK)

BERG was set up by the British government in 1985 to review the effects of acid rain on building materials. On physical dose-response functions the BERG report asks how buildings and materials damage have responded to reductions in S02 levels in the UK. It concludes that:

> the evidence favours the view that pollution does accelerate weathering;

> but as far as historical buildings are concerned, damage may be unrelated to current pollution levels, being due instead to past pollution (the "memory effect") and other weather events.

> other metals have not experienced any discernible change in weathering.

The BERG report also addresses the issue of measuring the stock at risk. For cultural buildings it concludes that an inventory is required while for modern buildings a probability distribution approach is recommended.

The report casts considerable doubt on the feasibility of estimating reliable dose-response functions. The group is unable to say which pollutants are the major sources of decay (moisture, frost, salt , sulphur dioxide, polluting particles , and oxides of nitrogen are among those implemented). It is unable to state whether further curbs on the emission of pollutants, such as sulphur dioxide and oxides of nitrogen, would be cost effective in terms of minimising the problem, and it is unsure whether there are "safe" levels of potentially damaging pollutants or weathering agents. There is evidence, however, that pollutants act synergistically.

The "memory" effect would mean that past exposure could be important. If the interest is in what damage has been done then the "memory" effect is relevant. However, if the interest is how to adjust current pollution control policy the memory effect suggests that the benefits of control may be less than otherwise might be thought. Effectively, damage could be mainly due to events in the past over which there is no control. The BERG Committee concluded it necessary to wait the outcome of National Materials Exposure Programme (NMEP) which commenced in 1987 and which is attempting to identify the dose-response effects in 29 sites in the UK before saying more on the dose response relationship. This programme is linked to the International Cooperative Materials Exposure Programme of UN ECE which also commenced in 1987.

The BERG report discusses the alternative methodologies for measuring economic cost. The authors regard the analysis of clean and dirty expenditures as an alternative approach to estimating a damage function. A figure of £2.50 per capita is quoted as a benefit of a 30% reduction in S02 in Birmingham. This value appears to relate to the ECOTEC [1986] study - see below. As with other commentaries and surveys, the BERG report focuses on costs of repair and maintenance.

Heinz [1980], BMU [1986] (Germany).

Heinz carried out Germany's first nation-wide materials damage valuation study. The Heinz study is summarised and up-dated (to 1983) in a report by BMU (1986). Heinz estimated the additional costs for maintenance, replacement and cleaning in so-called "deposition areas", as compared to "clean air areas". Primarily, these higher costs are due to the higher frequency with which these tasks have to be performed. Damage categories under consideration are buildings, steel constructions and windows (cleaning).

The total annual monetary damage for these categories in the FRG is estimated to be DM [1983] 2.3 billion. Nearly half of this figure is due to facade painting. Damage is due to sulphur dioxide and other pollutants.

Table 8.1 presents the results of Heinz's study.

Isecke [1990] (Germany)

Isecke et al. [1990] investigate those materials susceptible to damage which, in terms of quality and quantity, exhibit the greatest damage from air pollution and for which dose-response relationships have been documented in scientific studies. Materials include zinc, galvanised steel, natural stone, organic coatings, concrete and brickwork. Impacts are based on the 1987 annual mean value of SO2 emissions. The territory of the FRG was divided into to high deposition areas (urban\industrial areas) and low deposition areas (rural areas) in order to estimate the impact costs for buildings and materials. Due to the lack of data on actual material stock, material damage caused by air pollution in polluted regions was based on numerous enquiries submitted to appropriate institutions, authorities and associations.

Additional, deposition-related burdens in material maintenance were calculated as follows:

$$K_n - K * \sum_{i-1}^{n} S_i * \left(\frac{1}{L_i} - \frac{1}{L_t} \right) \qquad (1)$$

K_n = additional material maintenance costs in high-deposition areas (DM per year).
K = specific maintenance costs
S_i = surface area or number of exposed material assets in deposition region i (m²).
L_i = maintenance interval in the area subject to deposition impact (year).
L_r = maintenance interval in clean air area (year).

The study establishes a correlation between air-borne pollution concentrations and material damage. Expenditure on maintenance, corrosion protection and cosmetic repairs on building structures and material property in emission impact areas are higher than those in unpolluted areas.

The damage categories are not complete because for some categories a lack of sufficient base data and dose-response research did not allow for accurate valuation.

Remarkably, the results of Heinz's study and Isecke's study are very similar - see Table 8.1.

Table 8.1

Monetary Estimates of Materials and Buildings Damage by Air Pollution in the FRG.

Property group	Heinz/1983	Isecke et al./1990
Residential buildings	2,122	1,780 - 3,120
Window cleaning costs	142	250 - 443
Mineral oil deposits	-	13
Digestion towers		2
Overhead power transmission pylons	6	5
Motorway bridges	21	–
Railway bridges	6	7.2
Railway contact line systems	11	4
Total DM million	2,308	2,061 - 3,594

Related to SO_2 depositions of 1,077,000 tonnes in West Germany in 1987/1988 the Isecke estimates suggest damages of 1914 DM to 3337 DM per tonne or, at 1.8 DM in 1987 and 1 tonne = 2205 US lb, $0.48 to $0.84 US lb. The split between buildings and materials is 0.41 - 0.73 $/lb and 0.07 - 0.11 $/lb.

ECOTEC [1990]

ECOTEC carried out an extensive project on the assessment of damage of acid deposition to buildings in England, focusing on:

> the development of an inventory methodology to determine the numbers and kinds of buildings and building components and materials at risk;

> the assessment of damage in terms of the impact upon buildings and building components rather in terms of material loss or corrosion;

> the assessment of the costs damage and savings from air pollution abatement in terms which recognise that building components and buildings are, in any case, regularly maintained and have a finite life.

ECOTEC [1990] estimate the benefits in terms of reduced buildings corrosion from a 30% reduction in SO2 in England. A unit cost saving per m^3 of exposed surface is estimated. Aerial surveys were used to estimate the buildings stock and each building is converted to an 'external envelope' - i.e. exposed surface. The total benefit is then:

> No. of buildings * average envelope * unit cost saving.

The resulting savings are shown in Table 8.2.

Table 8.2
Buildings Damage in England [2]

Building Type	Total Buildings	Unit Costs £/m³ [2]	Total Cost Savings (£m) 1990 prices[2] (PV at 5%)
Houses (No)	18.6m	1.08	8049
Schools (No)	53,640	1.59	104.9
Shops (m²)	76.1m	1.75	164.7
Offices (m²)	48.2m	2.30	101.1
Govt. Bdgs (m²)	48.8m	1.65	196.2
Factories (m²)	225.7m	1.44	607.6
Warehouses (m²)	128.3m	0.77	274.9
Total			9498.4
Historic Buildings			2000.0
Total			11498.4

Source: ECOTEC [1990]

Taking these figures at face value, the present value (at 5% over 30 years) is £11.5 billion. This is consistent with an annual flow of £748 million p.a.

A 30% reduction in SO2 depositions in <u>Great Britain</u> would amount to some 324,720 tonnes SO2. Hence the 'buildings adder' is £2304 per tonne, or 0.23 p/g SO2. Applying this figure to the emission factors in Chapter 3 suggests adders as follows:

existing coal	3.22 p/kWh
new coal	0.28 p/kWh
oil	3.77 p/kWh
gas	0.11 p/kWh

Differentiating between buildings and historic buildings, the adders are:

buildings	0.19 p/g
historic buildings	0.04 p/g
	0.23 p/g

The ECOTEC reduction is higher than the other European estimates, but the stated confidence interval is wide at +/- 80%.

There are additional problems with the ECOTEC study. Pollution levels will obviously not change uniformly across the country; the source of the dose-reponse functions used is far from clear; and the relationship betwen repair and maintenance costs and willingness-to-pay to avoid damage is not explored in the study. As a result, there must be some doubt about the validity of the ECOTEC study. It is, however, the only recent study available relating to the UK.

8.4 Historic Buildings and Monuments.

Valuation of historic assets (buildings, monuments, works of art, books and archives) is best estimated using contingent valuation. If historical buildings and monuments could be reasonably described and quantified then it would be feasible to ask people to value various states of repair and disrepair through questionnaires using photographs of "typical" monuments.

Although it is possible to measure a dose-response relationship for a historical building, the next stage of applying a measure of valuation to a "unit" of damage is not meaningful. In the case of historic buildings and monuments, there is no necessary relationship between (maintenance and repair) costs and benefits, as the damage to a work of art is likely to diminish its aesthetic value far more than the simple loss of materials would indicate, this phenomenon is borne out in the following observations.

Historic buildings and monuments are irreplaceable.

Being part of the cultural heritage, they are also valued by non-visitors for their "existence" or "bequest" value.

Decisions on the level of repair and maintenance are arrived at by non-market processes.

Benefits of the maintenance of the building do not only accrue to the occupants of the building, but to all visitors to the building or the monument.

The measurement of preferences for restoration requires the estimation of user and existence values. User values for historic monuments could be estimated using the travel cost method (TCM). In terms of evaluation for policy purposes, however, TCM is unlikely to be of significant use because it is not clear how it could be adapted to a valuation of changes in the quality of historical buildings. One possible approach would be to combine a survey with TCM by asking visitors whether they would travel to the site if there was an improvement in the building quality. TCM might then be used to value the travel behaviour. In general, however, TCM would seem of limited use in the historic building context. Existence values are likely to be far more important and these would require the use of CVM.

For some types of material, e.g. paper and glass, cultural property is the main victim of pollution. It is estimated that 50% of the books printed between 1900 and 1940 are in need of conservation, while the most serious damage to glass is occurring to stained glass windows. Sulphur dioxide, soot and dust cause damage to artwork and structures. Damage to buildings and statutes is severe in many areas and increasing. SO2 has been shown to be responsible for much of the damage.

Feenstra [1984], (Netherlands)

Feenstra carried out a study on the damage of air pollution on cultural goods in the Netherlands. This study is the first attempt to give a comprehensive estimate of the damage of air pollution to monuments, objects of art, archives and buildings in the Netherlands. Apart from the problem of valuing unique and irreplaceable assets, the author notes a lack of data as to the objects at risk and the proportion of damage that can be attributed to air pollution.

Damage figures were arrived at using data on costs of preventative and restorative measures. Along with actual costs, the cost of urgent restoration and prevention measures which were not carried out because of lack of money were also considered.

Table 8.3 gives the damage categories considered and the corresponding damage figures.

Table 8.3

Damage to Historical Assets in the Netherlands

Damage category	Basis of damage estimate	Percentage of damage due to air pollution	Damage estimate (in million Dfl)
Monuments	actual restoration costs	30-50%	15-30 per year
Monuments	applications for restoration subsidies	30-50%	120-200
Stained - glass windows	preservation costs (outer glazing)	100%	20
Carillons	restoration costs	50%	0.25 per year

Museums, archives and libraries:
   -textiles
   -paper
   -paper
	restoration costs
	restoration costs
	prevention costs
		40%
		20%
		100%
			20
			620
			10
			per year

Source. Feenstra (1984).

The Feenstra study is one of the few European studies (another example is an Italian study by Muraro [1974]; a Norwegian study is currently being carried out) which tries to assess monetary damage to cultural goods.

As discussed, the cost of repair and maintenance approach has obvious drawbacks in the case of the valuation of damage to unique historic buildings. It may be incompatible with the requirements of cost-benefit analysis in that the amount spent by governments on restoration and protection of cultural property reflects the preferences of the authorities rather than those of the individual citizens. However despite obvious flaws, the study attracted much publicity in the media and has contributed to public awareness in the Netherlands of the negative effects of acidification on historic buildings and monuments (Kuik et al., [1991]). Feenstra's restoration costs for monuments translates to some DFL 695 - 1158 per tonne. At a 1984 exchange rate of 3.2 DFL = $1, this is equivalent to $0.1 - $0.16 per U.S. lb.

ECOTEC [1990]

ECOTEC uses the travel cost method in the case of historic buildings and monuments in England. Together with a 'priority evaluator technique' they estimate total savings in damage to historic buildings at £2 billion for a 30% reduction in SO2.

One study that actually used the travel cost method to assess damages to cultural materials due to acid rain, concluded that this approach can only be applied to sites where acid rain threatens to erode the value of the whole site (Charles River Associates, 1983). "The method is incapable of separating the potential loss in value caused by acid rain damage from the value of the site as a place of historical significance. Such a value could be quantified only in contingent valuation survey that asked people how they would behave if the outdoor art were threatened lost".

Navrud [1990]

Navrud describes an interesting project currently underway in Norway attempting to estimate the existence and bequest value of one specific historic building, the stone church of Nidarosdomen. A CV method is used to elicit people's willingness to pay to preserve the original church and not a restored one, i.e. what is being valued is authenticity.

Losing the original church due to corrosion from air pollution would be an irreversible loss, and increased maintenance cots will only provide a lower-bound estimate of the economic damage to historical buildings and monuments.

8.5 Household Soiling

Watson and Jaksch [1982].

Air pollution, notably from particulate matter affects household cleaning. Watson and Jaksch [1982] estimated household welfare losses arising from increased cleaning of walls and windows and increased painting of surfaces. Their national estimates for the U.S. are shown in Table 8.4.

Table 8.4
Household Soiling Damage in the USA

Improvement in existing TSP to (ug/m^3).	Benefits (1971 $) 10^6
100	613
75	1547
60	2656
55	3167

They argue that these benefits may well outweigh other benefit components, indicating the importance of estimating soiling damage.

8.6 Aggregate Estimates.

Some figures are available for Europe as a whole, for the Netherlands and Germany separately, and for the United States with respect to aggregate damages , i.e. undifferentiated by buildings, materials etc.

For Europe the information has been conveniently assembled by the Economic Commission for Europe [ECE 1982]. This provides broad relationships for sulphur compounds, and their impact on carbon steel, zinc and galvanised steel, nickel and nickel-plated steel copper materials and aluminium. The available evidence for damage to sandstone and limestone is given. The nature of damages to painted surfaces is not known with any precision and the ECE team report that even less is known about damage to plastics and rubber. After reviewing various economic assessments of material damage, the ECE team concluded that sulphur damage to materials other than historical buildings is of the order of $3-14 per capita per annum in $1983.

Netherlands Ministry of Housing and Environment [1983].

In the Netherlands, materials damage from air pollution, excluding some restoration expenses, was estimated at $8-15 per capita per annum 1983$.

Heinz [1986].

In Germany, materials damage to buildings and steel structures, but excluding monuments, was estimated by Heinz to be around $15 per capita per annum in 1983$.

Freeman [1982].

For the U.S. Freeman obtained a figure of about $28 per capita. This includes material damage from sulphur compounds, NOx and oxidants.

Taking these estimates and updating them we have:

ECE $3 - 14 per capita 1983
FRG $ 15 per capita 1983   or $16.8 in 1991
Neth $8 - 15 per capita 1983   or $ 8.5 - 16 in 1991
USA $ 28 per capita 1983   or $33.7 in 1991

The German figure translates to

$$\frac{\$16.8 \quad * \quad 61.3 \text{ million people}}{1,077,000} = \frac{\text{TOTAL DAMAGE}}{\text{SO2 DEPOSITIONS}}$$

$$= \quad \$956 \text{ per tonne or } \underline{\$ 0.42 \text{ per US lb}}$$

The Dutch figures translate to

$$\frac{\$ (8.5 \text{ to } 16) \quad * \quad 14.8 \text{ million people}}{172,600}$$

$$= \quad \$ 729 \text{ to } 1372 \text{ per tonne, or } \$0.33 \text{ to } \$0.71 \text{ per lb.}$$

8.7 Non-Monetary Studies.

Harter [1986]

Harter's 1986 review is extensive but also relies on other reviews of the literature, notably the surveys by Feenstra, Economic Commission for Europe, and Altshuller et al. The only UK study was that of the Programmes Analysis Unit in 1972. This study used a cross sectional damage function in which costs of painting , cleaning, replacement etc. were calculated for "clean" and "dirty" areas. The difference was used as an approximation of the addition costs arising from pollution.

On the basis of the international evidence, Harter concludes that:

Economic studies have used unrealistic assumptions in both the materials and atmospheric quality data. Cost data are fragmentary.

Damage to cultural property is "considerably more problematical". Harter's reasons for saying this are confused, however, since she refers to the disparity between the "intrinsic" value of such property and the value people place on it. It is of course only the latter that is relevant to monetary valuation.

Harter does not produce any estimates of probable buildings and materials damage for the UK.

Cambridge Decision Analysts and Environmental Resources Ltd [1988].

CDA and ERL reviewed the state of knowledge on damage functions in 1988. Experts were also interviewed in an effort to obtain additional evidence. Dose-response functions were reviewed for: zinc and galvanised steel, stone, paint, concrete and brickwork

The CDA/ERL study did not attempt a monetary valuation of materials damage, preferring instead to estimate "extended lifetimes" for several categories of materials arising from pollution control policies. This reflects the decision theoretical framework for the analysis - i.e. the interest is more in targeting actions which have the most significant effect.

8.8 Conclusion: A Building/Materials Adder

Valuation studies to date have concentrated on the effects of sulphur dioxide on materials. There is uncertainty of the role of NOx, though it is generally assumed that the effects are small.

There is still a large degree of uncertainty on the actual physical process. However there seems to be no reason not to use recent dose response functions which represent the state of the art at this time. It is reasonable to assume that the benefits which the owner/ occupant receives from maintaining and repairing his building are at least equal to the costs of doing so, provided these repairs are undertaken. Therefore, increased repair and maintenance costs is a fair minimum estimate of air pollution damage for the owners/ occupiers. However this argument does not necessarily hold for publically owned buildings and other outdoor structures. Bias may be created by the rental part of the housing market. It is not at all clear that tenants and landlords share the same preferences with respect to repair and maintenance. None of the studies has taken this, or other behavioral factors into account. In obtaining aggregate estimates, there are also serious problems of obtaining an accurate inventory of the materials that are exposed to air pollution.

If results are to be transferred to other countries or regions the following issues should be kept in mind;

* climate conditions may differ and therefore dose response relationships will differ;
* buildings materials used may be different in different countries
* the exposed areas of the various materials may be different;
* maintenance/repair costs may be different;

Especially with respect to historical buildings and monuments there may be a large difference in societies' valuation or willingness to pay for preservation, due to economic and cultural differences.

In most cases the total damage due to air pollution is assessed. To be able to assess the damage of a certain increase in ambient levels or to assess the benefits of a reduction of those levels, a complete damage function should be specified. This has rarely been done.

It is not easy to secure damage estimates for materials. Sulphur dioxide appears repeatedly as a significant man-made agent of damage, but the effects of NOx, ozone and other pollutants have not been properly evaluated for most materials. Several important sources of materials damage are yet to be quantified, such as damage to concrete structures, automobiles, electric components and plastics and rubber.

Table 8.5 summarises estimates of materials and buildings damage. The European estimates show some consistency at around 120 - 240 pence/kg, supported also by the aggregate estimates. However the UK estimate is 3-4 times higher at 430 pence/kg.

TABLE 8.5

SUMMARY ESTIMATES OF MATERIALS/BUILDINGS DAMAGE.
U.S. cents / U.S. lb (1989 prices)
(U.K. pence / kg 1991 prices)

	MATS c/lb	RES BUILDS c/lb	HIS BUILDS c/lb	HSEHOLD SOILING c/lb	TOTAL c/lb	p/kg
SO₂ U.S.A 1990	2-34[a]				>36	>36
GER 1990	7-11	41-73			>48-84	>62-109
NETH 1990 (NEPP, Feenstra aggregate).	33-71[a]		10-16		>43-87	>55-113
NOR 1988 (Glomsrod)	9				>9	>12
UK 1990 (ECOTEC)		146	31	-	>177	>230
DEN (Fenger)	27	-	-	-	>27	>35

[a]   Represents an aggregate range for materials and residential buildings.

Note: conversion from U.S.cents/U.S.lb to pence/kg as follows - adjust 1989 cents to 1991 prices at 1% p.a. Netherlands; 3% p.a. Germany; 4% p.a. U.S.A; 5% p.a. Norway; convert cents/lb to pence/lb at $1.7 = £1; convert lb to kg at 1lb = 0.454 kg.

CHAPTER 9   LAND DAMAGE

9.1   Introduction.

Fossil fuel and nuclear power plants require significant amounts of land for plant sites, fuel storage, transmission lines, and waste disposal. Although the cost of the land is incorporated into the capital cost, a number of external land use costs remain. Plant sites, combustion waste dumps, fuel piles and power lines often have the effect of lowering surrounding land values, due to the aesthetic impacts of construction, operation and maintenance. Much of the solid waste produced from power generation and transmission is disposed of in landfills, which may have a negative environmental effect on land and water. Renewables also have land use requirements, but their impacts vary greatly in degree from conventional power technologies.

Damages to land are highly site specific (they will depend on the nature of the surrounding geography, demographics, and wildlife needs). The valuation literature related to land is small, and it has not proved possible to derive an externality adder for land damage.

9.2   Power Plant Land Requirements.

The U.S. Department of Energy estimates that a typical 500 megawatt coal-fired plant will occupy 849 acres for coal storage, fuel preparation, solid waste disposal, and power plant. Oil fired plants require an estimated 96 acres for an 800 megawatt plant.

Facilities may be located so as to consume open space or agricultural land, which may impact upon wildlife and diminish present and future local food production. Fossil fuel plants are often located on or near waterways due to their need for cooling water, however, because rivers, streams and lakes typically provide much of the natural beauty of the area, scenic and recreational values are undoubtedly reduced by power plant construction and operation.

Combustion wastes, particularly from coal fired units - must be landfilled. This consumes landfill space that would otherwise be devoted to municipal waste disposal, and accelerates the need for additional land fill sites.

Wind farms require substantial land areas for their operation (between fifteen and forty-five acres per megawatt of capacity). The best sites are areas with little ground cover such as hill tops, shorelines or arable land, therefore, windfarms may conflict with other land uses such as farming and nature conservation. All major obstructions such as trees must be removed and a road must usually be constructed to allow maintenance access to the turbines.

Hydroelectric dams may damage land. When the land behind a dam is inundated, sediments previously carried downstream may become trapped behind the dam. Water flowing downstream at higher than normal velocities may cause erosion of river beds and banks as well as distant coastal lands such as deltas, estuaries and seashores.

9.2.1 Valuation Studies.

This section uses a representative selection of land valuation studies to illustrate the difficulty in deriving a general externality adder for land.

PACE cites The New York Public Service Commission (NYPSC) as the sole attempt to determine a generally applicable externality cost figure for land. However, this estimate is based on control and mitigation costs, rather than on estimates of damage. NYPSC assigns 0.4 cent per kilowatt hour for land-use related impacts. This figure was extrapolated from a case study of land use related social costs of a nuclear power plant, which estimated to range from 0.1 to 0.44 cents per kWh.

Ferguson [1990] attempts to estimate the amenity value of land. Starting with a value of a statistical life of £1-10m per person he supposes that the 'benefits provided by a high-quality environment may crudely be valued an order of magnitude less than life itself,' i.e. £0.1 - 1.0 m per person. He then concludes that 'based on population densities, the environment in the U.K. may be crudely valued using this approach at £20 - 200 m'. It is not clear whether this figure is the present value cost or the annual cost to society, although the context suggests that it is a present value.

This cost is higher than that given in other studies and is arbitrarily derived. There is no justification for the procedure used. Willis and Whitby [1985] found that the most highly valued land is greenbelt land, as it provides amenity to the largest number of people. Their study gives a maximum figure of £8.8m for London green belt land (based on hedonic property prices), and £4.8 m for Tyne-Tees green belt - based on a contingent valuation survey (these figures are based on estimates of £62,368 per hectare for London greenbelt and £34,086 per hectare for Tyne-Tees greenbelt at 1984 prices.) Their minimum figures are an order of magnitude lower.

Willis and Benson [1990], conducted a travel cost analysis of visits to the Upper Teesdale National Nature Reserve. They find that the total consumer surplus, per km², is £25,100 (year of prices not given). Assuming a discount rate of 5%, this is £0.5m/km² in present value, at a discount rate of 1%, it is £2.5m/km². This is much lower than the greenbelt estimate. However, it does not allow for existence value, and is partly explained by the distance of this land from a major conurbation.

Michael and Pearce [1989] use a CVM-iterative bidding technique to examine the costs and benefits of land reclamation in the U.K. They use the Higher Folds reclamation scheme in Lancashire, N.W. England as a case study. Different payment vehicles were employed to measure the WTP for reclamation which provided evidence of vehicle bias. The contingent valuations of £8.3 - 9.0 per person p.a (in increased rent/rates or electricity bills), and £18.5 per person p.a (user charge) were used to estimate a one-off aggregate bid for reclamation. Estimates of the effect of reclaimed and unreclaimed land on house prices were obtained from a survey of professional valuers working in local estate agents. From this information it was assumed that residents living within 250 metres of the site were likely to be affected. From 1981 population census returns the number of households within 250 metres of the site was estimated to be approximately 2,000. Therefore, aggregate, once and for all WTP for reclamation through rents/ rates or electricity bills ranged from £17,000 -18,000 (1988 prices) while the remaining vehicle used in the CV approach - the hypothetical user charge - suggested an aggregate bid of £37,000 p.a. Over a 20 year time horizon, at 5% discount rate this suggests a present value of some £480,000.

It is possible that the questions relating to rent/rates and electricity bills did not adequately capture the one-off nature of the payment. For this reason the authors place a higher degree of confidence on the user charge estimates.

The benefit figure is significantly less than the reclamation costs by some £2.5 m. Therefore on economic efficiency grounds, the reclamation was not justified. Furthermore, observations of post-reclamation land values revealed that land valuations were significantly less than the costs of acquiring land. Such a result is consistent either with the land having being purchased at an excessive price or with negative environmental benefits from reclamation.

It is possible that other benefits of reclamation might justify the scheme. These include the increased attractiveness of the area to business and potential developers, enhanced civic pride and social benefits in an area of above average unemployment and below average incomes.

The aesthetic improvement resulting from reclamation was the most commonly mentioned benefit, followed by recreational walks. Respondents were also willing to pay for benefits in site safety and health. These included the prevention of spoil heaps collapsing into back gardens, the elimination of sulphurous smoke from burning spoil heaps which caused stomach aches and other health problems. it is therefore difficult to separate the benefits of increased land amenity from the other benefits of reclamation such as health and safety which are included in the aggregate estimate.

Howard [1971] estimates the benefits from reclamation in eastern Kentucky between 1962-67. Aesthetic damages to land are arbitrarily valued at $1.00 per acre. Losses incurred by owners of surface rights to land (in a region where mineral rights are commonly severed from and dominant to surface rights) are estimated arbitrarily at a value of $1000 per incident, and the number of incidents is 'indicated' by Kentucky Reclamation Division personnel. Losses incurred by off-site land owners, as a result of landslides exacerbated by improper deposition of overburden, were estimated arbitrarily at $50 per incident.

Randall et al [1978] present a detailed study of the costs and benefits of reclaiming surface coal mines. They found that for the Central Appalachian region as a whole, the social benefits of reclamation exceed its private costs.

Surface mining particularly affects the quality of land. External costs are imposed upon owners of land adjoining the mine site, residents of the mining region, downstream users of water impacted by mining, and non-regional residents who visit the region in the future or may suffer disutility from knowledge that the regional environment is being damaged.

Five broad categories of environmental degradation were identified:

1. water pollution as it affects domestic, commercial and industrial uses of water.

2. degradation of life support system for fish, wildlife and recreational resources.

3. increased frequency and intensity of flooding.

4. damages to land, and buildings.

5. aesthetic damages.

Randall et al, consider land and buildings damages jointly. Damages to land involves changes in the quality of the land resource. Surface mining causes on-site and off-site damages to land and buildings, as a result of land disturbance and incomplete deposition and stabilization of the soil. In the absence of proper practices, landslides may destroy buildings and damage land off the mining site.

A personal survey of 1% of households in the study region was carried out collecting, among other things, data on the value of off-site damages to land and structures owned by the respondents. Data was aggregated across all regional households to estimate total damages. A problem with this approach is that self-reporting of information by damaged parties may lead to bias.

The on-site losses in agriculture or forest productivity of mined land during mining are very small since agricultural and forest productivity of land overlying coal reserves in the study region is typically low, and are more or less included in the private costs of mining since the surface mine operator customarily pays the surface right holder a small 'access fee' per acre disturbed.

For the private purposes which are advanced by land ownership, properly reclaimed land is valued in the market more highly than unmined land, which in turn is valued more highly than mined but unreclaimed land. This is because reclaimed land is usually a plateau (following mountain-top removal) or a flat bench (following contour mining), while unmined land is mostly steep hillsides carrying a cover of scrub timber.

The market values of the different land categories were determined through a telephone survey of region realters. The present value of the increment in the market value of mined and reclaimed land in the study region was calculated, and treated as an on-site benefit (a negative cost) of surface mining under existing Kentucky regulations. The net value of the damage to land and buildings due to surface mining in the study region was calculated, by subtracting the increase in value of reclaimed mine sites from the value of damages to land and buildings, to be $1,837,000.

Thayer [1981] employs CVM to estimate the benefits derived from the preservation of the Jemez Mountains, in the Sante Fe National Forest. This region possesses one of the few geothermal resources in the U.S. actively being developed, and recreational visitors were asked their maximum WTP in terms of increased entrance fees to prevent geothermal activities in the region. Consumer welfare losses imposed as a consequence of geothermal development are estimated at $2.56 for daytrippers and $2.48 for campers (1976 prices).

9-4

Walsh et al [1984] estimate the preservation value of increments in wilderness protection in Colorado using the CV approach. A reason for performing such a valuation is that without information on preservation values insufficient land may be protected and energy development, may irreversibly degrade the land. If potential development were to result in permanent or long-run loss of scarce natural environment because of the inability or prohibitively high cost to restore natural conditions, then future generations would be denied amenities provided by the natural environment.

Respondents were shown four maps of the state of Colorado depicting the current wilderness areas and the hypothetical increases in amount. They were then asked the maximum they would be WTP annually for the protection of current wilderness, and for hypothetical increases in wilderness depicted in the maps. Table 9.1 presents the results of this survey. These estimates include option, existence and bequest values, i.e they represent total economic value.

Table 9.1

Total Annual Consumer Surplus from Recreation Use and Preservation Value to Colorado Households from Increments in Wilderness Designation, Colorado, 1980.

	Wilderness areas, 1980, 1.2m acres	Wilderness areas, 1981, 2.6m acres	Double 1981 wilderness areas, 5m acres	All potential wilderness areas, 10m acres
Total annual recreational use value and preservation value to Colorado households, millions.	$28.5	$41.6	$60.9	$93.2

Adapted from Walsh et al [1984].

We would expect valuation of wilderness areas to be high as developments in these areas are more likely to result in irreversible losses. The questionnaire did not specifically refer to energy development, the prevention of which may be valued differently. Due to the site specific nature of land impacts it is difficult to transfer these estimates for the preservation of wilderness in Colorado to other areas.

9.3 Solid Waste

Apart from radioactive waste, solid waste is produced in significant quantities only by coal-fired power stations, (approximately 1% of utility fossil fuel wastes are from oil-fired generation, the remainder being attributable to coal-fired generation).

According to the CEGB, the 70-75 * 10^6 tonnes of coal burnt every year in England produces about 13 *10^6 tonne of ash, of which 80% is pulverised fuel ash (small non-combustible particles entrained by exhaust gas system), and 20% bottom ash or clinker (large particles that settle to the bottom of the boiler) (CEGB [1988]). In addition FGD plants will produce large quantities of gypsum or sulphuric acid, depending on the FGD technology (House of Commons [1990b]). Disposal costs are of course 'internal' to generation costs but any environmental impacts will be external. 50% of pulverised fuel ash is disposed of as landfill or in surface impoundments, at or away from the plant, while much of the rest is sold to be used as construction fill. All of the furnace bottom ash is sold, and is used for brick-making, construction fill, etc.

In so far as the waste ends on or under ground, without a liner, or collection system, there is a danger that toxic trace materials in the waste (arsenic, barium, cadmium, chromium, lead, mercury, selenium) may leach out into either surface water or ground water.

9.4 Conclusions

From the literature reviewed it is not possible to derive a externality adder to account for the non-internalised damage caused to land by energy production.

CHAPTER 10   WATER DAMAGES.

10.1 Introduction.

There is an enormous valuation literature related to water. However, it is not possible to relate a large part of this literature to the damages that might be caused by fuel cycles. This chapter focuses on the European damage studies to illustrate the problems in this area.

The production of energy has the ability to damage water environments by the following means:

acid deposition damages biotic communities in lakes, rivers and streams;

coal storage piles, plant site run-off, and waste water discharges of acids, organic, suspended solids and metals pollute surface waters;

coal, oil and nuclear power plants generate a wide variety of solid wastes from power generation and maintenance operations. Solid wastes disposed of in landfills may have a variety of adverse effects on surface water, and ground water;

cooling systems used by thermal electric power stations can have adverse effects on fish populations and other aspects of aquatic systems.

Deriving externality adders for water is complicated by the difficulties in accounting for the numerous routes through which energy production could affect the various water environments. Also, these effects tend to be highly site specific, i.e. the potential for groundwater contamination by combustion wastes may depend on local hydrogeologic conditions, and the impacts of thermal discharges vary with the size of the receiving water body, cooling water volume and plant operation schedules. Therefore it is very difficult to determine a generally applicable externality cost figure.

10.2 Valuation Studies Related to Fisheries.

10.2.1   Recreational Fisheries.

Recreational benefit estimation has been studied the most in the context of water. The importance of water based recreation is indicated by Freeman [1982] who suggests that 80% or more of the of the benefits of cleaner water would accrue to recreationists.

The travel cost method [TCM] still represents the most prevalent method for obtaining recreational benefits, although non-behavioral based studies of recreation, such as contingent valuation [CV], are frequently used in conjunction with travel-cost. CV studies mostly value quality dimensions of the recreational resource. CV methods are particularly appropriate when the impact of the quality characteristic is difficult to capture in a recreation demand model. If there is no good way of observing the variable then there is no means of econometrically capturing its effects on behaviour. Desvousges, Smith and McGivney [1983] ask hypothetical questions to elicit valuations for improvements in water quality from boatable to swimmable levels. These are subjective water quality criteria that individuals can understand. However they are not criteria that can be easily measured by the researcher, and as such have limited use in the recreational demand setting.

The most compelling reason for using CV is that in some settings no behavioural models can be used to value the service flows of interest - e.g. existence value.

From the individual's perspective, recreation takes place at specific sites that exhibit observable characteristics and measurable travel costs, and so recreational service flows are described as site specific. Transferability of results is therefore questionable.

Table 10.1 presents Norwegian and Swedish studies concerned with the recreational value of freshwater and saltwater angling.

Table 10.1

Review of Norwegian and Swedish Studies on the Recreational Value of Freshwater and Saltwater Angling 1990-Nor Krone

Author	River	Species	Method	Recreational value per fishing day [1990- NOK]
Strand [1981b]	River Gaula	Salmon/sea trout	TC	325
Rolfsen [1990]	River Gaula	Salmon/sea trout	TC CV	424-484 309
Singas [1991]	River Gaula	Salmon/sea trout	TC	209-326
Navrud [1988]	River Vikedalselv	salmon/Sea trout (acidified)	TC CV	134-183 126-180
Navrud [1990]	River Audna	Salmon/sea trout (acidified)	TC CV	206-234 90-263
Ulleberg [1988]	River Stordalselv	Salmon/sea trout	TC	226-299
Navrud [1984]	River Hallingdalselv	Brown trout	TC	165
Scancke [1984]	River Tinnelv	Brown trout	TC	165
Navrud [1991b]	Lake Lauvann	Brown trout	TC CV	114-145 73-99
Navrud [1991b]	Gjerstadskog Lakes	Brown trout	TC CV	82- 91 42- 63
Navrud [1991c]	Sea area near River Audna	Salmon/sea trout	TC CV	55 40- 65
Silvander [1991]	All Swedish salt and brackish water.	Most saltwater species.	CV	25

All studies are Norwegian except Silvander [1991] which is Swedish. TC and/or CV is used to calculate the recreational value of the fish stock in its current condition. When both the TC and CV methods are used in the same study , these independent methods seem to yield similar results.

The TC and CV models used in the Norwegian studies are quite similar, except for Strand [1981] and Scancke [1984]. While the TC-models in the other Norwegian studies are based on anglers' own statements of numbers of visits, travel costs, income, preferred substitute river etc, these two studies construct the data needed on the basis of secondary data (especially fish licences) and strict assumptions about anglers' behaviour.

Although multipurpose visits might not be a large problem in the specialised activity of salmon fishing, it could be a serious bias in trout fishing. Neither of these two studies nor Singsaas [1991] have tried to correct this potential bias. Strand [1981], Scancke [1984], and Navrud [1984] base their calculations on zonal observations, while the others use individual observations. By aggregating several individual observations of different variables to zonal averages, the model 'conceals' much of the actual variation in the data, and appears to fit the data better than it actually does. Although all the TC-models might be subject to misspecification, all of them have tried to include independent variables, other than travel cost, that might affect the visitation rate.

There seems to be a clear tendency that the recreational value of freshwater fishing is higher than for saltwater fishing, and that the atlantic salmon and sea trout species are valued the most. Of the salmon and sea trout rivers, those with the largest stocks of salmon have the highest recreational value per fishing day. In salt water, salmon and sea trout seem to have a recreational value per day twice the average of all saltwater species.

On the basis of these studies it should be possible to construct a WTP function of how recreational value per angling day varies with the characteristics/quality of the water body (e.g. salt or freshwater, lake or river, fish species present etc), availability of substitute fishing areas and /or recreational activities, and demographic/ socioeconomic variables of the regional population and the anglers. In other European countries the anglers' preferences might be different. If the potential differences could be identified, it should be possible to transfer the WTP function from this meta-analysis (see chapter 14) to other countries.

For these results to be usable for fuel cycle valuation purposes a connection needs to be made between the impacts of energy production and recreational fishing. As yet this has not been done.

10.2.2 Commercial Fisheries

Table 10.2 summarises the European commercial fisheries studies.

Table 10.2

European Commercial Fisheries Studies.

Study	Type of valuation.	Result	Comment
Ewers and Schulz [1982]	Estimate the benefit of increased commercial fishing due to water quality improvements from reduced phosphorous emissions in Lake Tegler.	The annual increase in producer surplus from improving the water level 7 to level 4 through to 1 (the best water quality) estimated at 12 400 - 44 000 DM [1980].	Price changes modeled. Value the effects of increased water quality, while the fuel cycle cost studies look at reduced water quality. Dose-response functions unreliable.
Baan [1983]	Estimates the beneficial effects on commercial fisheries of improving the quality of Dutch surface water.	Annual value of the increased catch in the commercial fishery estimated at 2 -4 Dfl [1983]	Uses market prices. unreliable dose-response functions.
Rasmussen et al [1991]	Estimates the costs to commercial and freshwater fisheries due to reduced water quality in Western Germany.	Social cost estimated at 245m DM [1987] annually.	This figure is found by taking the total lost income of commercial fisheries in the period 1905-82 due to water pollution and other anthropogenic impacts (e.g. over fishing) and subtracting the decrease in marginal harvesting costs due to the decreased harvest.

Rasmussen et al [1991] include the effects of reduced water quality on deep sea fishing, coastal fishing in the North and Baltic Seas, river fishing, lake fishing and aquaculture (ponds). The study illustrates the difficulty of separating the effects of pollution from the effects of changes in fishing techniques and policies, when using historical harvest data. Also, since this is an ex-post analysis; the uncertainty of the fishermen is not accounted for. It is not then possible to place a high level of confidence in these results.

In fuel cycle evaluation what is required is the value of the effects of marginal changes in the catch rates for commercial fisheries. It is possible therefore to use market prices rather than calculating changes in producer and consumer surpluses. One multiplies the lost net income per tonne fish, i.e. market price minus harvesting costs, and minus the additional costs, with the expected decrease in the catch per ton, calculated from the dose response functions. If this approach is accepted the main obstacle to valuation is the lack of reliable dose-response functions for different pollutants (covering the expected range of concentrations), different species, different hydrological and climatic conditions etc.

10.2.3 Fisheries/Non-Use Values.

Fisheries studies related to non-use values are presented to Table 10.3.

Table 10.3

Non-Use Values and Fisheries.

Study	Type of valuation	Result	Comment.
Navrud [1989]	Estimates the benefits of reduced acidification(30 - 70% reductions) on fish stocks in Norway.	390 per household per year [1990 NOK] (246-343 represents non-use value; the rest is use value).	Present a detailed description of the increased number of trout lakes and salmon rivers with restored stocks in Southern Norway.
Navrud [1991b]	WTP to avoid extinction of current salmon and sea trout stocks in River Audna	WTP per individual per year - 115 NOK [1990]	
Navrud [1991a]	WTP to avoid the extinction of current trout stocks in the Gjerstadskog lakes. (local)	WTP per individual per year 46 NOK [1990]	
Amundsen [1987]	WTP to avoid an unspecified 'reduction' of current trout stocks in Oslomarka lakes. (local).	WTP per household per year 360 NOK [1990]	Commodity misspecification seems to be a problem.
Carlsen [1985]	WTP to avoid 'some' and 'considerable' reductions in the salmon stock in River Numedaslagen. (local)	WTP per household per year 41-85 NOK [1990] (only 24-25% of the households were WTP 165-340 per household) (includes both use and non-use values).	Value changes in fish stocks due to different operating schemes of hydroelectric dams. Serious commodity misspecification appears to be present.
Strand [1981a]	WTP to avoid extinction of all freshwater fish stocks in Norway through acidification.	WTP per household per year 1650-2650 NOK [1990]. (1000-1600 is non-use value the rest is use value)	

Silvander [1991]	WTP to avoid extinction of species most popular for consumption, in all Swedish saltwater areas caused by eutrophication due to the leaching of nitrogen.	WTP per individual per year 310 NOK [1990]	To use theses results we need to know if the fuel cycles external effects on fish are perceived to be the same or different from the effects of eutrophication.

All studies use CV and are Norwegian except Silvander [1991], which is Swedish. Silvander [1991] looks at saltwater fish stocks, while the others look at freshwater fish stocks. He also uses a mail survey, the other studies were in-person interviews -which in most cases yield the most reliable results.

Of the Norwegian studies, all but one, Carlsen [1985], looked at the total WTP (non-use values included) of changes in the fish stocks due to acid rain. These studies should be relevant to calculating the external costs of fuel cycles.

All studies except Navrud [1989] look at the WTP to avoid decreasing fish stocks. Navrud looks at the WTP for increased fish stocks. We are interested in the external cost of an increase in pollution i.e. decreased fish stocks, thus the results from the Navrud study cannot be used directly. However, this is the only study where the changes are based on dose-response functions. It links European emissions of SO2 and the depositions in Norway, the depositions' effects on water quality, and the resulting effects on fish stocks using linear dose response functions. The other studies have rather vague descriptions of the changes in fish stocks.

Four of the studies give the total WTP i.e. both use and non-use values (Navrud [1989], Amundsen [1987], Carlsen [1985],Strand [1981a]). It is important to recognise this to avoid double counting. In two cases the two categories have been divided (Strand [1981a] and [1989], however, all the procedures used for such disaggregation are questionable, and there is no acceptable way of doing this.

The estimates have been produced both per household and per individual, making comparison difficult. WTP amounts per individual can often be close to or equal to the WTP per household, because individuals often think in terms of household budgets, and act as representatives of households.

In those studies that estimate the WTP to avoid extinction of fish stocks, the extinction threat might have caused very high WTP amounts which cannot then be used directly to estimate the damage costs of marginal increases in acid deposition, which is what would be relevant to the fuel cycle study.

Little is known about if and how non-use values can be transferred. However, unlike recreation, non-use estimates do not appear to be location specific. How these estimates can be used in the fuel cycle costs is unclear.

10.2.4 Studies Reviewed by PACE [1990].

The acid rain studies related to water in the USA reviewed by PACE [1990] are shown in Table 10.4. These studies are generally relevant to fuel cycle evaluation, but missing data do not allow pence per kWh to be derived.

Table 10.4.

Acid Rain Related Aquatic Studies Reviewed by PACE [1990](USA)

Study	Type of Valuation	Result	Comment.
Crocker and Regans [1985]	Estimate the benefits of a 100% reduction in acid deposition in Eastern U.S.	$250m [1978$]	Uses the same approach as Menz and Mullen [1984] with scaling up assumptions.
Forster [1984]	Estimates the benefits of reduced acid deposition in Ontario and Quebec under various scenarios.	$28 - 100m [Canadian $?]	Assumes that liming is effective and measures the benefits of reduced acid depositions by the cost of liming and effects on tourist revenue.
Menz and Mullen [1984]	Study recreational sites with a ph < 5 in the Adironacks. Estimates the cost of a 5% loss in lake area.	$1.7 - 3.2 m [1982$]	Uses TCM. Assumptions: Substitution only possible within the fishery. Only recreation and licensed fishermen considered.
Morey and Shaw [1990]	Estimate the effects of a 25% change in catch for a few lakes in the Adirondacks.	Average WTP$3.56/ per person per season.	Uses a share model. Estimate only use value.
Navrud [1989]	Estimates the WTP for a 30% - 50% reduction of sulphur emissions in Europe for Norway.	$16 - 48 per household.	Uses CV.
Violette [1985]	Estimates changes in consumers surplus of anglers due to reductions in catch rates and fishable acreage.	$7m - 12m [1984$]	Uses TCM and participation model.
Welle [1985]	Values moderate to severs changes in acid deposition in Minnesota.	$30 - 36 (non-use) $91 - 120 (use) per year.	Uses CV

Source: adapted from PACE [1990].

In the U.S. the specifics of the linkages between acid deposition and stock size are not well known, but Brook and Lake trout are believed to be the species most affected.

NAPAP [1991] estimates the economic effects of acid deposition damages on recreational fishing in the Adirondack lakes, based on the work of Violette [1985]. This analysis used a participation model and a varying-parameter TCM (Vaughan and Russell, 1982) to estimate changes in the consumer surplus of anglers due to reductions in catch rates and fishable acreage. The Adirondack lakes were selected because the impacts of acid rain are well documented, and the region is an important centre of freshwater game fishing. The two approaches produced comparable results. Estimates of the annual value of economic damages range from $7m to $12 m per year.

For a number of reasons these values should be viewed with caution. The estimates apply only to the Adirondack lakes and they do not include rivers since key data on streams were unavailable. The aggregation procedure used may not have captured important localised impacts such as those in high altitude lakes. In the TCM, the treatment of fishing behaviour does not account for anglers' ability to switch to substitute fishing locations - a change that would presumably result in lower total economic damages. The estimated changes in fishable acres and catch rates used in the analysis contained unquantified uncertainties not incorporated in the economic damage estimates. Morey and Shaw [1990] specify and estimate a characteristics-based utility-theoretic model of site-specific recreational fishing demand. They conclude that the consumer surplus fishermen associate with the availability of fish species varies extensively across fisherman as a function of their species preference, ability level, location of residence, value of time, and fishing budget, i.e. the individual consumer surplus for a simultaneous 25% increase in the catch rates for sites averaged $3.56, but varied from zero to $159.46 as a function of all the above factors. This illustrates the danger of just reporting averages or aggregates, although attempts to do so are common in the literature, e.g. Mullen and Menz [1985].

The model is linked to acid rain through the catch rates of different species at different sites. Acid rain impacts on the stocks of the different species at the different sites, which in turn affects the catch rates. Once these biological links are modelled, the model can be used to estimate lower bounds on the CVs that each fisherman would associate with different amounts of reduction in the level of acid deposition.

Morey and Shaw [1990] conclude that the benefits recreational fishermen would receive from reduced acid deposition are significantly positive but possibly quite small. The magnitude of the aggregate benefit measure is small, and reflects the fact that only those fishermen who target trout have a positive WTP to pay for trout, the species most likely to be affected by acid rain.

10.3 Recreation Studies Excluding Fishing.

Table 10.5 surveys European recreation studies not concerned with fisheries.

Table 10.5
Non-Fishery Recreational Values (Europe)

Study	Type of valuation.	Result	Comment
Hjalte et al [1982]	Uses the TCM to value the current and future recreational value of Lake Vombsjon in Sweden.	Recreational value per visitor per year is valued at approx 4SEK [1982]	In general the figures seem very low. The study was undertaken more as an example of how the model could be applied than to estimate precise figures. The results are not therefore particularly useful.
Kanerva and Matikainen [1972]	Use HP to estimate how water quality affects the average value per meter of shore areas in Lake Saimaa, Finland.	The mere awareness of water pollution reduces real estate value by 60% (compared to unpolluted water) This reduced value is independent of the change in water quality.	Descriptions of water quality changes were vague. (see Kyber study)
Kyber [1981]	Uses HP to estimate how water quality affects the average value per meter of shore areas in the Valkeaskosia area of Finland	Reducing the water level from level 2 - good to level 3 - satisfactory, 4 - passing, and 5 poor, reduced market value of on-shore real estate by 30%, 45% and 50% respectively.	The general problems of HP apply: misspecification and the possibility of the value estimate covering aspects other than changes in water quality.
Mantymaa [1991]	Uses CV to value improved water quality in lake Oulujarvi - the fourth largest lake in Finland.	Mean WTP per person per year to improve the water quality by one level - 836 FIM, mean WTP to avoid the water quality to be reduced by one level - 965 FIM.	Commodity misspecification could be present i.e what does it mean that water quality changes by one level. The WTP/WTA disparity is partly supported by these results.
Green and Tunstall [1990]	CV used to measure the prevailing state of beaches at 11 coastal site in England.	The recreational value of the prevailing state of the beach varied from £3.06 - £10.50 per visit. The loss in recreational value due to beach erosion was valued at an average of £3.34 - £4.37 1989-£.	This result may not be relevant to fuel cycle analysis as coastal erosion is not a significant external cost of energy.

WRC/FHRC [1989]	Use CV to value water quality improvements of river corridors at several sites in England.	Users WTP £19.56 Non-users WTP £13.60 per person per year [1987£]	see discussion below.
Turner and Brooke [1988]	CV of local and non-local users to value parts of the benefits of the Alderburgh sea - defence scheme.	Value to the nation was estimated at £186 137. The mean annual WTP to retain the existing recreational experience was £15 per household for local users and £18.87 for non-local users without alternative sites.	Again, this is a study of coastal recreation which may not be relevant.
Heiberg and Hem [1978]	CV study of improved water quality in the Kristian fjord in Norway	Mean average WTP per local household for users and non-users - 430 NOK [1990] (weighted average)	Only local WTP, Households living outside these areas might also be WTP something for increased water quality.
Aarskog [1988] Heiberg and Hem [1988]	CV study of improved water quality in the Inner oslo fjord in Norway.	Mean average WTP per local household [1990] NOK: users 906 non-users 589 weighted average 837.	WTP estimates refer to rather large improvements in water quality, from the prevailing state to a 'nearly unpolluted' state.
Dlagard [1989]	CV study of improved water quality in the Drammen fjord in Norway.	Mean average WTP per local household [1990] NOK: users 846 non-users 416 weighted average 563	see discussion below.
Magnussen and Navrud [1991]	Estimate the WTP, using CV, for increased water quality in all rivers, fjords, and coastal areas (due to a 50% reduction in the Norwegian emissions of nitrogen and phosphorous to the North Sea) in the South and Southeastern part of Norway (known as the North Sea Plan Area)	In the national survey the mean annual, average WTP per household varied between 600 - 5000 [1991 NOK]. This includes both user and non-user benefits. When corrected for CV biases this narrows to 1000 - 2000.	The improvements in water quality are described in great detail (using colour coded maps, colour photos, verbal descriptions). The described changes were closely linked to a physical dose-response model developed by the Norwegian Institute for Water Research. Both continuous and discrete choice valuation techniques were used.

Hervik, Rinces and Strand [1987]	Estimate the WTP for preserving Norwegian rivers from hydroelectric development.	The WTP of policy makers was in the range of 160 - 730 [1990-NOK] per household per year. Employing CV for Norwegian households the mean, annual WTP per household was estimated to be 800 - 1600 NOK.	It is not possible to divide these benefits into use and non-use benefits.
Strand and Hrevik [1991]	Study of policymakers' implicit WTP for river preservation, deriving implicit costs associated with each of the different user interests.	WTP per energy unit kWh of expected energy production is estimated at: conservation 0.015 outdoor recreation 0.027 wildlife 0.005 fish 0.016 water supply 0.017 cultural heritage preservation 0.028 agriculture 0.017 reindeer farming 0.015 local economic interests 0.109. [1982 NOK]	A basic assumption for such implicit valuations to be valid is that policy makers are well informed and aware of the economic and environmental trade offs involved.

Methodologically, considering both the linkages to physical damage functions and the constructed CV models, Magnussen and Navrud [1991] is probably the best Norwegian CV study on user and non-user benefits from water quality changes. However, only one quite large improvement in water quality improvement is valued. How these estimates could be transferred to value marginal reductions in water quality caused by changes in pollutants other than nutrients is unresolved.

The study by Mantymaa [1991] is of interest as it considers the effects of diminished water quality which is of more relevance to the costing of energy impacts. However for the average values presented in the study to be any use, we must know how the valuations vary with the different initial levels of water quality stated. These figures were not available in the original report. We also need to know how the water quality levels 1-5 correspond with our damage functions from the fuel cycles.

WRC/FHRC [1989] found that people were better at recognising indicators of pollution than indicators of good water quality. This indicates that valuation of reduced water quality has a higher correlation with the physical damage, than the valuation of the opposite change. In the fuel cycle study, increased pollution is of more interest. This study went on to estimate WTP for a more detailed description of water quality improvement. Water quality was classified as good enough for:

1. water birds (official river class 3);
2. supporting many fish including trout, dragonflies and many plants (official river class 2);
3. to be safe for children to paddle and swim (official river class 1).

Among those living in the river corridor the mean WTP per person per year to get the improved water quality was £546, 562 and 582 respectively. Thus people do not perceive differences in water quality. This is confirmed by a survey of all user benefits, where the recreational value per visit was £0.51, 0.60 and 0.52 for the water quality levels 3,2,1. These amounts are not significantly different. On average, each of the 1000 households using river corridors indicated an annual WTP of £6 (in water rates) for water quality improvements.

In the Drammens Fjord study the respondents were asked explicitly about both current and future number of user days. However, the answers were given in ranges, and some assumptions have to be made to calculate the average number of additional user days, which was 9 per respondent. This adds up to a total increase of 900,000 user days, while the total increase in use value can be estimated at approx 6.5 m 1990 - NOK (assuming that the total aggregated WTP could be divided into 1/3 use value and 2/3 non-use value, however, this ratio could vary from location to location). The recreational value per day increase in the Drammn Fjord is then approximately 7.20 1990-NOK.

The studies by Hervik, Rinces and Strand [1987] and Strand and Hrevik [1991] should be relevant to the external costs of hydro power. The relevance of the other studies to the social cost pricing of energy is unclear.

10.4 Ground Water.

Table 10.6 reviews European ground water valuation studies.

Table 10.6
Groundwater Valuation.

Study	Type of Valuation.	Result	Comment.
Baan [1985]	Values the benefit of reduced soil pollution on 3 groundwater impact groups, using avoided costs.	1. Effects on public water supply 50-200m annually in the year 2020 2. Effects on the service/ industrial sectors 10-40m. 3. Effects on cattle watering 1-11m. [1985 Dfl]	These aggregate estimates are uncertain, and no unit values can be deducted for different ground water pollutants. The use of these estimates is therefore limited.
Hubler et al [1991]	Estimates the external cost of soil pollution in West Germany. One of the components was the effects on groundwater.	The annual costs of contaminated groundwater due to soil pollution in Western Germany was estimated at 4.1 - 6.9b DM.	This 'national' estimate is based on available monetary estimates in only a few polluted areas. The aggregation is based on the available non-monetary information and expert judgement - this kind of method is questionable. The data for the areas where we do have monetary estimates could be used to provide unit values, if they are detailed enough to give values for different pollutants.
Hanley [1989]	Uses CV to estimate the WTP for reduced nitrate pollution of ground water. Ask respondents ' WTP to be sure that their nitrate concentration in their drinking water was below the WHO threshold of 50 ml nitrate/1.	Average WTP approx £13 per person per year.	Commodity misspecification bias might be present since this is an environmental effect that people have little information about. Due to a very low response rate, the results should be treated with care. Do not consider health effects.

Silvander [1991]	WTP for reduced health risks due to reduced nitrate levels in drinking water.	Average WTP per person per year of 332 SEK to decrease the risk of methhaemoglobinaemina in infants, and an additional 190 SEK to reduce the cancer risks of nitrate in groundwater to adults and infants.	Problems in perceiving marginal differences in the nitrate content of groundwater - 84% of the respondents didn't know if there were subject to nitrate concentrations above the threshold or not. The reduced risks of the two diseases were not described in detail

It is difficult to come up with a unit value of reduced nitrate level in groundwater, because of the differences between studies. Thus, Silvander [1991] assumes that 50% of nitrogen leaching is due to agricultural production, and estimates the social benefit of reducing the nitrate concentration in groundwater to be approx 5-51 SEK [1990] per kg nitrogen leached. This must be seen as more of an example, rather than an actual value estimate.

10.5 Surface Water.

European studies related to the non-ecological use of surface water are presented in Table 10.7.

Table 10.7
Surface Water Use Values.

Study	Type of Valuation	Results	Comment
SPCA [1991]	A cost effective analysis of different measures to get a 50% reduction in Norway's emissions of Nitrogen N and Phosphorous -P to the North Sea.	The discounted costs (discount rate 7%) of the different measures for reducing emissions of N and P by 1 ton is estimated to be : -0.02 - 1.15 NOX [1990] for N -6.95 - 30.90 for P.	Linear programming model used. Negative estimates indicate net benefits of implementing the measures.
Ewers and Schulz [1982]	Estimates the value of improved water quality (reduced eutrophication due to reduced emissions of phosphorous) in Lake Tegeler, Germany.	For drinking water, quality improvements from the present levels to 4,3,2, and 1 (1 being the highest) were valued in the range of 4.7 - 6.9 m DM annually. For catering firms the corresponding estimate was 0.4 - 4m DM	Drinking water benefits valued by the associated cost reductions of improved water quality. Benefits to catering firms valued through the generation of value added.
Winje et al [1991]	Calculates the total costs of treating different pollutants in the sectors: Public drinking water supply (pesticide residuals, chlorinated hydrocarbons, and nitrate), Privately owned water supply (nitrate), Industrial water supply. For Germany.	The total annual costs of pollution on the 'public water supply', which uses both surface and underground water, in 1983 708.3m DM. Privately owned water supply - 1000 - 2000 m. Industrial water supply - 120m DM.	
Baan [1983]	Estimates the social benefits from improving the quality of Dutch surface water level from the 1983 level to the 'natural state'.	Valuations in m Dfl per year [1983]. Public water supply: avoided cost of purification - 15 - 30. avoided costs of softening 16 - 20. avoided costs of dumping purification sludge 2-9. Industry: avoided costs of softening and demineralization 11.	As for the German studies the quantification of the reduced pollution in physical units seems rather vague.

If unit values for treating different water pollutants (and how these values vary with different levels of pollution) could be calculated from the data, the values for selected pollutants could be used for the fuel cost studies. Thus, Ewers and Schulz [1982] give no unit value - e.g. DM per ton of phosphorus reduction - but if the physical data on phosphorus reduction are available this could be calculated.

10.6 Environmental Effects of Cooling Systems.

Thermal electric power stations use large amounts of water in their cooling systems. The most common method is once-through cooling which continuously draws water from a nearby water source. This once-through process can have three major environmental impacts the cost of which are largely external to the cost of electricity:
1. impingement/entrainment
2. thermal pollution
3. water use

10.6.1 Impingement and Entrainment Effects.

Impingement and entrainment impacts can significantly affect populations of fish in the source water body. The water drawn from lakes, rivers, estuaries or the ocean, must be screened to prevent debris from entering the condenser/heat exchange system. Impingement occurs when aquatic animals are pinned against the screening device and killed or injured.

Organisms, primarily eggs and small larval fish too small to be excluded by the screens, can be drawn through the heat exchange and suffer often fatal thermal, mechanical and pressure shocks. Such entrainment has the potential for adversely affecting fish populations by destroying the underlying food sources of adults and entraining eggs and early juveniles of species whose survival rates are typically marginal.

As an example of the possible magnitude of these effects, in the Hudson estuary of the U.S, impingement is estimated to reduce the annual stock of white perch by 20% or more. At the Indian point 2 and 3 reactor on the Hudson River, fish impingement for 1987 totalled 848 fish per 1,000,000 cubic meters of water.

In the absence of damage estimates regulatory authorities in the U.S have attempted to account for these losses through a range of control or mitigation-based externality costs. Maryland regulatory authority requires operators of cooling water intake structures to derive a level of mitigation expenditure from a formula which multiplies the number of fish impinged by a set of factors ranging from $.75 to $1.00 per fish, depending on the nature of the fish. Greater value is assigned to commercial and recreational fish, and less to forage species. As part of the Hudson River Power Plant Settlement, utilities with plants in the vicinity of Indian point, began a stripped based hatchery program in an attempt to compensate for impingement losses. Expenses and stocking quantities were analyzed in order to determine an average cost per fish stocked.

This cost was then applied to estimates for fish impinged per kWh. This is an illustration of compensatory costing of the damage inflicted by a once-through cooling system.

For entrainment, no cost estimates methodology appear to exist. Models have been developed which can predict the added conditional mortality imposed on fish populations by entrainment. The conditional mortality is the fraction of the initial population that would be killed by entrainment during the year if no other sources of mortality operated. Further research into the valuation of individual species stocks could be applied to these conditional mortality rates to estimate the cost per kWh of electricity.

10.6.2 Thermal Discharges.

The water released from the cooling system is substantially warmer, 40 degrees celsius, than when collected from the source. The heat discharged can upset the normal balance of aquatic life in the receiving waters by destroying vegetation, causing nitrogen embolisms, oxygen depletion. The effect on fish populations may be positive or negative (it may create more favourable feeding and breeding conditions for some fish). Fish may also be subjected to fatal cold shocks when the system is closed down for maintenance or refuelling.

The site specific nature of the effects of thermal discharges make generalisations very difficult. Effects are dependent upon the characteristics of the water body into which the effluent is being discharged (eg the size of the water body, water flow rates, water temperature, and make up of the plant and animal community), the volume and temperature of the discharged effluent, and plant operation schedules. The effects of thermal discharge remain largely unquantified.

10.6.3 Water Consumption.

Water consumption primarily occurs through evaporation losses from the cooling system. In order to estimate a cost for water consumption, an average cost per gallon of untreated water from the local source could be applied to these gallon per kWh figures. In some areas where water may be in short supply the water supply may be a significant externality. No study was found which attempts to apply such prices to develop an externality cost for water consumption.

PACE [1990] concludes that the best cost factor to apply in the absence of proof of accurate assessment of these impacts, is that associated with the cost of the most effective mitigation technique - closed-cycle cooling system. Closed-cycle cooling systems function on 2 to 4% of the water required for a once- through system. Because the costs associated with a closed-cycle cooling system are high, it represents what industry generally considers to be the upper bound of control costs for impingement and entrainment impacts.

TCM could be employed to estimate impingement and entrainment effects on the basis that increased travel costs could result from the necessity of recreational and commercial fisherman having to travel further to catch fish because of reduction in stocks. Alternatively, CV responses are expected to increase in value as power plant mortalities require increased effort and expense to engage in a continuous level of fishing success. If data are available on the catch-rate of the particular fishing site, and some correlation exists between the catch rate and the value of the fishing site, then on could arrive at a cost for impingement and entrainment by determining a percentage reduction in population resulting from these effects.

10.7 Conclusions.

According to PACE [1990] the New York Public Service Commission (NYPSC), appears to have made the only effort to determine generally applicable external cost figures. NYPSC adopted water pollution externalities figures for use in new capacity bidding programs, and assigns 0.1 cent per kWh to water related impacts. These figures were derived from studies by the Bonneville Power Authority (BPA) based on the cost of controlling or mitigating residual water discharges. PACE [1990] values damage to aquatics from acid deposition at zero.

It is not possible to derive a externality adder for water from the current available valuation literature as there is no generally applicable damage based externality cost for any water effects.

CHAPTER 11 VISIBILITY AND AMENITY.

11.1 Introduction.

Visibility does not have a precise universally accepted definition. The US EPA defines visibility impairment as 'any humanely perceptible change in visibility (visual range, contrast, coloration) from that which would have existed under normal conditions'. Visual range is commonly interpreted as the distance an observer would have to back away from an object for it to disappear. Energy production can affect regional visibility through sulphur dioxide and the resulting sulphate and fine particulates emitted from power plants. The aesthetic impact of the plume from the power plant may also be important. However, the effects of the plume are very site specific.

The fundamental physics of the relationship between visibility and air pollutants is fairly well established (NAPAP [1991]). 'Visibility reduction' or 'haziness' is directly proportional to reduction in atmospheric light transmission. Light transmission in the atmosphere is attenuated by scattering and adsorption from both gases and particals. The scattering of fine particles is generally accepted as the dominant contributor to adverse visibility. The most uncertain aspect of visibility science is with human perception and values, i.e. the second link in the chain from air pollutant concentrations to atmospheric optics to human evaluations.

11.2 Valuation Methodologies

Often in the case of atmospheric visibility the environmental impact is aesthetic in nature. Aesthetic impacts are associated with sensory experiences, not physical affects on the body or possessions. The absence of physical effect differentiates aesthetic impacts from health, recreation, or materials damages. The requirement of a sensory connection differentiates aesthetic values from 'non-use' values based on knowledge rather than experience.

Valuation typically requires the following steps:

1. the identification of the sensory channels affected by the stimuli;
2. the selection of indirect or surrogate reactions from which the worth of the unobservable sensory reactions can be inferred;
3. the use of the appropriate statistical and theoretical constructs for data analysis.

The approaches most employed to measure the change in visibility in a recreational or residential setting are the CVM and hedonic pricing. One of the earliest uses of CV was the Randall et al [1974] study of haze from a power plant development in the southwestern U.S. Subsequently, a literature has developed describing the special challenges that aesthetics pose in CV survey design. The issues include:

1. Creating a real familiarity with the object of the study. This is essential to CV and often particularly difficult for intangible aesthetic goods. Fischoff and Furby [1988] discuss how this problem has been addressed in studies of visibility. Their framework was to treat

valuations of policies affecting visibility as being like any other transaction, involving (a) a good (b) a payment (c) a social context within which the transaction is conducted. They argue that features of each of these components of the transaction can introduce difficulties in interpreting CVM valuations.

2. Describing the aesthetic good. A CV instrument presents a description and elicits a response. Because aesthetic goods are often qualitative in nature, description is difficult. The very effort to capture an aesthetic good in words or pictures may cause a respondent to value it differently than he or she would based purely on his own prior experience. The extent to which visibility as an aesthetic good can be properly portrayed to the respondent is therefore an open question.

Attempts at making definitions of aesthetic goods more compelling include:
a) supplementing words with aids that are explicitly sensory - e.g illustrating the range of outcomes with photographs - Brookshire et al [1981] and Tolley and Randall et al [1986];

b) establishing a familiar point of reference and describing the aesthetic goods as they relate to that point of reference. Clearly specifying the reference and the target states resulting from a specific policy can be very complicated (Fischoff and Furby [1988]).

3. Quantifying the good. To obtain an economic value for visibility the question of quantifying the 'good' or commodity called visibility arises. It is necessary to link the visibility depicted in the set of colour photographs presented to actual distances seen.

Visual range cannot be measured directly, nor is it necessarily representative of what the observer 'sees'. Visibility involves human perceptions which could differ from scientific measures. Perception tests, however, suggest the existence of a linear relationship between perceived visual quality as quantified by individuals (1 to 10 rankings of visual air quality as represented in colour slides) and the scientific measure of apparent target contrast measured by a multiwave teleradiometer (Shulze et al [1983]).

4. Often aesthetic benefits from environmental improvements are intertwined with nonaesthetic benefits such as health , soiling, or ecological effects. Separating these intertwined effects presents additional analytical challenges.

Hedonic property pricing assumes that residents' preferences toward air quality will be reflected in the market prices for homes and property. Unlike CV, hedonic analysis must rely on available data although surveys of house price estimates and property characteristics are possible. Since few aesthetic goods are readily measurable, there are limited occasions when hedonics can be used. The use of proxy data, such as a particulate count for visibility, can introduce confusion because the proxies may be associated with other impacts; for example particulates are associated with respiratory problems and soiling.

In a study of the effects of visibility and suspended particles on land values, Graves et al [1988] found that the estimate for visibility was highly sensitive to a number of different model specifications. The issues explored were measurement error, functional form, error distribution, and variable selection and treatment, particularly regarding the size of the lots. Overall, Graves et al conclude that there is simply not much in the literature that yields convincing values for aesthetic goods in light of these difficulties. Brookshire et al [1982] also question the use of hedonic methods. CV seems to be the best method to employ, and one approach that has appeared in the literature is the iterative bidding technique which directly estimates individuals' economic value for a unit reduction in visibility.

The advantages of CV in visibility valuation include its ability to :

1. more sharply distinguish the aesthetic dimension of the policy-induced change;

2. generate data rather than relying upon remote proxies;

3. impose fewer behavioural assumptions, with the important exception of presuming that intentions accurately portray actions.

4. yield results that are at least plausible when the studies are conducted carefully, particularly in applications to visibility.

Methods requiring direct consumption responses, such as the travel cost method for recreational demand, have limited usefulness. The exception to this is a study by Tolley and Randell et al [1986]. One of their approaches to valuation involved paid trips to sky scraper viewing-decks in Chicago. These data were used to value the effects of information of current visibility conditions.

11.3 Valuation Studies.

Table 11.1 surveys the valuation studies related to visibility.

Table 11.1
Visibility Valuation Studies.

Study	Type of Valuation	Result	Comment
ECO [1987]	Estimates the value of lost visibility from a generic plant	Total visibility losses for the generic plant estimated at $1.38 m	Does not attribute visibility loss to particular pollutants.
ECO [1984]	Models the visibility loss due to each pollutant from the Frederickson generation facility. Estimate visibility effects from various distances from the plant.	Annual losses due to SO2 - $142,350. [1982$] Annual losses due to NOx (under the oil-fired scenario) - $115,000 [1982$]	Use a value of $10 per lost km-year per person.
Brookshire, Ives and Shulze [1976]	Values the possible visibility reductions from the proposed Kaiparowits power plants overlooking Glen Canyon National Recreation Area - Colorado.	Uses three scenarios of visibility and plant siting ranging from best (a) to worst (c). Aggregate bid of $727, 600.	Uses CV - iterative bidding techniques. Their vista is limited to that over lake Powell. Uses photographs. 15 national recreational areas can be found within a radius of 1000 miles from the proposed plant - an aggregate bid from all areas would be substantially larger.
Schulze et al [1983]	Measures the economic value of visibility in the national parklands of the Southwest of the U.S. and the Grand Canyon. Focuses on coal-fired power plants.	Average household WTP per month for the preservation of the current 'average' air quality and corresponding visibility in the Grand Canyon - $3.72 - $5.14. Average bids for the entire southwest parklands region - $6.61 - $9.64. Prevention of the visible plume seen from the Grand canyon - $2.84 - $4.25. [1980$].	Uses CV - Iterative bidding game. value use and preservation value. Interview over 600 households in Denver, Los Angeles, Albuquerque and Chicago. Payment vehicle: increased park fees/electric bills.

Rowe, d'Arge and Brookshire [1980]	Examines the proposed visibility reductions in the Four Corners of the Southern U.S.	Change in visual range from hypothetical baseline visibility of 75 miles to: 1. -25 miles residents: $3.97 [1990$/person/ month] non-residents: $2.97. [1990$/person/ day] 2. -50 miles residents: $5.46 non-residents: $3.39 3. -50 miles plus visible power plant. residents: $5.71 non-residents: $3.81.	Uses CV. No link to pollutants. Photographs used. Information and strategic bias found to be up to 40%.
Randall, Ives and Eastman [1974]	Measures the economic value of visibility reductions caused by coal fired generating plants in the Four Corners region of the Southwest of the U.S. Examine 3 scenarios: C - power plant with limited visible emissions and very little visibility reductions. B - moderate emissions and moderate visibility reductions. A - extensive emissions from power plants, extensive visibility reductions, unreclaimed soil banks and transmission lines.	Yearly mean bids of: $85 A - C $50 B - C.	Uses iterative bidding techniques. Damages illustrated with photographs of various states of visibility, topographical alterations, and transmission line corridors. concerned visibility as it related to emission abatement.

Hylland and Strand [1983]	Value marginal changes in visibility, both locally and nationally, due to air pollution in the Greenland area of southern Norway.	National survey: WTP of 1060 - 1855 NOK [1990] Local survey: annual WTP per person 900NOK [1990] This is the WTP for the largest improvement in air quality	Uses CV National survey: crude approach used. Short and incomplete description of air quality improvement. Commodity mis-specification bias might be present. Local survey: uses survey photographs to depict different visibility levels. Respondents had difficulty in distinguishing between visibility levels. Considerable starting point bias.

PACE [1990] concentrates on the ECO studies. ECO [1987] in their generic coal plant study use an average value of $10 per lost km-year per person [1987$] for the study region chosen from a range of $1-$79 per lost km-year per person reported in the studies reviewed (in these studies residents of, or visitors to an area are asked how much they would be WTP to improve visibility from one level to another (e.g. from 5km to 10km). A value 'per person-km-year' can then estimated). A linear relationship is assumed across all visibility ranges. The visibility effect (in lost km of visibility) was crudely stated as 0.1 km loss for the first 50km from the plant and 0.1km loss thereafter (out to 187 km). Multiplying the population at various distances from the plant by these differences gives the number of person-kms by which visibility will be reduced. The results of this study are not well supported.

ECO [1984] employ a more rigorous model to value lost visibility due to each pollutant emitted from a particular plant. At a value of $10 per lost km-year per person for visibility (estimated after a survey of WTP and CV studies), ECO [1984] estimate annual losses due to SO_2 to be $142,350 for emissions of 630 tons, or $0.11/lb SO_2 [1982]. In 1989$ this estimate would be closer to $0.14/lb SO_2, excluding regional population growth. The annual visibility losses due to NO_x emissions from the particular plant studied were put at about $115,000 [1982$]. Based on NO_x emissions of 440 tons/year, the cost of visibility loss due to the plant is $0.13/lb NO_x [1982$] or about $0.17/lb in [1989$]. ECO [1984] estimate that 10,000 person-kms will be lost annually due to particulate emissions. Valued at $10/person-km [1987$] or $10.80/ person-km [1989$] this translates to a cost of $0.83/lb particulates [1989$].

Schulze et al [1983] consider pollutants from coal-fired power plants. Their survey is designed to capture the two components of preservation value - user value and existence value. One-third of the respondents were asked a pure user value question - how much they would be WTP in higher entrance fees for visibility protection at the Grand Canyon and other parks, while the rest were asked how much they would be WTP in the form of higher electricity bills to preserve visibility in the parklands - a total preservation value question. Existence value is represented by the difference between the user and total preservation estimates.

Participants in the survey were shown sets of photographs of a particular national park vista with five different levels of visual air quality. In valuing WTP to prevent a plume being seen from the Grand Canyon National Park, two photographs were used one with a dark plume in the sky and one with no plume at all.

Extrapolating the bids to the nation Schulze et al [1983] estimate the preservation value of the Grand Canyon to be approximately $3.5 billion per year. Extension of visibility preservation to the entire southwest parklands region increases the annual benefits to nearly $6.2 billion per year. Plume avoidance has an aggregate annual value of approx $2b. The annualized preservation benefits for the nation came to $7.4 billion [1980$] while the annualized costs of control came to $2.8 -3.1 billion.

Rowe et al [1980] explore the conceptual difficulties associated with iterative bidding techniques. One area of emphasis was the linkage of the physical parameters of visibility e.g. prevailing visibility in miles, to a verbal and pictorial depiction of the good to individuals for valuation purposes. Randall et al [1974] and Brookshire et al [1976] use a series of pictures to depict the varying levels of the environmental good under question, however, no well-defined linkage existed between the picture and the actual parameters of visibility. Clearly, differing levels of visibility and other aesthetic effects were depicted, but the question remains as to the relation of economic value to the level of visibility and to the level of emissions from power plants. The study estimates the value individuals place on being able to see long distances and not have the vista or scene impeded by air-borne residuals where there is a direct connection between photographs and physical parameters of air quality. The good i.e. visibility, is described in quantity and quality terms to the respondent, i.e. the current situation is established for the respondent. This includes detailing the contributing factors for the current quality and quantity information i.e. if energy is a factor then the current level of generation and location will be stated. Then a series of possible future conditions ie increased levels of energy development and the resultant impact on the good is depicted, i.e. the respondent receives additional information which construct a contingent market. A price is posited for each contingent market which represents a starting point ($1,$5,$10) and the respondent bids via a bidding vehicle e.g. utility bill or payroll deduction.

It is not possible to derive an externality adder from this study as no link is made to pollutants. The cause of the visibility impairment is important, haze caused by natural vegetation or humidity may be valued differently from haze caused from industrial development. The visibility impact must be explicitly tied to energy production, and transferability of results related to other contexts is not possible.

The only European visibility study cited is by Hylland and Strand [1983]. As already mentioned, a problem that all visibility studies face is that value estimates often include WTP for reduced health effects as a result of reduced air pollution. Hylland and Strand do not include morbidity effects in their WTP survey questions, but a direct question at the end of the local study revealed that a large part of the respondents' stated WTP was due to the expected reduced health risks: only 14.5% stated reduced visibility as the largest negative effect of air pollution in the area, 50.1% stated that health effects were the largest problem, 18.6% bad conditions for raising children (which can be interpreted as belonging to the health risk category), and 16.8% smell and a dirty/dusty environment. It is likely therefore that the estimates in this study overestimate the value of a marginal change in visibility. Also an increment in visibility is being valued, while we are interested in a decrement. There is evidence that people value these opposite changes differently. Without emission factors for the area under study it is not possible to derive an externality adder.

11.4 Visual Amenity.

The effect of a power plant on visual amenity is site specific, it probably matters more that a station is located on a stretch of coastline rather than in an industrial area. As with visibility the impact is aesthetic in nature and the same challenges to valuation apply. There are virtually no valuation studies concerned with the losses to visual amenity related to energy production and so externality adders for this impact cannot be derived.

Ferguson [1990] attempts to estimate the visual impacts of the proposed Capel Cyon wind-farm in Wales. He calculates total amenity value to the local residents of land areas to be about $20 - 200 m/sq. km accounting for low population densities. The assumption is made that wherever the power station is 'significantly visually obtrusive', the amenity of land is reduced to zero. Based on the Environmental Statement for Capel Cyon, Ferguson concludes that the area of land reduced to a zero value per 330 wk wind turbine is about 0.2 sq km., with a value of £4 - 40m. This results in a very large cost of about 20 - 200 p/kWh. As there is no scientific basis for the estimate, however, we do not consider the estimates to be at all reliable. No such analysis has been performed for fossil fuel or nuclear plants.

11.5 Conclusions.

Particulates are strongly implicated in visibility decline. On PACE's analysis, particulate damage is mainly due to visibility impairment which contributes $0.83 per lb (ECO [1984]) to the total starting point estimate for particulates of $1.19 per lb (this total includes particulate damage to health, buildings and materials, crops and forests). PACE suggests an externality adder of $0.14 per lb of SO2 [1989$] and $0.17 per lb of NOx. Generally, visibility studies estimates are not transferable, atmospheric conditions are different for different areas as are population densities and people's preferences.

Although few estimates of adders are available there is some evidence that particulate-induced visibility impairment may be significant external cost of energy.

CHAPTER 12   NOISE NUISANCE

12.1 Introduction

Noise nuisance afflicts all societies in the workplace and in the open where the main causes
are construction and repair work, noise from domestic premises, traffic noise and aircraft
noise. Attempts to value people's preferences for peace and quiet have centred on the use of
the hedonic price approach whereby an analysis is made of the determinants of house prices.
A residential property price will vary with the characteristics of the property - its location,
size, neighbourhood, nearness to the business district and shopping, and so on. In this way
the house is seen more as a 'bundle of attributes' rather than bricks and mortar. By
statistically analyzing the prices of different properties according to their attributes it is
possible to separate out the factors influencing prices, factors that will include the local noise
level. The CVM can also be applied but no case studies using CVM were found.

12.2   Valuation of Noise Nuisance

Table 12.1 shows the results of various studies of the relationship between noise levels and
house prices. They are presented in terms of a 'price elasticity' -i.e. for each unit change in
the noise level, measured in standard noise units, the percentage change in property price is
shown. For aircraft noise the estimates suggest that for every unit change in NEF (noise
exposure forecast) property prices might change by around 1%, and for every unit change
in NNI (noise and number index) the change is around 0.5%. For traffic noise, measured in
Leq, a one unit change again produces property price depreciation of 0.5-1.0%. These results
are remarkably consistent, suggesting that 'benefits transfer' may well be feasible for noise
nuisance. No meta-analysis (see chapter 14) has yet been carried out on noise nuisance, but
the absence of significant variance about the mean suggests that transferability looks justified.

Clearly, using property price changes to measure preferences for reducing noise nuisance
does not encompass all the benefits of noise reduction. Night-time and continuous levels of
noise are probably associated with health impairment through stress, for example. It is
unlikely that individuals will be sufficiently aware of health risks to 'capture' their value in
the form of house location choice. None the less, the hedonic property price approach offers
a reasonable approach to the valuation of the dominant benefit of noise reduction - reduced
irritation and nuisance.

Noise in the energy context is most likely to relate to wind farms, but may also arise in
respect of any transportation of fuels. Because the results for aircraft noise relate to a noise
measure that includes the number of aircraft, the usefulness of the mean WTP results for

transferability to energy-related noise is very limited[1]. The measures for traffic noise are more relevant since they are related to a measure of noise based on loudness (Leq, a measure of constant sound in dBA which would have the same sound energy over a given period as the measured fluctuating sound under consideration). Transferability would then depend on the nature of the energy-related noise - a subject that requires further investigation.

---

[1] The 'Noise and Number index' is represented by the formula:
$$NNI = PndB + 15 \ln.N - 80$$
where PndB is perceived noise decibels, and N is number of aircraft take-offs/landings. Changes in the noise exposure forecast (NEF) are approximately equal to 2.25 changes in NNI (Walters [1975]).

Table 12.1

The Value of Reducing Noise Nuisance

Study:	Percentage Impact of 1 Unit Change on Property Price	
	NEF	NNI
Aircraft Noise		
USA		
Los Angeles		0.8
Englewood		0.8
New York	1.6-2.0	
Minneapolis	0.6	
San Francisco	0.5	
Boston	0.8	
Washington DC	1.0	
Dallas	0.6-0.8	
Rochester	0.6-0.7	
Canada		
Toronto		0.2-0.6
Edmonton	0.1-1.6	
UK		
Heathrow		0.2-0.3
Manchester		0.0-0.4
Australia		
Sydney	0.0-0.4	
Switzerland		
Basel		0.2
Netherlands		
Amsterdam		0.3-0.5
Norway		
Bode		1.0 (per dB)
Average:	0.6-1.3	0.2-0.5

Traffic Noise	Leq
USA:	
Virginia	0.1
Tidewater	0.1
N.Springfield	0.2-0.5
Towson	0
Washington DC	0.9
Kingsgate	0.5
North King County	0.3
Spokane	0.1
Chicago	0.7
Canada:	
Toronto	1.0
Switzerland	
Basel	1.3
Norway	
Oslo	0.8
Average	0.5

CHAPTER 13 ENERGY CONSERVATION

13.1 Introduction

If energy production and consumption have external effects then the 'negative' of production and consumption - namely, conservation - will <u>avoid</u> those external effects. Ostensibly then, any externality adder can be treated as an externality <u>credit</u> for conservation. Conservation may, however, involve its own externalities. Increased household insulation, for example, can increase exposure to natural and man-made sources of radon.

13.2 Analytics of Conservation

Figure 13.1 adapts a diagram from Bates [1991] to show the analytics of energy conservation versus energy supply. MCes is the marginal cost of energy supply and is very elastic at prevailing world prices of energy. D_cD_c is the demand curve for energy assuming all optimal energy conservation measures are undertaken. $D_{oc} D_{oc}$ is the demand curve <u>without</u> conservation. At any energy price, then, more energy is demanded without conservation than with conservation. The amount of conservation undertaken is the horizontal distance between $D_c D_c$ and $D_{oc} D_{oc}$. At all points on $D_c D_c$ conservation investments have been undertaken such that

$$\Delta I_{ec} = \Sigma \ P_t \ \Delta Q_{ect} \quad . \ (1+r)^{-t} \qquad \qquad \dots\dots(1)$$
where

ΔI_{ec} = extra investment in energy conservation
P_t = price of energy
ΔQ_{ec} = extra quantity of energy conserved
r = discount rate.

---

1 Conservation here means reduced energy consumption per unit of final product. It is not for example equal to reduced energy consumption if that involves a loss of benefits.

The marginal cost of energy conservation (MCEC) is given by
$$\frac{\Delta I_{ec}}{\Delta Q_{ec}} \quad . \ C_{n/r} \ = \ MCEC \qquad \qquad \dots\dots(2)$$

Where $C_{n/r}$ is a capital recovery factor equal to

$$\frac{r}{1 - (1+r)^{-n}}$$

Hence energy conservation is undertaken up to the point where P = MCEC. If energy conservation itself is subject to rising marginal cost, then $\Delta I_{ec}/\Delta Q_{ec}$ will rise as energy conservation increases. More energy conservation therefore requires higher prices. Lower prices will mean <u>less</u> conservation. $D_{oc} D_{oc}$ thus has the relationship to $D_c D_c$ seen in Figure 13.1, i.e. the horizontal distance between the two curves declines as the price of energy falls.

FIGURE 13.1
THE ANALYTICS OF ENERGY CONSERVATION

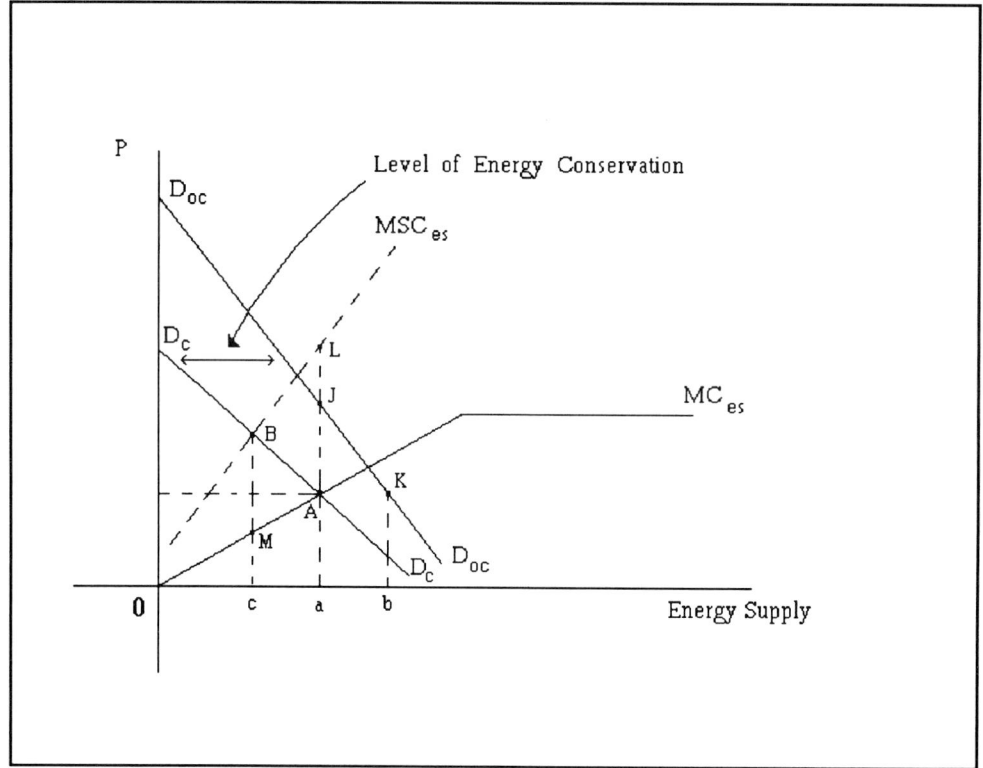

D_cD_c is the demand for energy <u>with</u> conservation
$D_{oc}\,D_{oc}$ is the demand for energy <u>without</u> conservation
MCes is the marginal cost of energy supply
MSCes is the marginal <u>social</u> cost of energy supply
(MCes + externality adders)

A is the private optimum with energy supply Oa and conservation ab. B is the social optimum with energy supply Oc and conservation is Ca.

Now consider the effect of adding an externality charge to energy supply. MCes will shift to MSCes, the vertical distance between the two being the externality adder. The new energy supply is O_c with intersection of $D_c D_c$ and MSCes at B. More energy conservation is now undertaken than previously. Less energy is consumed due to two effects: (a) the rising price of energy alters the conservation investment rate of return, and (b) income and substitution effects operate.

13.3   Conservation Adders

In terms of Figure 13.1, the effect of an externality adder on energy supply is to increase the level of conservation by

$$BJ - AK$$

The inverse of the statement is that a conservation level of BJ=AK avoids some externality, namely

$$AL - MB$$

AL - MB should then be credited to any policy resulting in increased conservation of BJ - AK.

13.4   Estimates of Conservation Adders

Few studies exist of the monetary value of conservation adders. Herz, Hohmeyer and Jochem [1991] correctly identify the benefits of conservation as avoided fuel cycle damages. They suggest that conservation measures will themselves involve some damages, mainly:

- accidents during installation of conservation measures;

- harmful fibre emissions from insulation materials;

- CFC emissions from insulation foam production;

- Emissions from glass, cement and steel production of insulation materials.

Table 13.2 shows estimates from Herz et. al. [personal communication] for insulating a 1 family house.

Table 13.2

Conservation Adders for a German 1 Family Household
(Costs = +; Benefits = - 1987 pfennig/kWh)

Option:	(1) Thermal Insulation	(2) Electric Space Heating	(3) Net Conservation Adder (1) -(2)
Damage Caused:			
- crops, timber	<0.01	0.4-0.5	-0.4 to -0.5
- livestock	<0.01	<0.01	0
- building	<0.01	0.01	0
- materials			
- health	<0.01	0.06-0.23	-0.05 to -0.22
- climate	0.02	2.55	-2.53
- depletion costs	<0.01	<0.06	-0.05
- GDP(net)	-2.38	-	-2.38
- employment(net)	-1.52	-	-1.52
(a) Hertz et.al. estimate	3.86	3.08-3.35	-6.49
(b) Omitting GDP	-1.48	4.56 to -4.31	

Source: Herz et al. (personal communication)

There are several problems with the estimates in Table 13.2:

    a) GDP should not be added to employment - one is a surrogate for the other;

    b) the depletion cost figure is suspect - see chapter 16.

The detailed methodology for deriving the costs adders for conservation is not available. Taking the figures at face value, and ignoring GDP/employment and the depletion cost estimate, the adders are less than 0.06 pfennig/kWh. This suggests a 'conservation adder' of around 0.01 - 0.02 pence/kWh. In the absence of more detailed information it is difficult to attach a confidence level to this figure.

CHAPTER 14 META-ANALYSIS

14.1 Meta-Analysis and Benefits Transfer

Meta-analysis involves the statistical analysis of different empirical studies of environmental values in attempt to explain the variation in the results of those studies. Thus, if there are, say, 10 studies of the demand for tobacco, a meta-analysis would treat each demand equation as a datum and would pool the equations. Econometric analysis would then be applied to the new pool of data in an effort (a) to elicit the most important factors determining tobacco demand, and (b) explaining the variation in the factors of importance across the different studies (Smith and Kaoru [1990a, 1990b], Smith [1991]). While meta-analysis may serve a number of functions, its primary purpose in the current context is to determine the validity of <u>benefits transfer</u>, i.e. to establish the extent to which an estimate of economic value in one location can be applied to another location. Thus, if meta-analysis established that an average of mean estimates was X, but that a 10% downward deviation from X could expected if characteristic y was present, then a site with characteristic y might have a value of 0.9X attributed to it.

Meta-analysis has, to date, been applied in only two spheres of environmental valuation - recreational demand and air pollution, although Chapter 12 reports something akin to a crude meta-analysis for noise nuisance.

14.2 Recreational Demand

The demand for recreational sites is of potential significance for externality adders in an energy context. Possible connections relate to the impact that air pollution may have on leaf cover in forests and on acidification of waters with consequent loss of commercial or sporting fish. However, to be of value, such estimates need to be combined with dose-response functions that show how pollution-induced site degradation impacts on recreational demand. Typically, recreational studies investigating this link have been very few. In a meta-analysis one would expect to see the 'quality of site' variable showing up as statistically significant if the linkage is potentially important.

Two studies of recreational demand meta-analysis exist, by Smith and Kaoru [1990a, 1990b] and by Walsh, Johnson and McKean [1989].

The Smith and Kaoru studies involved an analysis of 200 individual recreational demand studies prepared from 1970 to 1986. Various functional forms were applied to test the link between the dependent variable - visitor-days - and the independent variables: type of survey, type of recreation activity, type of recreation site, price of substitute site, a measure of opportunity cost (e.g. value of time), specification of the demand function, the year of the estimate, and the type of statistical estimator used. Note that the <u>method of study</u> enters the analysis, as well as factors directly influencing recreational demand. An R^2 of 0.43 was obtained for the authors' preferred functional form and a mean of $25.2 per trip or per activity day was found. Analysis of the 't' statistics for the preferred model shows that the nature of the site is significant, as are the substitute price, opportunity cost of time, model specification and some specific econometric attributes of the original studies.

Walsh, Johnson and McKean [1989] report a meta-analysis of 287 estimates of the net value of a recreation day based on 156 TCM estimates, 129 CVM estimates and 2 hedonic price estimates over the period 1968 to 1988. In 1987$ the mean value of a recreation day was $34 and the median (which they prefer) is $27. The highest values are reported for hunting, fishing, boating, hiking and winter sports. The study did not, however, seek to explain the variation in benefit estimates, so that it is of limited value for benefits transfer. Site quality was found to be significant as an explanator, as were regional factors, mixed public and private sites, the role of open-ended questions and the existence of hunting and saltwater fishing.

14.3 Air Pollution

Smith and Huang [1991] report a meta-analysis of US studies of air pollution using hedonic property price models. They review 37 studies giving rise to 167 estimates. Their findings are that there is a definite inverse relationship between air pollution and property prices, in contrast to the more cautious findings of Graves et al. [1988], and that the resulting estimates may be useful for benefit transfer. However, they observe that the last study they investigated was for 1980, there having been no further US studies since that date. All the studies are therefore 'out of date'. The meta-analysis showed that the 'price' of air quality (slope of the hedonic price function) was significantly related to the number of housing characteristics, a measure of air pollution (TSP), and real income. Actual property prices were not significant - i.e. use of variation in sales prices were found to be less likely to detect the impact of air pollution.

14.4   Conclusions

Meta-analysis is at an early stage of development in economics. Nonetheless, its development is likely to be critically important for the use of externality adders in the energy context. Essentially, if meta-analysis shows that variation in estimates cannot be reasonable fully explained, then the process of benefit transfer involves unknown risks of error. If meta-analysis does enable explanations of variance to be made, then the process of benefit transfer, while complex, becomes feasible.

Cline's estimates for increased mortality relate to specific causes of death from higher mean temperatures in the USA. It is instructive to look at possible health impacts elsewhere. These are likely to occur through:

o   changes in the availability of food
o   changes in the availability of drinking water
o   changes in the level of communicable diseases
o   mortality and disease from coastal flooding

Table 15.3 shows impacts of global warming on agriculture, but excludes any risks to life, but the estimates for sea level rise are based on sea defence costs. It might therefore be argued that coastal flooding impacts are allowed for in the estimates since it is presumed that they are prevented. Unfortunately, no quantifiable estimates of likely deaths from reduced food availability, communicable disease increase or reduced drinking water availability appear to have been made. The available reviews tend to support the view that the <u>direction</u> of change will be for the worse. i.e. increased morbidity and mortality. The net direction will be the result of two offsetting effects: probable reductions on winter deaths and disease as mean winter temperatures rise, but higher summer deaths from cardiovascular, cerebrovascular and respiratory disease. For the USA the evidence is probably to the effect that net deaths will increase, but there is considerable uncertainty in the literature. Communicable disease will almost certainly increase. The present distribution of many diseases such as malaria/trypanosomiasis/onchocerciasis and hookworm are temperature related. As temperature increases one might expect the geographical zones of these diseases to expand. Droughts may increase deaths through starvation, but may reduce communicable diseases as water-related insect havens are reduced (Haines and Fuchs [1991]).

Overall then, human health effects <u>could</u> be very large under a climate warming scenario. Much depends on the extent of acclimatization, on other behavioural responses (e.g. migration), and on the relative balance between positive and negative effects. The issue for damage estimation is whether the net adverse effects lie within the range of damage estimates of the order of 1-2% of GWP. The tentative conclusion is that the effects probably support a higher damage estimate of up to 3% of GWP.

Cline estimates an impact on forests whereas Nordhaus finds no such impact. It seem fair to say that Nordhaus's analysis rests very heavily on the US EPA[1980] impacts study, whereas Cline ranges more widely for his sources. The presumption that forest loss would occur is supported by Shugart et al [1986].

Cline observes that Nordhaus's estimates for agricultural damage come from the US EPA[1989] study, but he believes Nordhaus has confused $2xCO_2$ with $2xCO_2$ equ. Moreover, Cline believes that global agricultural effects will net out to be markedly negative at around 6% of world output, or some $40 billion. In 2250 the estimates are $95 billion for the USA and $212 billion for the world. General equilibrium work by Tobey, Reilly and Kane [1990] (quoted in Nordhaus [1990]) suggests a range from a pessimistic 0.3% world output loss (with China losing 5% of GDP) to a 0.1% increase in world real income. US Department of Agriculture [1990] estimates are shown in Table 15.3. These compute welfare changes in consumers' and producers' surpluses) in a globally disaggregated but partial equilibrium model ('SWOPSIM' - Static World Policy Simulation Model). SWOPSIM has certain disadvantages besides its lack of general equilibrium characteristics: it works with assume crop yield changes rather than with given climatic change assumptions, although the estimates in Table 15.3 are effectively for a CO_2 doubling: and it does not model farmer response nor, more importantly, CO_2 fertilisation. The latter aspects almost certainly mean that it will <u>understate</u> gains. It does however incorporate the effects of price changes brought on by yield changes, something that 'crop effect' models do not (Parry, Carter and Konijn [1988]). Table 15.3 suggests that impacts on agriculture may well be very small indeed for a 'moderate' climate change. As far as Cline's 2050 estimate is concerned, therefore, the work suggests that his figures may be too pessimistic and that Nordhaus's interpretation of the situation is likely to be closer to the truth.

On sea level rise OECD[1990] has investigated the costs of adapting to sea level rise. To 2050 the study assumes a rise in sea level of 30-50 cms, and up to one metre by 2100. The main feature of the study is an extension of a Delft Hydraulics [1990] study which looks at the cost of protecting low lying areas. The overall results are summarised in Table 15.4. The figures shown suggest a cost of some $800 billion over the next 100 years, or around 0.1% of aggregate annual OECD national income. Costs for low lying developing countries would have to be added to this. The figure of 0.1% of GNP is for 1 metre sea level rise whereas this is very unlikely to occur before 2100. Thus, while the 0.1% appears wholly consistent with Cline's estimate of around 0.13% it suggests that Cline's estimate may be a little high.

Table 15.3

<u>Climatic Change Impacts on World Agriculture</u>

Country/Region	Welfare Change ($1986 million)	%of GDP
USA	+ 194	0.005(gain)
Canada	- 167	0.047(loss)
EC	- 673	0.022(loss)
N Europe	- 51	0.010(loss)
Japan	-1209	0.062(loss)
Australia	+ 66	0.038(gain)
China	+2282	0.141(gain)
USSR	+ 658	0.292(gain)
Brazil	- 47	0.017(loss)
Argentina	+ 95	0.120(gain)
Pakistan	- 50	0.153(loss)
Thailand	- 33	0.081(loss)
R.O.W.	- 67	0.002(loss)
World	+1509	0.01(gain)

Source: US Department of Agriculture [1990]

Table 15.4

Costs of 1 Metre Sea Level Rise over Next Century
on OECD Countries
($ billions)

Policy:	Accommodate	Retreat	Protect
Wetlands	425	400	500
Beaches	50	50	50+
Drylands	115	150	0
Harbours	20	20	20
Infrastructure	50	50?	0
Protect Cities	60	60	60
Protect Rural Areas	100	0	160
Totals	820	730	790

Source: OECD[1990]

Table 15.5

Implicit or Hypothesised Damage Functions

	Point Estimate for c2050 and +3°C	Growth Function of damage share of GWP	Implied Point Estimate for later years
Nordhaus:	0.25-2.0%GWP	0.0%(*)	0.25-2.0%GWP (any year)
Cline:	1.1% GWP	0.85%pa	c6.0%GWP (2250/80)
Peck and Teisberg	2.0% GWP	0.70%pa	4.0% GWP (linear hypothesis)
		2.10%pa	16%GWP (power function) (c2150=>6°C warming)

* damage rises at the same rate as GWP

15-7

15.2.5 Benefit/Damage Functions

As noted previously, Nordhaus [1991], Cline[1990] and Peck and Teisburg [1990, 1991] all have implicit or hypothesised damage functions. Table 15.5 above shows the functions. Not too much can be read into the figures since Nordhaus's damage function is partly an artifact of the model specification, while the Peck-Teisberg figures are the outcome of different specification function rather than damage estimates. Cline's implied functions is the result of two separate point estimates of damage.

Table 15.6 sets out the resulting damages allowing for various changes to Cline's estimates. Taking the lower end of the range, due to the uncertainty surrounding Cline's health impacts, we have a range of £5.8 to 17.3 per t C in CO2 equ.

Table 15.6

Summary Climate Damage Measures
£1991 per t C

Damage as % of GWP	Damage per t c (Nordhaus)[1]	Cline's Adjustment[2]	Revisions to Cline[3] Lower	Upper
			Lower	Upper
1%	5.0	5.5	5.9	8.3
2%	8.6	10.0	11.7	16.5
3%	12.9	15.0	16.5	24.7

Notes
1.   Table 15.1
2.   Table 15.2 i.e. column (2) x 1.1
3.   Due to the 'value of life' i.e column(2) x 1.06 to 1.50

15.3 Greenhouse Gas Externality Adders

On the basis of the previous analysis it is now possible to derive externality adders for all greenhouse gases. We use the following 'CO2 equivalents' based on Derwent [to be published] and referred to by Eyre [1990].

Table 15.7
Greenhouse Gas Emission Factors
kg C/GJ

Weightings[1]	COAL	MOD-COAL	OIL	GAS	NUC
CO_2 as C 1	81.6	71.7	74.7	34.0	3.2
CO_4 4.6	5.3	4.6	0.1	2.5	0.2
N_2O as N 106	1.1	1.0	3.8	0.1	0.1
NO_2 as N 21.4	9.4	5.0	4.5	1.8	0.4
CO as C 1.5	-	-	-	0.1	-
AMVOC 2.1	-	-	0.1	-	-
TOTAL	97.4	82.3	83.2	38. 5	3.9

Source: Eyre (1990)
1.From Derwent (to be published)

Taking the totals and applying to monetary values from Table 15.5 gives the greenhouse externality adders shows in Table 15.8.

Table 15.8

Greenhouse Gas Adders

	Coal	Mod-coal	Oil	Gas	Nuclear	
(1)GHGS[2]	97.4	82.3	83.2	38.5	3.9	KG/Cegu.GJ
(2)GHGS[2]	352	296	300	139	14	g/ Cegu kWh
(3)Adder[3]	0.20	0.17	0.17	0.08	0.01	p/kWh
	to	to	to	to	to	
	0.61	0.51	0.52	0.24	0.02	

Notes
1.   From Table 15.7
2.   Multiply x1000 for kg to g; divide by 278 for GJ to kWh   (1GJ=278 kWh)
3.   £5.8 to £17.3 per tonne C = 0.00058 p/gC to 0.00173p/gC
      These values are multiplied by the figures in row 2.

15.4 Conclusion

Even through the Nordhaus- Cline estimates of global warming damage are regarded by some commentators as being too low, they still produce fairly significant adders for coal-fired generating plant and not inconsequential ones for gas.

CHAPTER 16 USER COSTS

16.1 Introduction

Under the Hotelling rule (Hotelling [1931]) the rental, 'R', on a depletable resource rises at the rate of discount s; i.e.

$$R_t = R_o . (1+s)^t \qquad \ldots\ldots(1)$$

and the rental, royalty or <u>user cost</u>, is the difference between price and cost. At time T the resource price reaches a level where a 'backstop technology' comes into play or the resource runs out. In the long run energy future this may be fusion, in the shorter term it may be oil shales etc. In time T, then,

$$R_T = P_{B,T} - C \qquad \ldots\ldots(2)$$

Where P_B is the price of the backstop technology, and C is the cost of extraction.

Substituting (2) in (1) gives

$$R_o (1+s)^T = P_{B,T} - C$$

or

$$R_o = \frac{P_{B,T} - C}{(1+s)^T} \qquad \ldots\ldots(3)$$

More generally, the royalty in any period t will be:

$$R_t = \frac{P_{B,T} - C}{(1+s)^{T-t}} \qquad \ldots\ldots(4)$$

It follows that a measure of user cost can be obtained from equation (4). What is needed is knowledge of the cost of the backstop technology, its probable cost of extraction, the period at which it is likely to come into play (T), and the discount rate.

16.2 Estimating User Costs

To find T, it is necessary to solve the equation

$$\sum^{T} Q_t = V - K \qquad \ldots\ldots(5)$$

Where Q_t is the quantity of the resource consumed in period t, V is reserves and K is any commitment to 'premium' uses (e.g. gas for feedstock).

If K=O, T is given by the time at which existing reserves are exhausted, or when the backstop price is just equal to the resource price.

16.3 Estimates of User Cost

Estimates of user cost have been made, especially for developing economies with new gas reserves, where the issue of optimal pricing is important. Clearly, the user cost will be smaller the longer is the time period to the replacement technology, the lower is the cost of the replacement technology, and the higher is the discount rate. Estimates for Bangladesh (Julius and Mashayekhi [1990] suggest very low user cost components of 3-6% of overall economic cost of supply, but Munasinghe and Schramm [1983] estimate user costs of 38% of overall cost for Thailand. User cost can therefore be important in contexts where the energy resource in question is unlikely to be internationally traded. Moreover, as equations (3) and (4) show, user cost rises over time at the rate of discount.

Newbery [1985] has computed efficient gas prices for the UK using what is essentially the Hotelling equation but with user cost (rents) decomposed to rents relating to long run replacement costs and rents due to short-run supply constraints. He concluded that for 1984 ' present gas prices seem to be close to efficient prices'. How far this conclusion holds today (1992) is open to question. If it does hold, then there is no case for adding user cost components on to existing prices to reflect this temporal externality. Note that estimating a user cost component, as in section 16.2, does not mean an 'adder' is called for if existing prices already reflect user costs, as Newbery's work suggests.

16.4 Hohmeyer on User Costs

One reason for assessing user costs is that they play a fairly significant role in the influential work of Hohmeyer [1988][1989]. There they are referred to as 'depletion surcharges'. Table 16.1 shows their relevance to the overall adder derived by Hohmeyer.

Table 16.1
Hohmeyer's Externality Adders and User Costs
pfennig 1982/kWh, rounded

	Fossil Fuel	Nuclear	Wind*	Solar PV*
(a) Adder	4-9	10-21	0	-6 to -2
(b) Depletion Surcharge	2	6	0	0
(c) (b)/(a)%	11-50	29-69	0	0

Source: Calculated from Hohmeyer [1988]

Note: *Hohmeyer estimates net <u>benefits</u> from wind and solar-hence the negative entry for solar. However, he also confusingly includes the <u>avoided</u> damage from nuclear and fossil fuels. Use of his totals as adders would therefore amount to double counting. We have omitted these avoided costs here.

Hohmeyer's actual user costs are:

		% 1986 Price
natural gas	0.38DM/kWh	11.5
oil	0.058	25.2
hard coal(FRG)	0.033	18.9
imported coal	0.037	21.1
lignite	0.005	6.7
uranium	0.064 to 0.066	25.6 to 70.7

(Hohmeyer [1988]p.78)

In turn, these charges change over time but the graph showing these changes reveal that none of them changes at the relevant rate of discount. Indeed, several of them <u>decline</u> over time. While Hohmeyer discusses and estimates 'dynamic' depletion surcharges to allow for these affects over time, he concludes that the 'static' charges are the ones to be used. Despite this, the table recording the total fossil fuel surcharge indicates a surcharge of 2pf/kWh whereas the above figures suggest something closer to 4pf/kWh.

There are numerous problems with Hohmeyer's approach and interpretation is also made more complex by unclear exposition. A model that purports to have something to do with the Hotelling approach is presented. Reinterpreted it appears to compute user cost as

$$\frac{\Sigma Q_t}{V} (P_B - G)$$

Where the notation is as before, but G is the 'primary value' of the resource. However, the expression has no discount rate, and the multiplier is the cumulative extraction rate (ΣQ_t) as a proportion of the total stock (V). The expression is simply not an estimator of user costs.

CHAPTER 17   NON-ENVIRONMENTAL EXTERNALITIES

17.1   Introduction

Chapter 2 discussed the theoretical basis for including non-environmental externalities (NEEs) in externality adders. The <u>empirical literature</u> on NEES is, however, very sparse.

17.2   Energy Security

Governments frequently express a concern for <u>energy security</u>. Such concerns are motivated by:

(a)   <u>political</u> concerns, ie nation A wishes not to be at the mercy of nation B which supplies A with energy. An obvious example is the widespread concern to reduce dependence on Middle-Eastern oil;

(b)   <u>economic</u> concerns; nation A fears interruptions of supply which have costs in terms of the <u>welfare losses from un-met demand and from energy price-induced recession</u>.

Both arguments suggest that a "security adder" should be added to the price of any fuel that has to be <u>imported</u> from sources thought to be a security risk. Alternatively, a security subsidy should be deducted from the price of indigenous resources. It is important to distinguish security arguments from import substitution arguments. The latter is a false justification for indigenous supply and offers no basis for differentiating between energy sources on security grounds.

17.3   Oil Prices and Recession

There is an extensive literature on the role of oil price "hikes" in causing recession. Hudson and Jorgenson [1978a, 1978b] and Mork and Hall [1980] attribute some of the recession and inflation post 1973 to the 1973 oil price hike. Gisser and Goodwin [1986] similarly implicate oil prices in macroeconomic change. Burbidge and Harrison [1984] found that output and real wages fell in the post 1973 and post 1979 periods due to oil price rises, and prices rose. Hamilton [1985] similarly shows that, from 1948 to 1981 recessions in the USA were almost always linked to oil price "spikes". This literature suggests then, that reliance on imported oil increases the risk of income losses due to market-induced or monopolistic pressures on world prices. In turn it could be argued that these associated income losses could be avoided by investing in indigenous technologies at costs of supply above the border price. The maximum excess cost that would be justified on this argument would be the lost GDP associated with the imports divided by the level of imports.

Any argument of this kind needs to be used with great care. In the first place, if an import surcharge or indigenous fuel subsidy is warranted when prices are high and (some) GDP is lost, then a domestic tax or import subsidy would be justified when prices fell dramatically causing, presumably, GDP gains. Typically, the oil price/recession literature has looked at price hikes only. Second, some probability of future hikes and their associated damages would be needed. Nonetheless, governments clearly <u>do</u> make energy investment decisions partly on the basis of a desire to minimise both quantity and price restrictions from imported energy. Some part of the UK Non-Fossil Fuel Obligation (NFFO) would appear to be motivated by this concern.

17.4 The NFFO and Fossil Fuel Levy

Under the UK Electricity Act of 1989 the Secretary of State for Energy can require regional electricity companies (RECs) in England and Wales to secure a certain quantity of electricity from non- fossil fuelled sources. The cost of meeting this obligation is met through a levy on electricity consumers in England and Wales, the proceeds of which are used to help meet the unavoidable costs associated with existing nuclear stations and to encourage development of renewable forms of electricity generation. The levy and the associated Non Fossil Fuel Obligation (NFFO) are designed to help secure the fuel diversity and environmental benefits of nuclear and renewable generation. The present NFFO and levy arrangements are due to expire in 1998. The Government is considering introduction of NFFO-type arrangements in Scotland and Northern Ireland.

In 1990/91 the levy raised some £1.2 billion. The rate of levy was 10.6%, which, applied to the average price of electricity of around 5.5 p/kWh (including the levy) implies a levy amount of over 0.5p/kWh. Funds raised by the levy are distributed to the owners of existing nuclear stations (including Sizewell B) and to generators of electricity from renewable sources in accordance with the terms of contracts signed in fulfilment of the Non Fossil Fuel Obligation.

Under the present arrangements, levy funding of existing nuclear stations will tend to fall in real terms year by year and will cease after March 1998. There is no provision for generation from a new PWR to benefit from levy receipts and in any case it is most unlikely that any new PWR could be ready to supply power before the termination of the existing arrangements in 1998.

Levy funding of renewables is expected to rise over time as more projects contracted in fulfilment of NFFO come onstream. Under contracts already in place, renewables generators are expected to receive electricity prices some 2-8 p/kWh (depending on the type of technology) above market levels for output delivered up to 1998. Although the present arrangements for renewables also terminate in 1998, their extension beyond 1998 is being considered.

17.5 Oil and Defence Expenditure Subsidies

Hall [1991] has presented an interesting argument concerning a NEE arising from the defence expenditure of the USA and their role in protecting the sources of oil imports. Basically, the argument is as follows:

a)   oil imports impose risks of domestic economic losses
b)   hence military expenditures are made to protect "cheap" oil import sources;

c)   those military expenditures are an externality associated with oil;
d)   hence oil is subsidised through those expenditures, and
e)   the "true" price of oil is much higher once this NEE is accounted for.

Since all defence spending is not related to protecting oil sources, Hall [1991] estimates a model in which changes in US defence spending are explained by oil imports, lagged several periods. The model suggests that in 1985 every million barrels per day imports was associated with $2.96 billion defence spending per year, or a defence subsidy of $7.32 per barrel. (Hall estimates an additional $1.15-1.75 per barrel because of the costs of the US Strategic Petroleum Reserve).

This may be compared to the 1985 crude oil price of some $15 per barrel, ie it suggests that the "true" price of oil, ignoring all other externalities, but including the security adder, would have been some 50% higher at $22-23 bbl. Broadman and Hogan [1988] estimate a "willingness to pay for military protection of oil supplies" of just over $7.

Clearly, the Broadman-Hogan-Hall argument is highly significant. If the same expenditures apply today, the "adder" to a $20 bbl oil price would be around 35-40%, allowing for inflation. If the market price of oil was higher by this amount, the configuration of energy supply in the USA would probably be very different. Translating the adder into electricity prices would be complex but feasible. As an upper bound, $7 bbl is equivalent to US¢/kWh 1.4 for oil-generated electricity.[1]

No comparable exercise appears to have been carried out for the UK or Europe generally.

17.6   Subsidies

It is widely suggested that some energy technologies are underpriced because of subsidies to research and development (R and D). Past R and D expenditure subsidies are not relevant, however, as they represent sunk costs. Current subsidies are relevant. Hohmeyer [1988], for example, estimates that R and D "transfers" account for 10-20% of nuclear energy externality adders in Germany. By contrast, monetary subsidies (eg to the coal industry) are relatively unimportant. Hohmeyer acknowledges that the high "subsidy adder" for nuclear electricity partly reflects the availability of information. Other "induced public expenditures" include the liming of forests to counteract acidification damage; some proportion of disaster prevention costs; disaster occurrence costs (see Chapter 14) if private insurance payments by energy industry are "capped" due to liability restrictions (as in Germany), emission abatement costs; publicly born security costs (eg for nuclear installations); and infrastructure costs.

---

[1] 1 million bbl = 1700 GWh electrical energy or 500 GWh electricity produced. The latter conversion is the relevant one. Hence 1 bbl = 500 kWh.

Hohmeyer's treatment of R and D subsidies is unsatisfactory. Rather than take current expenditures he debits the energy industries with adders based on foregone income from past R and D expenditures. This he does by computing such expenditures and estimating an interest payment at 8%. No further justification is given for the procedure and there is no discussion of sunk/and current costs.

Table 17.2 shows Hohmeyer's estimate of NEEs for Germany.

Table 17.2

Hohmeyer [1988] Estimates of NEEs for Germany

(Pfennig/kWh 1982 prices)

	Coal	Oil & Gas	Nuclear
Public Provisions in Kind	0.066	0.066	0.107
Monetary Public Subsidies	0.229	0.005	0.137
R and D	0.039	neg	2.353
Accelerated Depreciation	←--------------	0.083	--------------→
Total	←--------------	0.901	--------------→

Source: Hohmeyer [1988], p94.

Taking Hohmeyer's estimates at face value, updating 1982 prices and converting at current exchange rates, the total "public expenditure adder" for conventional energy sources is

$$\frac{0.9 \times 1.16 \text{ (inflation)}}{3.13 \text{ (exchange rate)}}$$

$$= 0.33 \text{p/kWh}$$

Unfortunately, the methodology used by Hohmeyer is suspect.

Lockwood [1992] offers some preliminary estimates of subsidies in the UK. First, he estimates subsidies due to R and D. Lockwood notes that the UK Department of Energy, the Health and Safety Executive and the Department of the Environment all spend R & D monies in support of the energy sector. For 1990/1 Lockwood cites these sums as:

Coal	£ 7.6m
Renewables	£ 20.3m
Nuclear	£193.0m
Waste Management	£ 10.0m
	£231.5m

In fact, nuclear R and D expenditure in 1990/1 was some £112 million, and is planned to decline to £75 million in 1994-5. One problem is that these expenditures are subsidies to the fuel cycles if and only if the relevant sectors would have undertaken them if central government did not. Lockwood suggests range of £70m - £183 million as the 'displaced expenditure' from the nuclear industry. If so, the implicit subsidy to nuclear is 0.13 - 0.33

p/kWh. Lockwood's own range is 0.16 -0.43 p/kWh. He also cites Sweet and Sweet [1989] as supporting a range of 0.2 -0.4 p/kWh. As noted, however, Lockwood's figures are too high. They also relate to <u>existing</u> nuclear capacity than new capacity.

Lockwood's second NEE subsidy relates to the domestic coal premium. UK coal is purchased by the generating companies at prices above the border price of coal. Lockwood suggests the difference is of the order of 50 pence/GJ, or 0.14 - 0.71 p/kWh for an average coal plant and 0.13 0.65 p/kWh. This means that the retail price of coal-generated electricity is <u>higher</u> than the 'optimal' price. These sums are therefore <u>negative adders</u> (i.e. taxes). Lockwood scttlcs for a ccntral cstimatc of 0.5 p/kWh.

17.7   Restrictions on Nuclear Damage Liability

Where a restriction is placed on damage resulting from an energy facility, the effect is to subsidise the energy activity by the difference between "true" damage and the capped liability. Thus, a "liability adder" would take the form

$$LA = \frac{D_A - D_C}{kWh}$$

where D_A is actual damage and D_C is the capped damage. Such liability limits are widespread for nuclear power for example.

In the UK nuclear liability is restricted under the 1965 Nuclear Installations Act. This Act limits liability in form and amount. Thus, liability is only for personal injury and physical damage to property.[2] There is also an upper financial limit to these damages as well. Note, however, that if a nuclear accident adder is estimated, the liability adder would double-count the surcharge. Hence we ignore the liability adder.

---

[2]In Merlin and Others v British Nuclear Fuels, 1990, it was established that "property" does not include economic damage. In this case the economic damage was the reduced price the owners of a house sold at due to radionuclide contamination from Sellafield, Cumbria.

CHAPTER 18 DISCOUNTING

18.1 Intergenerational Concerns

A considerable literature is devoted to the problem of how to modify the discounting procedure to make it compatible, or more compatible, with intergenerational concerns. Some authors argue that this is a mistaken procedure because what is being done is to attempt to modify a procedure based on efficiency gains and losses for a major redefinition of the underlying objective - intergenerational fairness. An appraisal procedure that evolved from concerns with mainly localised and certainly marginal changes to the state of the economy is being modified to apply to issues that are global in the spatial sense and global also in a non-marginal sense - i.e. significant changes in wellbeing are involved. A tool for fine-tuning decisions is being applied to contexts where fine tuning is not the issue.

18.1.1 Sustainability

One way to avoid some of these concerns is to impose a <u>sustainability constraint</u>. Essentially, this amounts to formulating some rule which would maximise gains to wellbeing now provided this does not reduce the wellbeing of future generations below that of the current generation. This is a departure from benefit-cost analysis because it requires that wellbeing be constant or increasing over time. Benefit-cost analysis would be consistent with reducing current wellbeing if it yields a greater benefit for future generations, and <u>vice versa</u>. Rules of this kind have been formulated in terms of maintaining overall stocks of capital of all kinds - man-made, human and natural (Solow [1986], Pearce, Markandya and Barbier [1989]). In <u>practical</u> terms such rules would require monitoring and measurement of capital stocks and an investment policy that sought at all times to ensure that net investment offset depreciation ('compensating investments'). The main difficulties would lie in the issue of measuring capital since physical units would not be adequate due to the heterogeneity of capital (the 'adding up' problem). Hence a valuation procedure would be needed. As yet little advance in this area has been made beyond some attempts to recompute GNP to reveal net investment levels that allow for depreciation on natural capital assets (Repetto [1989]).

18.2 Modifying the Discount Rate

Four approaches to setting discount rates may be considered. These are:

   (a) setting the discount rate equal to zero

   (b) computing a consumer discount rate

   (c) computing a producer discount rate

   (d) computing some weighted average of consumer and producer rates.

18.2.1 Zero Discount Rates

The argument for zero discount rates is essentially as follows. The point in time at which an individual exists cannot affect that individual's wellbeing. There has to be 'impartiality' about time. Wellbeing at one point of time cannot count more than wellbeing at another point of time. This argument has a long tradition in utilitarianism (e.g. Sidgwick [1907]) and has been forcibly restated in recent work (e.g.Broome [1991]). One defence of impartiality with respect to time is given by Rawls [1972] in terms of his 'original position' argument. An imaginary group of people coming together to determine an allocation of individuals to social groups and to time would not choose to favour one group or one time period over another since they would not know to which group or time period they themselves would be allocated. Thus there must be no discrimination between time periods if there is to be a 'just' allocation.

One argument against zero discount rates has been advanced by Olson and Bailey [1981]. They argue that there are two sources of discounting. The first relates to the discounting of consumption streams and this would be justified by assumptions about diminishing marginal utility of income. The second relates to the discounting of utility itself. The latter they refer to as time preference, the former being due not to time but to differences in the levels of consumption. They then show that if time preference is zero and interest rates are positive (for the first reason) then any individual would rationally reduce consumption levels now to zero in order to make the marginal utility of such consumption infinite. Everything would be transferred to the future. Adopting a zero rate of discount for utility - which is what pure equality of treatment for generations would imply - would imply a policy of total current sacrifice.

The debate over zero discount rates continues. For the moment, it would appear that zero rates may have implications contrary to the purpose advocated by those who want them.

18.2.2 Consumer Discount Rates

The standard formula for discounting future consumption is:

$$d_c = \sigma + \mu.g$$

where d_c is the consumer discount rate, σ is the 'rate of pure time preference' (i.e utility discounting), μ is the elasticity of the marginal utility of consumption function, and g is the growth rate of per capita consumption. If the utility function linking utility to consumption is logarithmic, then $\mu = 1$. If, further, pure time preference is rejected on ethical grounds (but see the argument of Olson and Bailey above), then $\sigma = 0$ and we have

$$d_c = g$$

The discount rate becomes equal to the (expected) rate of growth of per capita consumption. As illustrations this would produce the following discount rates for some advanced economies:

Estimates of Consumer Discount Rates
(assuming $\sigma = 0$, $\mu = 1$)

(% p.a.)

Country	Growth of Real Private Cons- umption (1)	Growth of Population (2)	Discount Rate (%) (1) - (2)
USA	3.3	1.0	+ 2.3
UK	2.8	0.2	+ 2.6
Japan	5.0	1.0	+ 4.0

Table 1 suggests rates for industrialised and industrialising countries would appear to be in the range 2-4%. Estimates will, however, be conditioned by the past period used to make the calculation. Moreover, while the value of unity for μ is convenient some empirical work suggests values of around 1.5 (Scott [1989]). The effect of $\mu = 1.5$ in Table 1 is to raise the effective discount rates to 4% for the UK and USA and above 6% in Japan. The exclusion of σ from the estimates has also to be questioned. In so far as any evidence exists for pure time preference rates in the industrialised world, Scott [1989] has suggested a rate of 1.3% for the UK. Added to the rates in Table 1 this would suggest a consumer discount rate inclusive of 'pure' time preference of about 4% for $\mu = 1$ and 5.3% for $\mu = 1.5$.

18.2.3 Producer Discount Rates

If capital markets were perfect, rates of return on capital would be equal to the rate d_c above. In practice, a number of distortions in the market place give rise to divergences between d_c and the producer rate of discount d_p. Corporation taxes, for example, mean that a company must earn r% if it is to pay its shareholders s% where:

$$r = s/(1-t)$$

where t is the corporation tax rate. Company taxation necessarily makes the producer borrowing rate higher than the rate at which consumers discount the future.

Many economists argue that r% is the 'correct' rate of discount because it measures the opportunity cost of using up $1 in public expenditure -i.e. it is the forgone rate of return on the marginal investment in the private sector. To find r one might take the weighted rate of return on equity and debt. In practice, such calculations are complex. The problems are well rehearsed in Spackman [1991]. In the UK, real returns to debt are probably 3-4%. Real returns to equity comprise dividend yields plus the capital gains. This suggests a return to equity of 5-7%. The resulting long run weighted average cost of capital to the private sector would be no higher than 7% (Spackman [1991], p.4).

Clearly, if a discount rate of 7% is used, long term environmental damage would become insignificant in any benefit-cost comparison.

18.2.4 Synthetic Discount Rates

Any public expenditure on environmental controls would not simply be at the expense of private investment. It is more reasonable to suppose that it would be at the cost of some private investment and some consumption. If so, a 'synthetic' rate of the form:

$$s = w_p.d_p + w_c.d_c$$

would be appropriate. If it could be assumed that the weights for marginal investments are the same as the weights for existing expenditures, then the shares of consumption and investment in national income could be used. For the UK the result, using previous estimates of d_c and d_p would be:

$$\{0.18 \times 7\%\} + \{0.82 \times 5.3\%\}$$

$$= 5.6\%$$

If, on the other hand, a long term consumption growth rate of 1.5% is used together with $\sigma = 0$ and $\mu = 1$, then the synthetic rate becomes 2.50%. It is difficult to argue that it is any lower than this.

18.3 Negative Time Preference

Discounting at positive rates is consistent with a sequencing of events which the best occur first and the worst last. Effectively, costs are postponed, benefits are desired early on. But there is evidence to suggest that sequences in which the best is last and the worst is first are often preferred. If so, there is negative time preference and the resulting discount rate is less than zero Lowenstien [1987] and Pearce [1991].

Negative time preference has arisen in the following contexts:

a) preference for rising wage levels one time even when respondents were shown that a falling stream with savings behaviour would dominate the rising wage level stream;

b) preferences for brief sequences of decreasing discomfort, even when over all discomfort was higher - the dread phenomenon i.e. getting it over with;

c) preferences for sequences that 'end on a good note' the savouring phenomenon;

d) Loss aversion and assimilation (adaptation) induce preference for using levels of benefit over time as people assimilate new stimuli:

The overall result is that changes in assumption rather than levels of assumption often determine value.

The normative significance is that individual time preference is likely to be positive (the orthodox case) when individual decisions are viewed in isolation. When presented as a sequence, however, individuals may well adopt a more 'far-sighted' approach, showing more concern for higher benefits in the future. As yet, the relevant literature is small and inconclusive, but it raises fundamental questions about discounting.

18.4 Conclusions: Discounting and Energy

There are two options for accommodating the distant nature of the effects of global warming and other environmental costs. The first requires that some intergenerational criterion of sustainability be imposed, leaving the 'conventional' discount rate unmodified. The second involves seeking some quantitative adjustment to the conventional discount rate. The problem with the former adjustment is that, as yet, no specific rules for practical operation have emerged in the literature. The problem with the second approach is that it takes fairly heroic assumptions to make a quantitative adjustment that is other than arbitrary. The 'discounting problem' is not resolved either way. Rates of 1-2% can be justified if utility discounting is rejected as unethical - which seems valid given the whole idea is to account for intergenerational equity - if opportunity cost discounting is ignored, and if specific restrictions are placed on the nature of the income - utility function. Use of the opportunity cost rate alone does not appear justified, so that the appropriate range of estimates appears to be 1-5.5%.

CHAPTER 19   EXTERNALITY ADDERS FOR THE UK - A PRELIMINARY ASSESSMENT

19.1   Summary Adders

We now draw together the estimates of the various adders. **Once again, it is important to emphasise the illustrative nature of the figures. Much research needs to be done to firm-up the figures and, ideally, new plant adders require estimation of damages from first principles using an hypothetical plant location in the UK.**

Table 19.1 shows our provisional estimates for the adders. It is not possible to say when they are marginal damage estimates and when they are average estimates. By and large, however, averages dominate. Note that the adders have not been summed. This is because a number of impacts have not been estimated in this report, notably ' disasters' pertaining to the coal, oil hydropower and gas fuel cycles. Neither biodiversity nor noise is expected to be significant, but there may be some land contamination externalities for coal. Public perception of the nuclear waste disposal issue may also not be adequately captured in the health adders for nuclear power - the same issue of perceived and objective risk arises. Finally NEEs and user costs have not been estimated.

Table 19.1

Summary Environment Externality Adders for the United Kingdom

(p/kWh 1990/91 prices)

Fuel Cycle: EEs	Old	New Coal	Oil Coal	Gas		PWR	Sol	Win	Hyd	CHP
Health										
-mortality	0.32	0.32	0.29	0.02		0.01	0.07	0.04	0.03	0.03?
-morbidity	0.12	0.12	0.12	0.04		0.01	-	-	-	0.06
-disaster	NE	NE	NE	NE	(a)	0.02	-	NE	NE	NE
						0.05				
					(b)	0.27*				
Crops	0.10	0.05	0.05	0.02		NE	NE	NE	NE	0.02
Forest +	0.84	0.07	0.98	0.03		NE	NE	NE	NE	0.03
Biod	NE	NE	NE	NE		NE	NE	NE	NE	NE
Builds	3.22	0.28	3.77	0.11		-	-	-	_	0.14
Noise	NE	NE	NE	NE		NE	NE	NE	NE	NE
GHGs x	0.40	0.34	0.35	0.16		0.01	-	-	0.01	0.17
Visib	NE	NE	NE	NE		NE	NE	NE	NE	NE
Water	NE	NE	NE	NE		-	-	-	NE	NE
Land	NE	NE	NE	NE		NE	NE	NE	NE	NE

[Notes: * a) uses the Rocard-Smets function which is linear in the number of people affected; b) takes the 'square function' estimate for risk aversion and the value of a group accident; x takes the average of the range for GHG damage; - means zero; NE means not estimated and probably positive].

For <u>landfill gas</u> the EEs will tend to correspond to the values for natural gas.

For <u>geothermal</u> and <u>wave power</u> it has not proved possible in the time available to secure an overall adder profile.

For <u>tidal</u> a potential biodiversity adder of 0.8 p/kWh may be considered, although there is considerable uncertainty about this figure.

For <u>conservation</u> there is some evidence to suggest an adder of 0.01 to 0.02 p/kWh for the externalities associated with insulating materials and indoor pollution exposure problems.

19.2 Other Overall Adder Exercises

Several attempts have been made to secure overall estimates of adders. The most detailed estimates are those of Hohmeyer [1988, 1990, 1991] for Germany and PACE [1990] for the USA. Hohmeyer's estimates have been severely criticised by Friedrich and Voss [1991]. The work of Hall [1991] for the USA is important because (a) it is better founded in economic analysis and (b) it extends to NEEs. Hohmeyer's work also includes NEEs, whereas PACE [1990] does not. Lockwood [1992] provides a partial assessment for UK NEEs. Lockwood discusses PACE and Hohmeyer's estimates of EEs, but concludes that they cannot be borrowed for the UK context.

Comparing these overall estimates is hazardous. Different approaches are used, coverage varies substantially, and there are varying degrees of 'borrowing' of values from other studies. Nonetheless, we believe the comparison is useful provided, yet again, the right degree of caution is exercised.

Table 19.2 brings the results together.

Table 19.2

(p/kWh 1989-1991 prices)

	PACE[1]	HALL2[3]	HOHM[3]	F+V[4]
Old Coal	3.4	{	1.2-5.3	NE
		{0.4-3.8		
New Coal	1.5	{	{	0.2-0.4
Old Oil	{	NE	{	NE
	{1.6-3.9		{1.0-4.3	
New Oil	{	2.0-2.6	{	NE
Gas	0.6	0.2-1.9	{	NE
SolPV	0.0-0.2	-	<0.3	0.0-0.5
Wind	0.0-0.1	-	<0.1	0.0-0.1
PWR	1.7	1.1-1.6	1.3-7.8	0.0-0.2
Hydro	NE	NE	NE	NE
Langas	NE	NE	NE	NE
CHP	NE	NE	NE	NE
Geoth	NE	NE	NE	NE
Wave	NE	NE	NE	NE
Tidal	NE	NE	NE	NE
Cons	NE	-	NE	NE
Waste	1.7	NE	NE	NE

Notes to Table 19.2

1. PACE [1990]. 'Old coal' is 1.2%S. New coal is either fluidised bed or IGCC. PACE excludes all NEEs and is for generation only i.e. it does not incorporate life cycle impacts.

2. Hall [1990]. Hall's 'gas adder' is $0.3-2.85 MMBTU. At 1 MMBTU = 90 kWh, this results in 0.33 - 3.2 c/kWh. His 'oil adder' is $16.85-22.14 bbl, with the upper estimate including global warming costs. Taking 1 bbl = 500 kWh, this results in 3.4-4.4 c/kWh. Hall's coal adder is $13.68-$124.75 per ton, or $15.08-137.54 per tonne. 1 tonne = 2100 kWh.

3. Hohmeyer [1991] updates Hohmeyer [1988]. Pf/kWh have been converted to p/kWh at 3:1. Hohmeyer's estimates are for EEs and NEEs and incorporate a life cycle approach.

4. Friedrich and Voss [1991]. This unpublished document is designed as a critical comment on Hohmeyer and has limited coverage of EEs only.

There is some consistency in the coal, oil and gas figures given that total fuel cycle impacts are not being measured. Similarly, renewables show small impacts outside of Friedrich and Voss's higher upper figure for solar PV. There is a wide divergence of view of nuclear ranging from negligable or low estimates by Friedrich and Voss to very high estimates by Hohmeyer.

ANNEX 1

THE EC - US DOE STUDY ACCOUNTING FRAMEWORK FOR SOCIAL COST MEASUREMENT

The European Commission and US Department of Energy have commissioned a research programme on the social costs of fuel cycles. The researchers have established an <u>accounting framework</u> in order to order and analyse the relevant social costs.

This annex shows how the accounting framework is structured. It is clearly an 'ideal' system in that it attempts a comprehensive listing and framework for identification of externalities. Its use for the current overview purpose, however, is limited because of the considerable detail involved. We have therefore resorted in Chapter 3 to presenting a simplified version of the evaluation process based on:

fuel cycle stages
emissions or burdens
impact and valuations

The EC-US DOE accounting framework consists of a series of matrices that map each phase of the <u>fuel cycle</u> to a suite of possible <u>emissions</u>; each emission is a suite of <u>impact categories</u> and each category is an <u>external cost</u>. It presents a static measure of the broad range of external costs that arise from the incremental use of different fuel types. In the EC/DOE study, the accounting framework will be applied to eight fuel types - coal, oil, natural gas, nuclear, wind,biomass sources, hydro and photovoltaic. In addition, a number of conservation options will be examined to the extent that they represent alternatives to new investment in conventional fuel types.

The appropriate level of activity within any stage of the fuel cycle is determined by setting the scale and technology for electricity generation and the deriving all the requisite inputs and outputs to support that generating option.

A full account of all the external costs of all stages of all fuel cycles is beyond the scope of current information. For this reason, building the information base and indicating where information is lacking are recognised as essential features of current fuel cycle externality studies.

Table 1 presents the 'mappings ' [relationships] central to the analysis of external costs.

Broad-level mappings define the problem in the broadest terms. A second supporting mapping deals with more specific relationships and translations. These contain the necessary information on emission transport and dose-response that leads to the measurement of physical impact.

For each fuel cycle, eg. coal, each stage of the cycle is defined by its <u>activities</u>, eg the first stage of the coal fuel cycle is coal mining. The activities associated with coal mining are -

mine construction, the mining of coal, waste water management, solid waste management and post mining operations. Each activity of each stage of the fuel cycle is then characterised by its residuals, emissions and burdens, eg coal mining results in emissions to air and water and to solid waste residuals.

TABLE 1

Fuel Cycle Externality Mappings in the EC/US DOE Programme

Broad Level Mappings

Fuel cycle stages	-	activities
Activities	-	emissions and burdens
Emissions	-	physical impacts
Impacts	-	external costs

Supporting Mappings

Emissions	-	source terms
Source terms	-	concentrations
Concentrations		exposures
Exposures	-	doses
Doses	-	responses
Responses	-	physical impact endpoints
Impact endpoints	-	valuation startpoints
Valuation startpoints	-	external costs

The matrix format is used to display the relationship between fuel cycle activities and residual emission burdens. Focus is confined to residual emissions and burdens because abatement technology or waste management act to internalise the costs of physical impacts - therefore these costs are already reflected in market places. The next set of relationships for the framework is the mapping of emissions into physical impacts. Impacts are categorised under human health, ecological and socio-economic.

The ecological impact categories are defined in terms of biological resources valued by society, rather than by medium or path. Using this scheme, soil or water quality are intermediate impacts rather than resource categories because they affect the suitability of the environment for natural organisms or for other human uses.

The socio-economic impacts of interest include building materials, blight effect in land and water resources, visibility and visual insults, noise, public services (ie community services and public institutions that must resolve conflicts derived from the presence of other burdens), and other quality of life impact, eg increased traffic congestion. The scope of the impacts includes local regional and global consequences, however local and regional impacts will be examined first. The final mapping represents the translation of physical impacts into external costs.

Underlying the matrix entries are the necessary supporting mappings to match physical impacts and monetary values. This supporting mapping relies on information to define the appropriate valuation startpoints from the impacts literature. As explained above it is the various impacts caused by the emission and burdens of the fuel cycle, such as a deterioration in health caused by air pollution, which becomes the 'starting point' of the valuation procedure i.e. it is impacts which we seek to value. Once the appropriate valuation startpoint has been identified, valuation measures must be available to derive the external costs.

Emissions are mapped into source terms, ie the source of external costs, eg gaseous emissions, are characterised by their major constituents, their rates of release and their chemical form. Once emission characteristics are developed they are followed through their various pathways up to the point of exposure, where the issue of identifying the exposure-response relationship becomes paramount. Responses are mapped into physical impact endpoints, eg health impact endpoints include cancers and cardiovascular diseases, which become the valuation startpoints.

EXTERNALITY ADDERS IN PRACTICE:
THE EXPERIENCE OF THE USA

The US Approaches

In the United States the generation of electricity is pervasively regulated for economic, environmental and other government objectives at both the State and federal levels. A panoply of legislative and regulatory devices is employed to influence the acquisition of generation and fuel resources seeking to achieve environmentally sound selection. To date, 30 states have required, or are actively considering requiring, their utilities to include environmental externality costs in some manner in planning, bidding or some other resource acquisition procedure.

The methodologies used for the incorporation of environmental externality costs include the following approaches:

1. Quantitative
2. Qualitative
3. Rate of return
4. Avoided cost
5. Ranking

Palmer and Krupnick [1991] review the US experience in general terms and note that, while no state currently (1992) uses damage costs to derive externality adders, some are funding research to enable them to do this. Most use some arbitrary 'adder' or look to abatement costs for the source of the surcharge. Palmer and Krupnick simulate the effects of adders on the US utility system. They use the following <u>provisional</u> figures:

	NO_x c/lb	SO2
Damage Approach	25	50
Abatement Cost Approach	325	75
CO2 Tax	*25 - 100 tC	

The carbon tax is not based on any damage estimate but on numbers being generally discussed as possible carbon taxes. The resulting ratio of social costs to private costs of electricity generation is 1.5 on the damage cost approach (the theoretically correct approach).

A \$25 carbon tax raises the ratio to 1.6. The effect on utilities' behaviour depends very much on how utilities are expected to respond. The existing 'adder' regimes do <u>not</u> require the utilites to pay the social costs of energy. Rather, they are required to invest in <u>new</u> energy sources according to the <u>'ranking with grandfathering'</u>. This contrasts with the orthodox economics prescriptions which are:

> to tax <u>new</u> sources according to their marginal damage costs: <u>'taxation with grandfathering'</u>;

> or to tax <u>all</u> sources at marginal damage costs: <u>'complete emissions taxation'</u>.

The last approach means that not just investment behaviour is altered: so is the 'despatch' of generation units. Despatch will be in terms of unit social costs - or 'environmental despatch'.

The Palmer - Krupnick simulations with the US utility system produce the following provisional results:

> ranking with grandfathering produces little impact on despatch, so that private costs
of   electricity are not altered much (3%);

> taxation with grandfathering has a bigger effect on despatch, especially if CO_2 is taxed. But, perversely in respect of the intent of the adder, reliance on <u>existing</u> sources increases because new sources are taxed. If existing sources are mainly highly polluting coal-fired stations, <u>one effect may be to increase levels of pollution</u>;

> complete taxation results in little change to investment and operating behaviour unless the CO_2 tax is \$100 tC or the SO_2 and No_x taxes are raised substantially (by a factor of 10). Changes are then dramatic in favour of renewables (CO_2 tax) or closure of existing plant and a switch to new coal plant (high SO_2/NO_x taxes).

The analysis is important in suggesting that a complete damage-based taxation system may have little effect on investment and despatch behaviour. How far the conclusions would hold in the UK cannot be resolved without model simulation with appropriate European 'adders'. The ready availability of gas for new power plant may also make a difference.

Finally, the Palmer-Krupnick simulations show the effects on electricity prices for a base case of 5.2 c/kWh:

> ranking with grandfathering: add 0-0.1c,
> taxation with grandfathering: add 0-0.5c, the upper end of the range reflecting the high CO_2 tax
> complete taxation: add 1-3 c/kWh

In each case we have taken the damage-based taxes. The conclusion is that only a large carbon tax (\$100 tC) on new capacity, or a complete taxation system has any significant effect on electricity prices.

Quantitative Consideration

Quantitative consideration involves the establishment of dollar values for environmental costs by a commission or by a utility under commission order. The values calculated are either added to the cost of the resources in the selection process (an underlying externality adder) or may be deducted from cost in the case of less polluting resources (an underlying externality credit). Alternatively, the externality values calculated may be used in a resource rating system.

Qualitative Consideration

Qualitative consideration requires utilities to incorporate or consider environmental externalities, without specifying how these costs are to be calculated or employed.

Rate of Return Consideration

Rate of return consideration involves utility commissions awarding an increased rate of return to utilities based on:

      1.   Specific low polluting resource investment such as demand side management (DSM) or renewables,

or   2.   their total investment in low polluting resources,

or   3.   overall performance in utilising non-polluting resources.

Avoided Cost Consideration

Avoided cost is similar to opportunity cost; it is usually used to refer to the cost of new capacity which may be deferred as a result of some resource action. Avoided cost consideration requires utility commissions to value avoided cost at a premium over their calculated avoided power plant capacity and energy costs, to help account for environmental externalities, e.g. an avoided cost at 10% over a regional power pools energy billing rate may be established to reflect the potential cost savings to society from more environmentally benign sources.

Ranking Consideration

Ranking consideration assigns weights to various resources or pollutants to take into account environmental externalities to aid resource selection, e.g. a set number of total scoring points would be given to environmentally benign resources.

The term as used here applies only to ranking systems not based directly on quantified environmental costs, i.e. resources are weighed by their environmental impacts or by other criteria, not by their environmental costs - cost based rankings are categorized under 'quantified consideration'.

Collaborative Consideration

Collaborative consideration involves commission-ordered or voluntary collaboration between one or more utilities, and combination of State agencies and investors to establish environmental externality values and treatments.

Incorporation Methodologies Not Yet Applied In Any State

Environmental LCUP

Environmental least cost utility planning (LCUP) requires the establishment of emission reduction targets for pollutants that utilities must meet at least cost. The advantage of LCUP is that it avoids the necessity for calculating environmental externality costs and is designed to achieve specific emission reduction targets. It is readily adaptable to use in determination of hard-to-quantify resource damages, while more readily quantifiable resource damages can be incorporated using the various methodologies for quantified consideration, e.g. for hard-to-quantify climate change costs, a 20% CO_2 target could be required to be attained at least cost, while the remaining utility environmental costs were incorporated using traditional methods such as adders or credits.

The disadvantage of this methodology is that it requires calculation of the emission reduction targets, a calculation with which commissions may have difficulty. Commissions may also feel that they lack legal authority to establish emission targets.

Environmental Dispatch

Environmental dispatch requires utilities or a power pool to include environmental costs in a lest cost dispatch of existing resources. Environmental dispatch has the advantage of minimising environmental damages and costs by displacing production from _existing_ power plants, which are universally the most heavily polluting, and thus encouraging their early closure. All other methodologies presently adopted by States address only resource selection to meet new capital or energy needs.

Cost-charging

Cost-charging involves the environmental costs being charged to the resource-owner and the proceeds used to establish a pollution mitigation fund.

Set-asides

This methodology requires utilities to 'set-aside' a specified proportion of their capacity needs for designated resources considered to be relatively environmentally benign, e.g. a commission might specify that 20% of each utility's capacity needs had to be filled with demand side management (DSM) and/or renewable resources in order to account for environmental externalities. The advantage of set-aside is that it avoids the difficult problem of damage valuation; however, it runs the risk that the amount set aside will not relate in any meaningful way to environmental damages.

State-by-State Assessment

This section briefly summarizes information on the status of environmental externality treatment by State legislation and utility regulating commissions on a State-by-State basis categorized by externality incorporation methodology. It should be recognized that the status of environmental externality policies is rapidly changing. Consequently, the summaries are only a 'rough cut' of State endeavours. Thirty State public service commissions or legislatures have taken some action to incorporate environmental externality costs or have such action under active consideration.

Nineteen have issued orders or passed legislation requiring their utilities to take these costs into account in planning and/or bidding. Three States have such orders pending, seven States have them under active consideration, and two States have taken no action to incorporate environmental costs.

Orders:	AZ, CA, CO, ID, KA, MA, MICH, MN, MT, NJ, NY, OH, OR, PA, TX, VA, VT, WI, WA
Statutes:	ALK, NV
Pending:	CT, IA, MN
Consideration:	DC, HW, ME, MD, RI, UT
No consideration:	ALA, ARK, DE, FL, GA, IL, IND, KY, LA, MISS, MO, NB, NH, NM, ND, NC, OK, SC, SD, TN, WVA, WYO

The District of Columbia (DC) is considered as a State for purposes of this analysis.

Table 1 lists the 30 States which have acted to incorporate environmental externality costs or have such action pending or under consideration.

Table 1

Type of Action by States Acting to Incorporate Environmental Externality Costs

Legend

O - Incorp. Ordered
P - Incorp. Order Pending
U - Under Consideration
QN - Quantitative Consideration
QL - Qualitative Consideration
ROR- Rate Consideration

AC - Avoided Cost Consideration
ED - Environmental Dispatch
C - Collaborative Action
L - Legislative Action

State	QN	QL	ROR	AC	ED	C	Comment
ALSK				O			
AZ		0					
CA	OP				U	C*	*Collaboration ended
CO	O*						*by fuel type
CT	P		L*			C	*5% ROR adder
HW							
ID		O	O				
IA			P			C	
KA	P		O				
ME		U					
MD	U					C	
MA	P*						*DSM Evaluations
MICH	U			O			
MN*		O					*Law caps SO2
MT		U	L*				*2% adder for DSM
NV		L					
NJ	O			O			
NY	O		O	L		C	
OH		O					
OK			O*				*ROR, trash only
OR*	O	O					*Law caps CO_2
PA		O*					*Not implemented
TX		L					
VT	O*					C	*15% DSM
VA				O*			*15% DSM adder to
WA			L*				*2% ROR law for D
WI	O		O		U		

ANNEX 3 MONETARY VALUATION TECHNIQUES

There are four broad categories of valuation technique that have been developed to a sophisticated level. These are:

(a) Conventional Market Approaches. These approaches use mark
et prices for the environmental service that is affected, or, if market prices are not an accurate guide to scarcity, then they may be adjusted by shadow pricing. Where environmental damage or improvement shows up in changes in the quantity or price of marketed inputs or outputs, the value of the change can be measured by changes in the total 'consumers plus producers surplus'. If the changes are small the monetary measure can be approximated by market values. Two approaches may be distinguished:

> The dose-response approach. Under this approach a given level of pollution, say, is associated with a change in output and that output is valued at market or shadow prices.

> The replacement cost technique. This technique looks at the cost of replacing or restoring a damaged asset and uses this cost as a measure of the benefit of restoration. It needs to be used with some care - see below.

Examples of MP approaches include the costs of cleaning buildings made dirty by air pollution; the loss of crop output from air pollution; clean-up costs downstream from water pollution upstream.

Other valuation approaches use market values but they are classified separately here (e.g. the avertive behaviour approach).

(b) Household Production Functions (HPFs). In the HPF approach expenditures on commodities that are substitutes or complements for the environmental characteristic are used to value changes in that environmental characteristic. Thus, noise insulation is a substitute for a reduction in noise at source; travel is a complement to the recreational experience at the recreation site (it is necessary to travel to experience the recreational benefit). There are two types of HPF approach:

> Avertive Expenditures, by which expenditures on the various substitutes for the environmental change are added together;

> Travel Cost Method by which expenditures on the travel needed to reach the recreational site can be interpreted to give an estimate of the benefit arising from the recreational experience.

(c) Hedonic Price Methods (HPM). With HPM an attempt is made to estimate an implicit price for environmental attributes by looking at real markets in which those characteristics are effectively traded. Thus, 'clean air' and 'peace and quiet' are effectively traded in the property market since purchasers of houses and land do consider these environmental dimensions as characteristics of property. The attribute 'risk' is traded in the labour market.

High risk jobs may well have 'risk premia' in the wages to compensate for the risk. The two HPM markets of most interest, therefore, are:

> <u>Hedonic House (Land) Prices</u> for valuing air quality, noise, neighbourhood features (parks etc).

> <u>Wage Risk Premia</u> for valuing changes in morbidity and mortality arising from environmental (and safety) hazards.

(d) <u>Experimental Methods</u>

With experimental approaches a direct attempt is made to elicit preferences by questionnaire ('structured conversations'). Two kinds of questioning may take place:

> Eliciting <u>values</u>. Here a direct attempt is made to ask 'what are you willing to pay for X or prevent Y' and/or 'what are you willing to accept to forego Z or tolerate A'. This is the <u>contingent valuation method</u> (CVM).

> Eliciting <u>rankings</u>. Here the questioner is content to obtain a ranking of preferences which can later be 'anchored' by the analyst in a real price of something observed in the market. This is the <u>contingent ranking</u> (CRM) or <u>stated preference</u> (SP) method.

Some valuation procedures are widely used but their interpretation as changes in consumers/producers surplus is not straightforward. These are:

(a) <u>Replacement Cost</u>. The replacement cost approach is straightforward. If environmental damage is done, it is often possible to find out quite easily what the cost of restoring the damaged environment is. The replacement cost is often widely used to measure the damage. The approach is correct where it is possible to argue that the remedial work <u>must</u> take place because of some other constraint. Such situations will be quite widespread. For example, where there is a water quality standard that is mandatory, then the costs of achieving that standard are a proxy for the benefits of reaching the standard. This is because society can be construed as having sanctioned the cost by setting the standard.

There are risks in this procedure. If the remedial cost is a measure of damage then the cost-benefit ratio of undertaking the remedial work will always be 1: remedial costs are being used to measure remedial benefits. To say that the remedial work must be done implies that benefits exceed costs, whatever the latter are. Costs are then a <u>minimum</u> measure of benefits. If, to pursue the water quality example, the standard has clearly been set without thought for costs, then using replacement costs as a measure of minimum benefits could be misleading. A standard based on 'BATNEEC' tends to fit the replacement cost approach, but others may not. Judgement is required, as with many valuation problems.

Another situation where the replacement cost approach is valid would be where there is an overall constraint not to let environmental quality decline (sometimes called a 'sustainability constraint'). In these circumstances replacement costs might be allowable as a first approximation of benefits or damage. The so-called shadow project approach relies on such constraints. It argues that the cost of any project designed to restore an environment because of a sustainability constraint is then a minimum valuation of the damage done.

(b) Opportunity Cost Technique

On the opportunity cost approach no direct attempt is made to value benefits. Instead, the benefits of the activity causing environmental deterioration - say, a housing development - are estimated in order to set a benchmark for what the environmental benefits would have to be for the development not to be worthwhile. Clearly, this is not a valuation technique but, properly handled, it can be a powerful approach to a form of judgmental valuation. It has been particularly useful in evaluations of energy and mining developments.

Any environmental asset is capable of being characterised by several types of economic value. To ensure that the valuation exercise is carried out properly it is necessary to check that all components have been assessed. The components are:

USER VALUES + NON-USER VALUES = TOTAL ECONOMIC VALUE

User values, as the name implies, relate to the preferences that people have for using the environmental asset in question -e.g. value of fishing in a river, value of recreation at a beach site, value of breathing clean air, etc. Non-user values arise when the asset is valued by people who make no direct use of the asset. Many people care about the African elephant or an ecologically precious wetland without having seen either. If they value the asset because they think they would probably like to see it one day, then this is an option value - a kind of insurance payment to make sure the asset still exists at the time the individual decides he or she will exercise the choice of using it. Many people value things like elephants and wetlands even though they have not seen them in their 'natural' state, nor do they plan to see them. Such people have existence value.

Whether option value is regarded as a use or non-use value or not, matters little. The total economic value will therefore comprise:

TEV = User values + Option values + Existence values

When are option and existence values likely to be important ? The evidence suggests that they are potentially very important when the damage done or threat is to a unique or very well known environmental asset (a Grand Canyon, Broads area, Flow country, endangered species etc.). In such circumstances it is very important that non-use values be investigated. From the brief outline of techniques above, it will be evident that only the experimental market approach can capture non-use values. This is why so much recent valuation work has used CVM (and to a lesser extent CRM/SP).

<u>Valuation Techniques in Outline</u>

The following brief sections describe each technique and its pros and cons.

'Validity' might be assessed in the following terms:

<u>theoretical validity</u> - is the technique consistent with the underlying theory of surplus measurement?

<u>convergent validity</u> - do the results of studies using each technique have the expected relationship with the results of using other studies ? -e.g. different theoretically valid techniques should give similar estimates of WTP or WTA, but we have no particular reason to say any one technique is 'correct'. In the convergent validity test, then, we check to see if, say, HPM and CVM give similar results. If they do that should contribute to the credibility of the results.

<u>repetitive validity</u> - does the same technique applied to <u>similar</u> contexts yield broadly similar values? This test is weak in that there is no <u>a priori</u> reason why the value of, say, a wetland in the UK should be the same as one in Spain, even after correcting for income differences. Tastes may simply vary. Nonetheless, it offers a little more information. The extent to which values in one place can be <u>transferred</u> to another place is, as yet, under-researched.

<u>criterion validity</u> - does the technique yield results that bear a consistent relationship with real market behaviour ?

MARKET VALUE APPROACHES

Range of Applicability Extensively used where 'dose-response' relationships between pollution and output or impact are known. Examples include crop and forest damage from air pollution, materials damage, health impacts of pollution. Limited to cases where there are markets - i.e. cannot estimate non-use values. Replacement cost approaches also widely used because it is often relatively easy to find estimates of such costs. Replacement cost approaches should be confined to situations where the cost relates to achieving some agreed environmental standard, or where there is an overall constraint requiring that a certain level of environmental quality is achieved.

Procedure Dose-Response: take physical and ecological links between pollution ('dose') and impact ('response') and value the final impact at a market or shadow price. Most of the effort usually resides in the non-economic exercise of establishing the dose-response links. Multiple regression techniques often used for this.

Replacement Cost: ascertain environmental damage and then estimate cost of restoring environment to its original state.

Validity Dose-response : theoretically: a sound approach. Uncertainty resides mainly in the errors in the dose-response relationship: e.g. where, if at all, are threshold levels before damage occurs; are their 'jumps' (discontinuities) in the dose-damage relationship ? An adequate 'pool' of studies may not be available for cross-reference.
Criterion validity not relevant since presence of 'real' markets tends to be a test in itself -i.e. revealed preferences in the market place are being used as the appropriate measure of value.

Replacement Cost: validity limited to contexts where agreed standards must be met.

Expense Dose-response can be costly if large databases need to be manipulated in order to establish dose-response relationships. If D-R functions already exist, method can be very inexpensive and with low time demands.

Replacement cost is usually very inexpensive as standard engineering data often exist.

Case Material

US Environmental Protection Agency, <u>Costs and Benefits of Reducing Lead in Gasoline: Final Regulatory Impact Analysis</u>, EPA-230-05-85-006, Washington DC, February 1985.

HOUSEHOLD PRODUCTION FUNCTIONS I : AVERTIVE EXPENDITURES

Range of Applicability

Limited to cases where households spend money to offset environmental hazards, but these can be important - e.g. noise insulation expenditures; risk-reducing expenditures such as smoke-detectors, safety belts, water filters etc.

Has not been used to estimate non use values though arguable that payments to some wildlife societies can be interpreted as insurance payments for conservation.

Procedure

Whilst used comparatively rarely, the approach is potentially important. Expenditures undertaken by households and designed to offset some environmental risk need to be identified. Examples include noise abatement, reactions to radon gas exposure -e.g. purchase of monitoring equipment, visits to medics etc. Technique needs to be managed by experts as significant econometric modelling is usually required.

Validity

Theoretically correct. Insufficient studies to comment on convergent validity. Uses actual expenditures so criterion validity is generally met.

Expense

Econometric analysis on panel and survey data usually needed. Fairly expensive.

Case Study

M.Dickie, S.Gerking, M.Agee, 'Health benefits of Persistent Micropollutant Control: the Case of Stratospheric Ozone Depletion and Skin damage Risks', in J.B.Opschoor and D.W.Pearce (eds), Persistent Pollutants: Economics and Policy, Kluwer, Dordrecht, 1991.

HOUSEHOLD PRODUCTION FUNCTIONS II: TRAVEL COST METHOD

Range of Applicability

Generally limited to <u>site</u> characteristics and to valuation of time. Former tends to be recreational sites. Latter often known as <u>discrete choice</u> - e.g. implicit value of time can be estimate by observing how choice between travel modes is made or how choice of good relates to travel time avoided (last case has been used to value women's water collection time in developing countries).

Cannot be used to estimate non-use values.

Procedure

Detailed sample survey needed of travellers, together with their costs of travel to the site. Complications include possible benefits of the travelling, and presence of competing sites.

Validity

Theoretically correct, but complicated where there are competing sites and multi-purpose trips. Some doubts about 'construct validity' in that number of trips should be inversely correlated with 'price' of trips -i.e. distance travelled. Some UK studies do not show this relationship. Convergent validity generally good in US studies. Generally very acceptable to official agencies and conservation groups.

Case Study

K.Willis and J.Benson, 'Valuation of Wildlife: A Case Study on the Upper Teesdale Site of Special Scientific Interest and Comparison of Methods in Environmental Economics', in R.K.Turner (ed), <u>Sustainable Environmental Management: Principles and Practice</u>, Belhaven Press, London, 1988.

HEDONIC PRICING I : HOUSE PRICE METHOD

Range of Applicability

Applicable only to environmental attributes likely to be capitalised into the price of housing and/or land. Most relevant to noise and air pollution and neighbourhood amenity.

Does not measure non-use value and is confined to cases where property owners are aware of environmental variables and not because of them (as with avertive behaviour).

Procedure

Approach generally involves assembly of cross sectional data on house sales or house price estimates by estate agents, together with data on factors likely to influence these prices. Multiple regression techniques are then needed to obtain the first estimate of an 'implicit price'. Technically, a further stage of analysis is required since the multiple regression approach does not identify the demand curve directly. Often this stage of the analysis is omitted because of complexity.

Validity

Theoretically sound, although final estimate is not of a demand curve as such (see above). Markets often may not behave as required by the approach. Data on prices and factors determining prices often difficult to come by. Limited tests of convergent validity but reveals encouraging results.

Case Study

D.Brookshire et al., 'Valuing Public Goods: A Comparison of Survey and Hedonic Approaches', American Economic Review, Vol.72, No.1, 1982.

HEDONIC PRICING II: WAGE RISK METHODS

Range of Applicability | Limited to valuation of morbidity and mortality risks in occupations. Resulting 'values of life' have been widely used and applied elsewhere, e.g. in the dose-response approach.

Procedure | As with HPM, the approach uses multiple regression to relate wages/salaries to factors influencing them. Included in the determining factors is a measure of risk of accident. The resulting 'wage premium' can then be related to risk factors to derive a so-called value of a statistical life.

Validity | Theoretically sound. Convergent validity may be tested against CVM of risk reduction, but wage-risk approach measures WTA not WTP.

Case Study | A.Marin and G.Psacharopoulos, 'The Reward for Risk in the Labour Market: Evidence from the United Kingdom and a Reconciliation with Other Studies', Journal of Political Economy, Vol.90, 1982.

EXPERIMENTAL MARKETS: CONTINGENT VALUATION

Range of Applicability   Extensive since it can be used to derive values for almost any environmental change. This explains its attractiveness to 'valuers'. Only method for eliciting non-use values.

Procedure   The method involves setting up a carefully worded questionnaire which asks people their WTP and/or WTA through structured questions. Various forms of 'bidding game' can be devised involving 'yes/no' answers to questions and statements about maximum WTP. Resulting survey results need econometric analysis to derive mean values of WTP bids. Literature tends to suggest that most sensible results come from cases where respondents are familiar with the asset being 'valued'.

Validity   The literature has identified various forms of potential bias. 'Strategic bias' arises if respondents make bids that do not reflect their 'true' values. They may do this if they think there is a 'free rider' situation. But there is limited evidence of strategic bias. Hypothetical bias arises because respondents are not making 'real' transactions. Expense usually limits the number of experiments involving real money (criterion validity), but some studies exist. Convergent validity is good. Construct validity - relating values to expectations about values of other measures - is debated, especially the marked divergence in many studies between WTP and WTA.

Case Study   Case material is extensively reviewed in R.Mitchell and R.Carson, Using Surveys to Value Public Goods: the Contingent Valuation Method, Resources for the Future, Washington DC, 1989.

EXPERIMENTAL MARKETS II: CONTINGENT RANKING

Range of Applicability   Unknown but could be extensive. Limited number of studies exist for environmental context and are confined to 'private goods' -i.e. goods purchased in the market place. It is unclear how extensive the application could be for environmental goods but this is under investigation in the context of house location decisions.

Procedure   Individuals are asked to rank several alternatives rather than express a WTP. Alternatives tend to differ according to some risk characteristic and price. Idea could be extended to a ranking of house characteristics with some 'anchor' such as the house price being used to convert rankings into WTP.

Validity   Not widely discussed in the literature but appears theoretically valid. Too few studies to test other validity measures but initial results suggest CRM WTP exceeds CVM WTP.

Case Study   W.Margat, W.Viscusi, J.Huber, 'Paired Comparisons and Contingent valuation Approaches to Morbidity Risk Valuation'', Journal of Environmental Economics and Management, Vol.15, 1987.

THE SOCIAL COSTS OF FUEL CYCLES

SECTION THREE:

BIBLIOGRAPHY

This bibiliography has been classified according to the type of "**adder**" discussed in the main Report (Volume 3) and the Executive Summary (Volume 1).

The categories are:

Air Pollution

Buildings

Catastrophic Risks / Discount Rates

Crops

Energy and Environment Valuation

Forest Damage

General Principles of Monetary Valuation

Global Damage

Health

Land

Noise

Non-Environmental Externalities

Non-Use Values

Radiation Damage

Recreation

Transmission

UK Valuation Studies

Visibility and Amenity

Water Pollution

Wildlife, Biological Diversity

Air Pollution: General

HAIGH J, HARRISON D. and NICHOLS A. (1984), 'Benefit-Cost Analysis of Environmental Regulation Case Studies of Hazardous Air Pollutants', The Harvard Environmental Law Review, Volume 8, No 2, pp. 395-434

HALVORSEN R. and RUBY M. (1981), 'Benefit-Cost Analysis of Air Pollution Control', D C Health and Co, Lexington, Massachussets

KRUPNICK A.J, HARRINGTON W. and RADIN S. (1990), 'Externality Costs by Emission: Acid Deposition' in OTTINGER R. *et al*, eds, Environmental Costs of Electricity, New York, Oceana Publications Inc, pp. 229-263

MOREY E. and SHAW W. (forthcoming), 'An Economic Model to Assess the Impact of Acid Rain: A Characteristics Approach to Estimating the Demand for and Benefits from Recreational Fishing' in SMITH V. and WITTE A. eds, Advances in Applied Microeconomics Theory, Volume 8, JAI Press Inc, Greenwich, Connecticut

SCHULZE W. (1985a), 'Bessere Luft, Was ist sie uns wert? Eine Gesellschaftliche Bedarfs-Analyse auf der Basis Individueller Zahlungs-Bereitschaft', Technical University of Berlin, Germany

Buildings

ALTSHULLER A.P. *et al* (1983), 'Acidic Deposition Phenomena and its Effects: Critical Assessment Review Papers', US Environmental Protection Agency.

BMU (1986), 'Kosten der Umweltverschmutzung', (The Costs of Environmental Pollution) Symposium report, Bundesumweltministerium/Erich Schmidt Verlag, Berlin.

BUILDINGS EFFECTS REVIEW GROUP (BERG) (1989), The Effects of Acid Deposition on Buildings and Building Materials, HMSO, London.

CAMBRIDGE DECISION ANALYSTS and ENVIRONMENTAL RESOURCES Ltd, (1988), 'Acid Rain and Photochemical Oxidants Control Policies in the European Community', European Commission, Brussels.

CHARLES RIVER ASSOCIATES (CRA) (1984), 'Benefits and Costs of Externalities and Intangibles Associated with Southern California Edison's 1985 and 1986 Conservation and Load Management Programs,' CRA Report #792.

CROCKER T. and REGANS J. (1985), 'Benefit Cost Analysis of Acid Deposition Control: A Benefit-Cost Analysis: Its Prospects and Limitations,' Environmental Science and Technology, February 19, pp 112-6.

ECO NORTHWEST *et al* (1987), 'Generic Coal Study: Quantification and Evaluation of Environmental Impacts', Report commissioned by Bonneville Power Administration.

ECO NORTHWEST *et al* (1983), 'Final Report; Economic Analysis of the Environmental Effects of the Coal-Fired Electric Generator at Broadman, Oregon,' Report commissioned by the Bonneville Power Administration.

ECO NORTHWEST *et al* (1984), 'Economic Analysis of the Environmental Effects of a Combustion Turbine Generating Station at Frederickson Industrial Park, Piece County, Washington: Final Report', Report commissioned by Bonneville Power Administration.

ECONOMIC COMMISSION for EUROPE (1982), 'Effects of Sulphur Compounds on Materials, Including Historic and Cultural Monuments', Draft Report, ENV/IEB/WG1, UN ECE, Geneva.

ECOTEC (1990), 'Identification and Assessment of Materials Damage to Buildings and Monuments by Air Pollution', ECOTEC Research and Consulting Ltd

FEENESTRA J.F. (1984), Cultural Property and Air Pollution, Ministry of Housing, Physical Planning and Environment, Leidschendam.

FENGER J, JENSEN T, BRINCH MADSEN H, (n.d.), 'Forsuringsprojektet: Materialeskader (Acidification Project: Material Damage)', Miljominesteriet, Copenhagen,

FINK F.W, BUTTNER F.H and BOYD W.K. (1971), 'Technical-Economic Evaluation of Air Pollution Corrosion Costs on Metals in the US' Batelle Memorial Institute.

FREEMAN A.M. (1982), 'Air and Water Pollution Control: A Benefit-Cost Assessment,' Wiley, New York.

GILETTE (1975), 'Sulphur Dioxide and Materials Damage,' Air Pollution Control Association Journal.

GLOMSROD S. and ROSLAND A. (1988), 'Air Pollution and Materials Damages: Social Costs', Report 88/31, Central Bureau of Statistics of Norway.

HARTER P. (1986), 'Acid Deposition - Materials and Health Effects', IEA Coal Research, 14-15 Lower Grosvenor Place, London, SW1W OEX.

HAYNIE F.H. (1982), 'Economic Assessment of Pollution-Related Corrosion Damage,' Atmospheric Corrosion. New York, USA, Wiley-Interscience

HEINZ I. (1986), 'Zur okonomischen Bewertung von Materialschaden durch Luftverchmutzung' (On the Economic Valuation of Materials damages by Air Pollution). In: Kosten der Umweltverchmutzung, Umweltbundesamt, Berichte 7/86.

HORST R.L, MANUEL E.H, BLACK R.M, TAPIERO J.K, BRENNAN K.M. and DUFF M.C. (1986), 'A Damage Function Assessment of Building Materials: The Impact of Acid Deposition', Mathtech Inc, Princeton, New Jersey, Report prepared for the EPA, Washington, DC.

HORST R.L, ZANKEL K, KAMEN S, ROSSO D. (1990), 'Economic Assessment of Materials Damage in the South Coast Air Basin: A Case of Acid Deposition Effects on Painted Wood Surfaces Using Individual Maintenance Behaviour Data', MATHTEC Inc, Princeton, NJ.

ISECKE B, WELTSCHEV I, HEINZ I. (forthcoming), 'Volkswirtscaftlich Vreluste durch Umweltverschmutzungsbedingte Materialschaden in der Bundesrepublik Deutscland (Economic Losses Resulting form Material Damage Caused by Environmental Pollution in the FDR', Umweltbundesamt.

JANSEN H.M.A, OLSTHOORN A.A. (1982), 'Economische Waardering van de Nationale Schade door Luchtverontreiniging', in mozaiek van de milieuproblematiek, IVM-VU, Amsterdam.

JANSEN H.M.A, MEER G.J van der, OPSCHOOR J.B, STAPEL J.H.A. (1974), 'Een Raming van de Schade door Luchtverrontreiniging in Nederland in 1970', Instituut voor Milieuvraagstukken, Amsterdam.

KRAWIEC F, (1990), 'Economic Measurement of Environmental Damages', Golden Colorado, Solar Energy Research Institute.

KUIK O.H, JANSEN H.M.A. and OPSCHOOR J.B (1991), "The Netherlands" in: J.P Barde and D.W.Pearce (eds), <u>Valuing the Environment: Six Case Studies</u>, Earthscan, London.

KUIK O. and JANSEN H. (1991), '<u>On the Valuation of Air Pollution Damage to Buildings and Monuments and on Recreation in Forests and Parks</u>', Institute for Environmental Studies, Amsterdam, *mimeo*.

LANTINNG R.W. MOREE J.C. (1984), '<u>Aantasting van Materiallen door Luchverontreiniging (Effects of Air Pollution on Materials)</u>', TNO-G-1157, Delft, Netherlands, Instituut voor Milieuhygiene en Gezondheidstechniek.

LIPERT F. (1987), 'Effects of Acidic Deposition on the Atmospheric Deterioration of Materials', <u>Materials Performance</u>, July 1987, pp 12-19.

MIDWEST RESEARCH INSTITUTE REPORT (1970), reviewed in: National Academy of Science, "<u>Effects of Photochemical Oxidants on Materials Ozone and other Photochemical Oxidants</u>', Washington, DC, Chapter 13.

MINISTRY of HOUSING and ENVIRONMENT, NETHERLANDS (1986), "The Benefits of Environmental Policy in the Netherlands", <u>Journal of Political Economy</u>, Vol 90, No. 4.

MUELLER and STICKNEY (1970), '<u>Final Report on the Survey and Economic Assessment of the Effects of Air Pollution On Elastomers</u>,' National Air Pollution Control Association, Contract cpa 22-69-146. Battelle Memorial Institute, Columbus, Ohio.

NAVRUD S. and STRAND J. (1990), '<u>Valuation of Our Cultural Heritage-a Case Study on Historical Buildings and Monuments in Norway (Project Description)</u>', Centre for Research in Economics and Business Administration, University of Oslo.

OECD (1989), <u>OECD Environmental Data</u>, Compendium 1989, Paris.

PROGRAMMES ANALYSIS UNIT, '<u>An Economic and Technical Appraisal of Air Pollution in the United Kingdom</u>', Atomic Energy Research Establishment, Harwell.

SALMON R.L. (1970), '<u>Systems Analysis of the Effects of Air Pollution on Materials</u>', Midwest Research Institute, Prepared for Economic Effects Research Division, National Air Pollution Control Administration, Raleigh NC, Kansas City, Missouri.

SPENCE, J. and HAYNIES, F. '<u>Plant Technology and Air Pollution: Survey and Economic Assessment</u>', EPA-AP-103 Research Triangle Plant, NC, US EPA 72.

WADDELL T, (1974), '<u>The Economic Damages of Air Pollution</u>', US EPA Washington.

WATSON W. and JAKSCH J. (1982), 'Air Pollution: Household Soiling and Consumer Welfare Losses', <u>Journal of Environmental Economics and Management</u>, Volume 9.

Catastrophic Risks / Discount Rates

BIENZ A. and BOHNENBLUST (1988), 'L'Evaluation du Risque Comme Outil de Gestion Economique', in La Société Vulnerable, Presses de l'Ecole Normale Supérieure, Paris

BROOKSHIRE D. *et al* (1985), 'A Test of the Expected Utility Model: Evidence from Earthquake Risks', Journal of Political Economy, Volume 93, pp. 369-389

BROOME J. (1991), 'The Intergenerational Aspects of Climate Change', Report to the Economic and Social Research Council, Bristol, *mimeo*

FISCHOFF B. *et al* (1981), 'Acceptable Risk', Cambridge University Press, Cambridge

HUBERT Ph. et al (1991), 'Elicitation of Decision-Makers' References for Management of Major Hazards', Risk Analysis, Volume II, No. 2

OLSON M. and BAILEY, M. (1981), 'Positive Time Preference', Journal of Political Economy, Volume 89, No 1

RAWLS J. (1972), 'A Theory of Justice', Oxford University Press, Oxford

ROCARD P. and SMETS, H. (1991), 'A Socio-Economic Analysis of Controls on Land-Use Around Hazardous Installations', OECD, Paris, mimeo

SCOTT M. (1989), 'A New View of Economic Growth', Clarendon Press, Oxford

SIDGWICK II. (1970), 'The Methods of Ethics', seventh edition, Macmillan, London

SOLOW R. (1986), 'On the Intergenerational Allocation of Natural Resources', Scandinavian Journal of Economics, Volume 88, No 1

SPACKMAN M. (1991), 'Discount Rates and Rates of Return in the Public Sector: Economic Issues', Government Economic Service Working Paper No 113, HM Treasury, January

Crop Damage

ADAMS R.M, and CROCKER T.D. (1985), 'Economically Relevant Response Estimation and the Value of Information: Acid Deposition', in Economic Perspective on Acid Deposition Control, ed. T.D. Crocker, pp. 53-64. Boston: Butterworth Publishers.

ADAMS R.M, HAMILTON S.A. and McCARL B.A. (1985), 'An Assessment of the Economic Effects of Ozone on US Agriculture', Journal of the Air Pollution Control Association, Volume 35, pp. 938-943.

ADAMS R.M, CROCKER T.D, and KATZ, R.W. (1984), 'Assessing the Adequacy of Natural Science Information: A Bayesian Approach', Review of Economics and Statistics Volume 66, pp. 568-575.

ADAMS R.M. and McCARL B.A. (1985), 'Assessing the Benefits of Alternative Ozone Standards on Agriculture: The Role of Response Information', Journal of Environmental Economics and Management, Volume 12, pp. 264-276.

ADAMS R.M, CALLAWAY J.M. and McCARL B.A. (1986), 'Pollution, Agriculture and Social Welfare: The Case of Acid Deposition', Canadian Journal of Agricultural Economics, Volume 34, March, pp. 1-19.

ADAMS R.M, CROCKER T.D. and THANAVIBULCHAI N. (1982), 'An Economic Assessment of Air Pollution Damages to Selected Annual Crops in Southern California', Journal of Environmental Economics and Management, Volume 9, pp. 42-58.

ADAMS R.M. and CROCKER T.D. (1989), 'The Agricultural Economics of Environmental Change: Some Lessons from Air Pollution', Journal of Environmental Management Volume 28, pp. 295-307.

ADAMS R.M, HAMILTON S.A., and McCARL B.A. (1986), 'The Benefits of Pollution Control: the Case of Ozone and U.S. Agriculture', American Journal of Agricultural Economics Volume 68, pp. 886-893.

AED (1991), 'Economic Benefits of Improved Air and Water Quality on the Agricultural Sector: The Case of the Andulusian Region of Spain', Report Analysis Estadistico de Datos (AED).

BENEDICT H.M, MILLER C.J, and OLSON R.E. (1971), 'Economic Impact of Air Pollution on Plants in the United States', Menlo Park, CA: Stanford Research Institute.

BROWN D. and SMITH M. (1984), 'Crop Substitution in the Estimation of Economic Benefits Due to Ozone Reduction' Journal of Environmental Economics and Management Volume 11, pp. 327-346.

CALISH S, FLIGHT R.D, and TEEGUARDEN D.E. (1978), 'How do Non-timber Values Affect Douglas Fir Rotations', <u>Journal of Forestry</u> Volume 76, pp. 217-223.

CHAPMAN D. and KOHUT R. (1984), '<u>Ozone and Acid Deposition: An Economic Perspective</u> on Agricultural and Forestry Impact', Cornell Agricultural Economics Staff Paper No. 84-28.

CROCKER T.D. and REGANS J.L. (1985), 'Benefit Cost Analysis of Acid Deposition Control: A Benefit-Cost Analysis: Its Prospects and Limits', <u>Environmental Science and Technology</u> 19 February 1985. pp. 112-16.

CROCKER T.D. (1986), 'Economic Effects on Materials Degradation', in <u>Materials Degradation Caused by Acid Rain</u>, ed. R. Baboian, pp. 369-383. Washington: American Chemical Society.

CROCKER T.D. (1975), 'Cost-Benefit Analyses of Cost-Benefit Analysis', in <u>Cost-Benefit Analysis and Water Pollution Policy</u>, eds. H.M. Peskin and E.P.Seskin, pp 341-360. Washington: The Urban Institute.

EATON J.S. (1984), 'Theoretically Optimal Environmental Metrics and their Surrogates'. <u>Journal of Environmental Economics and Management</u> Volume 11, pp. 18-27.

EERDEN L.J. van der, TONNEIJCK A.E.G. and WIJNANADA J.H.M. (1987), '<u>Economische Schade door Luchtverontreiniging ann de Gewasteelt in Nederland</u>'. (Economic Damages due to Air Pollution to Crop Production in the Netherlands). Publikatiereeks Lucht 65, Ministry of Public Housing, Physical Planning and Environmental Management, Leidschendam.

ETSU/ITE (1992), 'Impacts of Sulphur Dioxide from the West Burton 'B' Coal-Fired Power Station on Yield of Wheat and Barley', *mimeo*

FEINERMAN E, and YARON D. (1983), 'The Value of Information on the Response Function of Crops to Soil Salinity', <u>Journal of Environmental Economics and Management</u> Volume 10, pp. 72-85.

FORSTER B.A. (1981), 'Separability, Functional Structure and Aggregation for a Class of Models in Environmental Economics', <u>Journal of Environmental Economics and Management</u> Volume 8, pp. 118-134.

FORSTER B.A. (1984), 'An Economic Assessment of the Significance of Long-Range Transported Air Pollutants for Agriculture in Eastern Canada,' <u>Canadian Journal of Agricultural Economics</u>, Volume 32, pp. 489-525.

FREEMAN A.M. (1982), '<u>Air and Water Pollution Control: a Benefit-Cost Assessment</u>', New York: John Wiley & Sons, Inc.

GARCIA P, DIXON B.L, MJELDE J.W, and ADAMS R.M. (1986), 'Measuring the Benefits of Environmental Change Using a Duality Approach: the Case of Ozone and Illinois Cash Grain Farms', <u>Journal of Environmental Economics and Management</u> Volume 13, pp. 69-80.

HOWITT R.E, GOSSARD T.W, and ADAMS R.M. (1984), 'Effects of Alternative Ozone Levels and Response Data on Economic Assessments: the Case for California Crops', <u>Journal of Air Pollution Control Association</u> Volume 34, pp. 1122-1127.

KAHN F.R, and KEMP W.M. (1985), 'Economic Losses Associated with the Degradation of an Ecosystem: the Case of Submerged Aquatic Vegetation in Chesapeake Bay', <u>Journal of Environmental Economics and Management</u>, Volume 12, pp. 246-263.

KOPP R.J, VAUGHAN W.J, HAZILLA M, and CARSEN R. (1985), 'Implications of Environmental Policy for U.S. Agriculture: the Case of Ambient Ozone Standards', <u>Journal of Environment and Management</u> Volume 20, pp. 321-331.

McGUCKIN J.T. and YOUNG R.A. (1981), 'On the Economics of Desalination of Brackish Household Water Supplies', <u>Journal of Environmental Economic and Management</u> Volume 8, pp. 79-91.

MENDELSOHN R. (1980), 'An Economic Analysis of Air Pollution from Coal-Fired Power Plants', <u>Journal of Environmental Economics and Management</u> Volume 7, pp. 30-43.

MJELDE J.W, ADAMS R.M, DIXON B.L, and GARCIA P. (1984), 'Using Farmer's Actions to Measure Crop Loss Due to Air Pollution', <u>Journal of the Air Pollution Control Association</u> Volume 34, pp. 360-365.

PAGE A, FABIAN and CIEKA (1982), 'Estimation of Economic Losses to the Agricultural Sector from Airbourne Residuals in the Ohio River Basin Region', <u>Journal of Air Pollution Control Association</u> Volume 32, pp 151.

PAGE W.P. (1981), '<u>Estimating Regional Losses to Agricultural Producers from Airbourne Residuals in the Ohio River Basin Energy Study Region, 1976-2000</u>', Ohio River Basin Energy Study, Urbana, IL., October 1981.

ROBERTS T. (1984), 'Long Term Effects of Sulphur Dioxide on Crops: An Analysis of Dose-Response Relations', <u>Philosophical Transactions of the Royal Society</u>.

SHORTLE, J.S, DUNN J.W and PHILLIPS M. (1986), '<u>Economic Assessment of Crop Damage due to Air Pollution: the Role of Quality Effects</u>', Staff paper 118. Department of Agricultural Economics, Pennyslvania State University, State College, PA.

WADDELL T.E. (1974), '<u>The Economic Damages of Air Pollution</u>', Office of Water Resources Research, U.S. Environmental Protection Agency, May 1974.

Energy and Environment Valuation: General

CANTOR R.A. *et al* (1991), 'The External Costs of Fuel Cycles: Guidance Document to the Approach and Issues', Oak Ridge National Laboratory, Tennessee.

EYRE N. and HOLLAND M. (1992), 'External Costs of Electricity Generation Using Coal', Energy Technology Support Unit, Harwell, *mimeo*

HOHMEYER O. (1989), Soziale Kosten des Energieverbrauchs, Springer-Verlag, Berlin.

HOHMEYER O. (1990), 'Social Costs of Electricity Generation: Wind and Photovoltaic versus Fossil and Nuclear', Contemporary Policy Issues, Volume VIII, No 3, July, pp 255-282.

HOHMEYER O. (1988), 'Social Costs of Energy Consumption: External Effects of Electricity Generation in the Federal Republic of Germany', Springer-Verlag, Berlin.

JULIUS D. and MASHAYEKHI A. (1990), The Economics of Natural Gas, Oxford University Press, Oxford.

KRUPNICK A.J. (1990), 'The Environmental Costs of Energy Supply: A Framework for Estimation', Paper given at the Workshop on Environmental Externalities Costs of Energy Resources in New York, Albany, New York, 6 April 1990.

MUNASINGHE M. and SCHRAMM G. (1983), Energy Economics, Demand Management and Conservation Policy, Van Nostrand, New York.

NEWBERY D. (1985), 'Pricing Policy' in BELGRAVE R. and CORNELL D. eds Energy Self Sufficiency for the UK?, Gower, London, 77-114.

OTTINGER R. *et al* (1990), Environmental Costs of Electricity, Oceana Publications Inc, Dobbs Ferry, New York 10522.

PALMER K. and KRUPNICK A. (1991), 'Environmental Costing and Electric Utilitics' Planning and Investment', Resources, Fall, No 105, 1-5.

RAINER F. and VOSS A. (1989), 'External Costs of Electricity Generation', Institut fur Energiewitschaft und Rationelle Energieanwendung, University of Stuttgart, mimeo.

STARR C. (1976), 'General Philosophy of Risk-Benefit Analysis' in ASHLEY H, RUDMAN R. and WHIPPLE C. eds. Energy and the Environment: a Risk-Benefit Approach, Pergamon, Oxford.

Forest Damage

BENSON J.F. and WILLIS K.G. (1990), 'The Aggregate Value of the Non-Priced Recreational Benefits of the Forestry Commission Estate', report to The Forestry Commission, Development Division, Edinburgh.

BROWN T.C, RICHARDS M.T, and DANIEL T.C. (1989), 'Scenic Beauty and Recreational Value: Assessing the Relationship', Fort Collins, CO, unpublished manuscript, USDA Forest Service, Rocky Mountain Forest and Range Experiment Station.

CALLAWAY J.M, DARWIN, R.F. and NESSE R.J. (1985), 'Economic Valuation of Acidic Deposition: Preliminary Results from the 1985 NAPAP Assessment', Draft Report for the National Acid Precipitation Assessment Program, USEPA, Washington, DC.

CALLAWAY J.M, DARWIN R.F, and NESSE R.J. (1986), 'Economic Effects of Hypothetical Reductions in Tree Growth in the Northeastern and the Southeastern United States', Pacific Northwest Laboratory, Richland, Washington.

CHRISTENSEN J.B. (1983), 'An Economic Approach to Assessing the Value of Recreation with Special Reference to Forest Areas', unpublished PhD Thesis, Department of Forestry and Wood Science, University College of North Wales, Bangor.

CROCKER T.D. (1985), 'On the Value of the Condition of a Forest Stock', Land Economics Volume 61.

CROCKER T.D. (1984), 'On the Value of the Condition of a Forest Stock', Unpublished manuscript, Department of Economics, University of Wyoming, Laramie, WY.

CROCKER T.D. and REGANS J.L. (1985), 'Benefit-Cost Analysis of Acid Deposition Control: A Benefit-cost Analysis: Its Prospects and Limits', Environmental Science and Technology, 19 February 1985, pp. 112-16.

EVERETT R.D. (1979), 'The Monetary Value of the Recreational Benefits of Wildlife', Journal of Environmental Management Volume 9, pp. 203-213.

EWERS H.J. et al (1986), 'On the Monetization of Forest Damages in the Federal Republic of Germany', in Kosten der Umweitverschmutzung, Umweltbundesamt, Berichte 7/86; pp.121-143.

GRAYSON A.J, SIDAWAY R.M, and THOMPSON F.P. (1975), 'Some Aspects of Recreational Planning in the Forestry Commission', in Searle G.A.C. (Ed), Recreational Economics and Analysis, Longman, London.

HOEN H.F. and WINTER G. (1991), 'Attitudes to Willingness to Pay for Multiple Use Forestry and Preservation of Coniferous Forests in Norway', draft, Department of Forestry, Agricultural University of Norway.

International Institute for Applied Systems Analysis (IIASA) (1991), 'European Forest Decline: The Effects of Air Pollutants and Suggested Remedial Policies'.

KNETSCH J.L. and DAVIES R.K. (1965), 'Comparisons of Methods for Recreation Evaluation', in Water Research eds A.V. Knesse and S.C. Smith pp. 125-142, Balitmore: John Hopkins University Press.

KRISTROM B. (1988), 'On the Benefits of Preserving Virgin Forests'. Paper prepared for the Conference on Multiple Use of Forests. Oslo, May 24-26.

LINDER J.W. van der and OOSTERHUIS F.H. (1988), 'The Social Valuation of the Vitality of Forests and Heath', Report VROM 80115/3 - 88 4850/101 from the Ministry of Public Housing, Physical Planning and Environmental Management.

LIPFERT F.W. (1987), 'Effects of Acidic Deposition on the Atmospheric Deterioration of Materials'.

NAVRUD S, SIMENSEN B, SOLBERG and WIND M.H.A. (1990), 'Valuing Environmental Effects of Different Management Practices in Mountainous Forests in Norway - A Survey of Recreationists' Preferences and WTP', Department of Forestry, Agricultural University of Norway. Paper presented at the XIX World Congress of the International Union of Forest Research (IUFRO) in Montreal, Canada, August 5-11, 1990.

NNM (1988), 'Forest Damage Scenarios: How Pollution Might Affect Norwegian Forests in a 25-30 years Perspective', Norwegian Ministry of Environment (NME) Oslo.

PETERSON D.C. et al (1987), 'Improving Accuracy and Reducing Costs of Environmental Benefit Assessments' Office of Policy, Planning and Evaluation, US EPA, Washington DC.

WILLIS K.G. and BENSON J.F. (1989b), 'Values of User Benefits of Forest Recreation: Some Further Site Surveys', report to The Forestry Commission, Development Division, Edinburgh.

WILLIS K.G. and BENSON J.F. (1989), 'Recreational Value of Forests', Forestry, Volume 62, No 2, pp. 93-110.

General Principles of Monetary Valuation

BANFORD N.D, KNETSCH J.L. and MAUSER G.A. (1979), 'Feasibility Judgements and Alternative Measures of Benefits and Costs', <u>Journal of Business Administration</u> 11, Nos 1, 2: 25-35.

BARDE J.P. and PEARCE D.W. (1991),'Valuing the Environment', <u>Earthscan</u>.

BENTKOVER J.D, COVELLO V.T. and MUNPOWER J. (1986), 'Benefit Assessment: The State of the Art', D. Reidel, Dordrecht.

BISHOP R.C, HEBERLEIN T.A. and KEALY M.J. (1983), 'Hypothetical Bias in Contingent Valuation: Results from a Simulated Market', <u>Natural Resources Journal</u> Volume 23, No 2, pp. 619-633.

BISHOP R.C. and HEBERLEIN T.A. (1979), 'Measuring Values of Extramarket Goods: Are Indirect Measures Biased?', <u>American Journal of Agricultural Economics</u> 61 (December 1979): 926-30.

BISHOP R.C. (1982), 'Option Value: An Exposition and Extension', <u>Land Economics</u>, Volume 58, No 1, pp. 1-15.

BISHOP R, HEBERLEIN T. and KEALEY M.J. (1983), 'Contingent Valuation of Environmental Assets: Comparisons with a Simulated Market', <u>Natural Resources Journal</u>, Volume 23, July, pp. 619-633.

BOYLE K, BISHOP R. and WALSH M. (1985), 'Starting Point Bias in Contingent Valuation Bidding Games', <u>Land Economics</u>, Volume 61, pp. 188-194.

BRADEN J. and KOLSTAD C. (1991), 'Measuring the Demand for Environmental Quality', North Holland-Elsevier, Amsterdam.

BROOKSHIRE D.S, RANDALL A. and STOLL J.R. (1980), 'Valuing Increments and Decrements in Natural Resource Service Flows', <u>American Journal of Agricultural Economics</u> 62, (August 1980): 478-88.

BROOKSHIRE D.S. and COURSEY D.L. (1987), 'Measuring the Value of a Public Good: An Empirical Comparison of Elicitation Procedures', <u>American Economic Review 77</u> (September 77): 554-66.

BROOKSHIRE D.S. *et al* (1982) 'Valuing Public Goods: a Comparison of Survey and Hedonic Approaches', <u>American Economic Review</u>, Volume 72, No 1, pp. 165-171.

COURSEY D.L, HOVIS J.L. and SCHULZE W.D. (1987), 'The Disparity between Willingness to Accept and Willingness to Pay Measures of Value', <u>Quarterly Journal of Economics</u> 102, (August 1987) pp. 679-90.

CUMMINGS R, BROOKSHIRE D. and SCHULZE W. (1984), 'Valuing Environmental Goods: A State of the Arts Assessment of the Contingent Valuation Method', Volumes 1A and 1B, Report to the Office of Policy Analysis, US Environmental Protection Agency, Washington DC.

CUMMINGS R.G, BROOKSHIRE D.S. and SCHULZE W.D. eds. (1986), 'Valuing Environmental Goods: A State of the Arts Assessment of the Contingent Valuation Method', (Rowman and Allanheld, Tototowa, NJ)

DEPARTMENT OF THE ENVIRONMENT (1991), 'Policy Appraisal and the Environment', HMSO, London.

ECO NORTHWEST et al (1984), 'Economic Analysis of the Environmental Effects of a Combustion-Turbine Generating Station at Frederickson Industrial Park, Pierce County, Washington: Final Report', Bonneville Power Administration.

ECO NORTHWEST. (1983), 'Economic Analysis of the Environmental Effects of the Coal-Fired Electric Generator at Broadman, Oregon', for Bonneville Power Administration.

ECO NORTHWEST. (1986), 'Estimating Environmental Costs and Benefits for Five Generating Resources', Prepared for Bonneville Power Administration, Portland, Oregon.

ECO NORTHWEST. (1987), 'Generic Coal Plant Study: Quantification and Valuation of Environmental Impacts', for Bonneville Power Administration, Portland, OR.

EYRE N. (1991), 'Environmental Burdens of Coal Technology', EC/US Study: External Costs of Fuel Cycles, Working Document.

FREEMAN A.M. (1982), 'Air and Water Pollution Control: A Benefit-Cost Assessment', Wiley, New York, 1982.

FREEMAN A.M. (1979b), 'The Benefits of Environmental Improvement, Theory and Practice', Johns Hopkins University Press, Baltimore.

FREEMAN A.M. III (1979), 'The Benefits of Environmental Improvement' (Baltimore: John Hopkins University Press for Resources for the Future, Inc).

FRIEDRICH R. and VOSS A. (1989), 'External Costs of Electricity Generation', Institut für Energiewirtschaft und Rationelle Energieanwendung, Stuttgart, mimeo.

GREGORY R. (1986), 'Interpreting Measures of Economic Loss: Evidence from Contingent Valuation and Experimental Studies', Journal of Environmental Economics and Management, Volume 13, pp. 325-337.

H M TREASURY. (1991), 'Economic Appraisal in Central Government: a Technical Guide for Government Departments', London.

H M TREASURY (1984), 'Investment Appraisal in the Public Sector: a Technical Guide for Government Departments', London.

HALL D. (1990), 'Preliminary Estimates of Cumulative Private and External Costs of Energy', Contemporary Policy Issues Volume VIII, No 3, July, 283-307.

HAMMACK J. and BROWN G.M. Jr. (1974), 'Waterfowl and Wetlands: Toward Bio-economic Analysis', Baltimore: Johns Hopkins Press (for Resources for the Future).

HANEMANN W.M. (forthcoming), 'Willingness to Pay and Willingness to Accept: How Much Can They Differ?', American Economic Review.

HANLEY N. (1990), 'Valuation of Environmental Effects', ESU Research Paper No 22, Industry Department for Scotland/Scottish Development Agency.

HARRISON D. Jr. and NICHOLS A.L. (1990), 'Benefits of the 1989 Air Quality Management Plan for the South Coast Air Basin', (Cambridge, Massachusetts: National Economic Research Associates, Inc.).

HEBERLEIN T.A. and BISHOP R.C. (1985), 'Assessing the Validity of Contingent Valuation: Three Field Experiments'. Paper presented at the International Conference on Man's Role in Changing the Global Environment, Italy 1985.

HICKS J.R. (1943), 'The Four Consumers' Surpluses', Review of Economic Studies Volume 11, February.

HOHMEYER O. (1990), 'Social Costs of Electricity Generation: Wind and Photovoltaic Versus Fossil and Nuclear', Contemporary Policy Issues Volume VIII, No 3, July, 255-282.

JOHANSSON P.O. (1987), 'The Economic Theory and Measurement of Environmental Benefits', Cambridge University Press.

KAHNEMAN D. and TVERSKY A. (1979), 'Prospect Theory: An Analysis of Decision under Risk', Econometrica 47 (March 1979): 263-91.

KAHNEMAN D, KNETSCH J. and THALER R. (1990), 'Experimental Tests of the Endowment Effect and the Coase Theorem', Journal of Political Economy 98, No 6, December, pp. 1325-1348.

KAHNEMANN D. and TVERSKY A. (1979), 'Prospect Theory: An Analysis of Decision Making Under Risk', Econometrica, Volume 47, pp. 263-291.

KNEESE A. (1984), 'Measuring the Benefits of Clean Air and Water', Resources for the Future, Washington DC.

KNETSCH J. and SINDEN J. (1984), 'Willingness to Pay and Compensation Demanded: Experimental Evidence of an Unexpected Disparity in Measures of Value', Quarterly Journal of Economics Volume 99, pp. 507-521.

KNETSCH J. (1989), 'The Endowment Effect and Evidence of Non Reversible Indifference Curves', <u>American Economic Review</u> 79, No 5 December, pp. 1277-1284.

KNETSCH J. (1990), 'Environmental Policy Implications of Disparities Between Willingness to Pay and Compensation Demanded Measures of Values', <u>Journal of Environmental Economics and Management</u>, 18, No 3, May, 227-237.

KRUPNICK A.J. (1991), 'The Valuation of Environmental Externalities: Guidance Document', Resources for the Future (*mimeo*)

KRUPNICK A. (1990), 'Environmental Externalities', Resources for the Future (*mimeo*)

LOCKWOOD B. (1992), <u>'The Social Costs of Electricity Generation'</u>, Report prepared for the Parliamentary Office of Science and Technology (POST), Centre for Social and Economic Research on the Global Environment, University of East Anglia and University College London.

MITCHELL R.C. and CARSON R.T. (1989), <u>'Using Surveys to Value Public Goods: The Contingent Valuation Method'</u>, Resources for the Future, Washington DC

PEARCE D.W. and NASH C.A. (1981), <u>'The Social Appraisal of Projects: a Text in Cost-Benefit Analysis'</u>, Macmillan, London.

PEARCE D.W, MARKANDYA A. and BARBIER E. (1989), <u>'Blueprint for a Green Economy'</u>, Earthscan, London.

PEARCE D.W. and MARKANDYA A. (1989), <u>'Environmental Policy Benefits: Monetary Valuation'</u>, Organisation for Economic Co-operation and Development, Paris.

REPETTO R. (1989), <u>Wasting Assets</u>, World Resources Institute, Washington DC.

ROWE R.D, d'ARGE R.C. and BROOKSHIRE D.S. (1980) 'An Experiment on the Economic Value of Visibility', <u>Journal of Environmental Economics and Management</u> 7 (March 1980): 1-19.

SCHULZE W.D, d'ARGE R.C. and BROOKSHIRE D.S. (1981), 'Valuing Environmental Commodities: Some Recent Experiments', <u>Land Economics</u>, Volume 57, pp. 151-172.

SELLAR C, STOLL J.R. and CHAVAS J-P. (1985), 'Validation of Empirical Measures of Welfare Change: A Comparison of Nonmarket Techniques', <u>Land Economics</u>, Volume 61, No 2, pp. 156-175.

SINCLAIR W.F. (1978), 'The Economic and Social Impact of Kemano II Hydroelectric Project on British Columbia's Fisheries Resources', Vancouver, Department of Fisheries and Oceans.

THAYER M. (1981), 'Contingent Valuation Techniques for Assessing Environmental Impacts: Further Evidence', Journal of Environmental Economics and Management, Volume 8, pp. 27-44.

TURNER R.K. and BATEMAN I. (1990), 'A Critical Review of Monetary Assessment Methods and Techniques', Environmental Appraisal Group, University of East Anglia.

US NATIONAL ACID PRECIPITATION ASSESSMENT PROGRAM (1991), 'Acidic Deposition: State of Science and Technology', NAPAP, Washington DC

WILKS L.C. (1990), 'A Survey of the Contingent Valuation Method', Resource Assessment Commission, Canberra, Research Paper Number 2, November 1990.

WILLIG R.D. (1976), 'Consumer's Surplus without Apology', American Economic Review 66 (September 1976): 589-97.

WILLIS K.G. and GARROD G.D. (forthcoming), 'Valuing goods' characteristics: an application of the hedonic price method to environmental attributes', Journal of Environmental Management.

WINPENNY J. (1991), Valuing the Environment: A Guide to Economic Appraisal, HMSO.

Global Warming

AYRES R. and WALTER J. (1991), 'Global Warming: Abatement Policies and Costs' and 'Global Warming: Damages and Costs', Environmental and Resource Economics, Volume 1, No 3, 237-270.

BROOME J. (1991), The Intergenerational Aspects of Climate Change, Report to the Economic and Social Research Council, Bristol University, *mimeo*.

CLINE W. (1991), Estimating the Benefits of Greenhouse Warming Abatement, Draft, Institute of International Economics, Washington EC, March, prepared for the Organisation for Economic Co-operation and Development, Paris.

CLINE W. (1992), The Economics of Climate Change, Cambridge University Press, Cambridge (forthcoming)

CROSSON P. (1989), 'Climate Change: Problems of Limits and Policy Responses', in N. Rosenberg, *et al* (eds), Greenhouse Warming: Abatement and Adaptation, Resources for the Future, Washington DC.

DELFT HYDRAULICS (1990), Sea Level Rise: a World Wide Cost Estimate of Basic Coastal Defence Measure, The Hague.

DONALDSON D. and BETTERIDGE G. (1990), 'Carbon Dioxide Emissions from Nuclear Power - a Critical Analysis of FOE 9', Atom, February, 18-22.

ENVIRONMENTAL PROTECTION AGENCY. (1989), The Potential Effect of Global Climate Change on the United States, Washington DC.

GLEICK P. and SASSIN W. (1990), 'Rates and Limits of Climatic Change: Discussion of Possible Targets', in Ribsberman, F. and Swart, R. (eds), Targets and Indicators of Climatic Change, Stockholm Environment Institute, Stockholm.

HAINES A. and FUCHS C. (1991), 'Potential Impacts on Health of Atmospheric Change', Journal of Public Health Medicine, Volume 13, No 2, pp 69-80.

IPCC (1990), Climate Change: the IPCC Scientific Assessment, Cambridge University Press, Cambridge.

JONES P. (1990), 'Social Costs of Energy', Atom, 403, May.

MORGENSTERN R. (1991), 'Toward a Comprehensive Approach to Global Climate Change Mitigation', American Economic Review, Volume 81, No 2.

MORTIMER N. (1991), 'Nuclear Power and Global Warming', Energy Policy, January-February, 76-78.

17

MURRAY J. (1990), 'Can Nuclear Energy Contribute to Slowing Global Warming?', <u>Energy Policy</u> Volume 18, No 6, July/August, 494-499.

NATIONAL ACADEMY OF SCIENCE. (1991), <u>Policy Implications of Greenhouse Warming</u>, National Academy Press, Washington DC.

NORDHAUS W. (1991a), 'The Costs of Slowing Climate Change: a Survey', <u>The Energy Journal</u>, Volume 12, No 1, pp 37-65.

NORDHAUS W. (1991b), 'Economic Approaches to Global Warming', in Poterba J. and Dornbusch R. (eds), <u>Economic Policy Responses to Global Warming</u>, MIT Press, forthcoming.

NORDHAUS R. (1991c), 'To Slow or Not to Slow: the Economics of Global Warming', <u>Economic Journal</u>, Volume 101, July, pp 920-937.

NORDHAUS R. (1991d), 'A Sketch of the Economics of the Greenhouse Effect', <u>American Economic Review, Papers and Proceedings</u>, Volume 81, No 2, pp 146-150.

OECD (1990), '<u>Climate Change: Annex 3 - Potential Costs of Adapting to Sea-level Rise</u>, Draft, November, OECD, Paris.

PARRY M, CARTER T. and KONIJN N. (1988), <u>The Impact of Climatic Variations on Agriculture: Volume 1: Assessments in Cool Temperate and Cold Regions</u>, Kluwer, Dordrecht.

PARRY M. (1991), <u>Climate Change and World Agriculture</u>, Earthscan, London.

PECK S. and TEISBERG T. (1990), 'A Framework for Exploring Cost Effective CO_2 Control Paths', Electric Power Research Institute, Palo Alto, *mimeo*.

PECK S. and TEISBERG T. (1990), 'CETA - A Model for Carbon Emissions Trajectory Assessment', Electric Power Research Institute, Palo Alto, *mimeo*.

RIJSBERMAN F.R. and SWART R.J. (1990), <u>Targets and Indicators of Climatic Change</u>, Stockholm Environment Institute, Stockholm.

SHUGART H.H. *et al* (1986), 'CO_2, Climate Change and Forest Ecosystems', in B. Bolin *et al*, <u>The Greenhouse Effect, Climatic Change and Ecosystems</u>, Wiley, New York.

US DEPARTMENT OF AGRICULTURE (1990), 'Climate Change, Economic Implications for World Agriculture', Resources and Technology Division, Economic Research Service, Washington DC 20005-4788

Health Damage

ARNOULD R. and NICHOLS L. (1983), 'Wage Risk Premiums and Workers' Compensation: A Refinement of Estimates of Compensating Wage Differential', <u>Journal of Political Economy</u>, Volume 91, pp. 332-340.

ACTON J.P. (1976 Autumn), 'Measuring the Monetary Value of Life Saving Programs', <u>Law and Contemporary Problems</u>, Volume 40, pp. 46-72.

ARNOULD R.J. and NICHOLS L.M. (1983), 'Wage-Risk Premiums and Worker's Compensation: A Refinement of Estimates of Compensating Wage Differentials', <u>Journal of Political Economy</u> 91(2), pp. 332-340.

BLOMQUIST G. (1981 January), 'Value of Human Life: An Empirical Perspective', <u>Economic Inquiry</u> 19, pp. 157-164.

BLOMQUIST G. (1979), 'Value of Life Saving: Implications of Consumption Activity', <u>Journal of Political Economy</u>, Volume 78, No 3.

BROOME J. (1979), 'Trying to Value a Life', <u>Journal of Public Economics</u>, Volume 9, pp. 91-100.

BROWN C. (1980), 'Equalizing Differences in the Labor Market', <u>Quarterly Journal of Economics</u> 94(1), pp. 113-134.

CHAPPIE M. and LAVE L. (1983), 'The Health Effects of Air Pollution: a Reanalysis", <u>Journal of Urban Economics</u>, Volume 12, pp. 346-376.

CHINN S. *et al* (1981), 'The Relation of Mortality in England and Wales 1969-1973 to Measurements of Air Pollution', <u>Journal of Epidemiology and Community Health</u>, Volume 35, pp. 174-179.

CONLEY B.C. (1976 March), 'The Demand for Human Life in the Demand for Safety', <u>American Economic Review</u> 66, 45-55.

COUSINEAU J.M, LACROIX R, GIRARD A.M, (1988), 'Occupational Hazard and Wage Compensating Differentials', Centre de Recherche et Développement Economique, University de Montréal.

CROPPER M.L. (1981), 'Measuring the Benefits from Reduced Morbidity', <u>American Economic Review Papers and Proceedings</u>, Volume 71, No 2, pp. 235-340.

DARDIS R. (1980), 'The Value of Life: New Evidence from the Market Place', <u>American Economic Review</u> December 1980, pp. 1077-1082.

19

DICKENS W.T. (1984), 'Difference between Risk Premiums in Union and Non-Union Wages and the Case for Occupational Safety Regulation', American Economic Review 74(2), pp 320-323.

DILLINGHAM A. (1985), 'The Influence of Risk Variable Definition on Value of Life Estimates', Economic Inquiry 24, pp. 277-294.

DORSEY S. and WALZER N. (1983), 'Workers' Compensation, Job Hazards and Wages', Industrial and Labor Relations Review 36(4), pp. 643-654.

FISHER A, CHESTNUT L.G. and VIOLETTE D.M. (1989), 'The Value of Reducing Risks of Death: A Note on New Evidence', Journal of Policy and Management, Volume 8, No 1, pp. 88-100

FRANKEL M. (1979), 'Hazard, Opportunity, and the Valuation of Life', unpublished manuscript, Department of Economics, University of Illinois, Champaign-Urbana (IL).

FRITZSCHE A. (1989), 'The Health Risks of Energy Production', Risk Analysis Volume 9, No 4, 565-577.

GARBACZ C. (1989), 'Smoke Detector Effectiveness and the Value of Saving a Life', Economic Letters 31, pp. 281-286.

GEGAX D, GERKING S, SCHULTZ W. (1987), 'Perceived Risk and the Marginal Value of Safety', unpublished, University of Wyoming, Laramie, (in Miller, Calhoun and Arthur, 1990).

GERKIN S. and SCHULZE W. (1981), 'What Do We Know About Benefits of Reduced Mortality from Air Pollution Control?', American Economic Review, Volume 71, No 2, May.

GERKING S. and STANLEY L. (1986), 'An Economic Analysis of Air Pollution and Health: The Case of St Louis', Review of Economics and Statistics, Volume LXVIII, No 1, pp. 115-121.

GERKING S, HAAN M. and SCHULTZ W. (1988), 'The Marginal Value of Job Safety: A Contingent Valuation Study', Journal of Risk and Uncertainty 1 (2), pp. 185-199.

GHOSH D, LEES D. and SEAL W. (1975 June), 'Optimal Motorway Speed and Some Valuations of Time and Life', Manchester School of Economic and Social Studies 43, 134-143.

HARRINGTON W, KRUPNICK A.J. and SPOFFORD W.O. Jr. (1986), 'The Economic Losses of a Waterborne Disease Outbreak', Journal of Urban Economics, Volume 25, No 1, pp. 116-137.

IPPOLITO P.M. and IPPOLITO R.A. (1984), 'Measuring the Value of Life Saving from Consumer Reaction to New Information', Journal of Public Economics 25, pp. 53-81.

JONES-LEE M.W. (1989b), 'Altruism and the Value of Other People's Safety', Newcastle University, Economics Discussion Paper Series.

JONES-LEE M.W, HAMMERTON M. and PHILIPS P.R. (1985), 'The Value of Transport Safety: Results of a National Sample Survey', <u>Economic Journal</u>, 95: 49-72.

JONES LEE M.W. (1979) 'Trying to Value a Life - Why Broome Does not Sweep Clean', <u>Journal of Public Economics</u>, Volume 10, pp. 249-256.

JONES-LEE M.W. (1989), <u>The Economics of Safety and Physical Risk</u>, Basil Blackwell Ltd.

KRUPNICK A.J. and CROPPER M.L. (forthcoming), 'The Effect of Information on Health Risk Valuations', <u>Journal of Risk and Uncertainty</u>, also RFF Discussion Paper QE 980-13.

LANDEFELD J.S. and SESKIN E.P. (1982), 'The Economic Value of Life: Linking Theory to Practice', <u>American Journal of Public Health</u> 72 (6), pp. 50-566.

LAVE L. and SESKIN E. (1973), 'An Analysis of the Association between US Mortality and Air Pollution', <u>Journal of the American Statistical Association</u>, Volume 68, No 342, pp. 284-290.

LAVE L. and SESKIN E. (1977), <u>Air Pollution and Human Health</u>, Johns Hopkins University Press, Baltimore.

LITAI D. (1980), <u>'A Risk Comparison Methodology for the Assessment of Acceptable Risk'</u>, PhD thesis, Massachusetts Institute of Technology.

LOW S.A. and McPHETERS L.R. (1983 April), 'Wage Differentials and Risk of Death: An Empirical Analysis', <u>Economic Inquiry</u>, Volume XXI (2), pp. 271-280.

MACLEAN A.D. (1979), <u>The Value of Public Safety: Results of a Pilot Scale Survey</u>, London Home Office Scientific Advisory Branch.

MAGAT W., VISCUSI K. and HUBER J. (forthcoming), 'Valuing Chronic Morbidity Damages', <u>Journal of Environmental Economics and Management</u>.

MAIER G., GERKING S. and WEISS P. (1989), 'The Economics of Traffic Accidents on Austrian Roads: Risk Lovers or Policy Deficit?', *mimeo*, Wirtschaftuniversität, Vienna.

MARIN A. and PSACHAROPOULOS G. (1982), 'The Reward for Risk in the Labor Market: Evidence from the United Kingdom and a Reconciliation with Other Studies', <u>Journal of Political Economy</u>, Volume 90, No 4, pp. 827-853.

MELINEK S.J. (1974), 'A Method for Evaluating Human Life for Economic Purposes', <u>Accident Analysis and Prevention</u>, Volume 6, pp. 103-114.

MELINEK S.J, WOOLLEY S.K.D. and BALDWIN R. (1973), <u>Analysis of a Questionnaire on Attitudes to Risk</u>, Fire Research Note No 962, Joint Fire Research Organisation, Herts, England.

MILLER T.R. (1990), 'The Plausible Range for the Value of Life - Red Herrings among the Mackerel', <u>Journal of Forensic Economics</u>, August.

MOORE M.J. and VISCUSI W.K. (1988), 'Doubling the Estimated Value of Life: Results Using New Occupational Fatality Data', <u>Journal of Policy Analysis and Management</u> 7 (3), pp. 476-490.

NEEDLEMAN L. (1979), 'The Valuation of Changes in the Risk of Death by Those at Risk', University of Waterloo, Working Paper 103.

NEEDLEMAN L. (1976), 'Valuing Other People's Lives', <u>Manchester School</u>, 44: 309-42.

PERSSON U. (1989), 'The Value of Risk Reduction: Results of a Swedish Sample Survey', *mimeo*, The Swedish Institute of Health Economics.

OLSON C.A. (1981), 'An Analysis of Wage Differentials Received by Workers on Dangerous Jobs', <u>Journal of Human Resources</u>, Volume XVI (2), pp. 167-185.

OSTRO B. (1983), 'The Effects of Air Pollution on Work Loss and Morbidity', <u>Journal of Environmental Economics and Management</u>, Volume 10, pp. 371-382.

OSTRO B. (1987), 'Air Pollution and Morbidity Revisited: a Specification Test', <u>Journal of Environmental Economics and Management</u>, Volume 14, No 1, pp. 87-98.

PICKLES J.H. (1986), 'Health Risks and Air Pollution - Error Analysis for a Cross-Sectional Mortality Study', <u>Risk Analysis</u>, Volume 6, No 2, pp. 203-212.

PORTNEY P.R. (1981), 'House Prices, Health Effects and Valuing Reductions in the Risk of Death', <u>Journal of Environmental Economics and Management</u>, Volume 8, pp. 72-78.

RICCI P. (1990), 'Mortality, Air Pollution, and Energy Production: Uncertainty and Causality', <u>Journal of Energy Engineering</u> Volume 116, No 3, December, 148-162.

ROSEN S. (1981), 'Valuing Health Risk', <u>American Economic Review: Papers and Proceedings</u>, Volume 71, No 2, pp. 241-245.

SESKIN E. (1979), 'An Analysis of Some Short-Term Health Effects of Air Pollution in the Washington DC Metropolitan Areas', <u>Journal of Urban Economics</u>, Volume 6, pp. 275-291.

SMITH R.S. (1979 April), 'Compensating Wage Differentials and Public Policy: A Review', <u>Industrial and Labour Relations Review</u>, Volume 32 (3), pp. 339-352.

SMITH V.K. (1983), 'The Role of Site and Job Characteristics in Hedonic Wage Models', <u>Journal of Urban Economics</u> 13 (3), pp. 296-321.

SMITH R.S. (1976), 'The Occupational Health and Safety Act', <u>American Enterprise Institute</u>, Washington DC.

SMITH V.K. and GILBERT C.S. (1984), 'The Implicit Valuation of Risks to Life: A Comparative Analysis', <u>Economic Letters</u>, Volume 16, pp. 393-399.

THALER R. and ROSEN S. (1976), 'The Value of Saving a Life: Evidence from the Labour Market', in <u>Household Production and Consumption</u> (N. Terlekyj, Ed) NBER Volume 40, pp. 265-298, National Bureau of Economic Research, Washington DC.

THIBODEAU L.A. et al (1980), 'Air Pollution and Human Health: a Review and Reanalysis', <u>Environmental Health Perspectives</u> 34, February.

ULPH A. (1982), 'The Role of Ex Ante and Ex Post Decisions in the Value of Life', <u>Journal of Public Economics</u>, Volume 18, pp. 265-276.

VELJANOVSKI C. (1978), 'The Economics of Job Safety Regulation: Theory and Evidence in the Market and Common Law', mimeo, Centre for Socio-Legal Studies.

VELJANOVSKI C. (1981), <u>'Regulating Industrial Accidents: An Economic Analysis of Market and Legal Responses'</u>, PhD thesis, University of York.

VIOLETTE D. and CHESTNUT L. (1983), 'Valuing Reductions in Risks: A Review of The Empirical Estimates', United States Environmental Protection Agency, Washington DC, <u>Report EPA</u> 230-05-83-002.

VISCUSI W.K. and MOORE M.J. (1987), 'Worker's Compensation: Wage Effects, Benefit Inadequacies, and the Value of Health Losses', <u>The Review of Economics and Statistics</u> 6912: 249-261.

VISCUSI W.K. and MOORE M.J. (1989), 'Rates of Time Preference and Valuations for the Duration of Life', <u>Journal of Public Economics</u> 38, pp. 297-317.

VISCUSI W.K, MAGAT W.A. and HUBER J. (1989), 'Pricing Environmental Health Risks: Survey Assessments of Risk Risk and Risk-Dollar Trade-Offs', <u>Estimating and Valuing Morbidity in a Policy Context: Proceedings of June 1989 AERE Workshop</u>, US Environmental Protection Agency, Washington DC.

VISCUSI W.K, MAGAT W.A. and FORREST A. (1988), 'Altruistic and Private Valuations of Risk Reductions', <u>Journal of Policy Analysis and Management</u>, Volume 7, No 2, pp. 227-245.

VISCUSI W.K. (1978b), 'Labour Market Valuations of Life and Limb: Empirical Evidence and Policy Implications', <u>Public Policy</u>, Volume 26, pp. 359-386.

VISCUSI W.K. (1978a), 'Health Effects and Earnings Premiums for Job Hazards', <u>Review of Economics and Statistics</u>, Volume 60, pp 408-416.

VISCUSI W.K. (1981), 'Occupational Safety and Health Regulation: Its Impact and Policy Alternatives', <u>Research in Public Analysis and Management</u> 2, pp. 281-299.

VISCUSI W.K. (1986), 'The Valuation of Risks to Life and Health: Guidelines for Policy Analysis', in BENTKOVER *et al* (eds) <u>Benefit Assessment: The State of the Art</u>, D. Reidel, Dordrecht.

VISCUSI W.K. (1980), 'Union, Labour Market Structure and the Welfare Implications of the Quality of Work', <u>Journal of Labor Research</u> 1(1), pp. 175-192.

WESTERN D.J. (1988), 'Proof of Evidence on Potential Site Effects of Radiation', <u>Hinkley Point C Power Station Public Inquiry</u>, CEGB, September.

WINSTON C. and MANNERING F. 'Consumer Demand for Automobile Safety: New Evidence on the Demand for Safety and the Behavioural Response to Safety Regulation', <u>American Economic Review</u> 74 (2).

Land Damage

HOWARD H.A. (1971), 'A Measurement of the External Diseconomies Associated with Bituminous Coal Surface Mining, Eastern Kentucky 1962-1967', <u>Natural Resources Journal</u> 11, pp 76-101

MICHAEL N. and PEARCE D.W. (1989), '<u>Cost Benefit Analysis and Land Reclamation: A Case Study</u>', IIED/UCL Environmental Economics Centre, London

RANDALL A. *et al* (1978), 'Reclaiming Coal Surface Mines in Central Appalachia: A Case Study of the Benefits and Costs', <u>Land Economics</u> Volume 54

THAYER M.A. (1981), 'Contingent Valuation Techniques for Assessing Environmental Impacts: Further Evidence', <u>Journal of Environmental Economics and Management</u> Volume 8, pp 27-42

WALSH R.G, LOOMIS J.B. and GILLMAN R.A. 'Valuing Option, Existence, and Bequest Demands for Wilderness', <u>Land Economics</u> Volume 60

Noise

NELSON J.P. (1978), 'Economic Analysis of Transportation Noise Abatement', Ballinger, Cambridge, Mass

NELSON J.P. (1980), 'Airports and Property Values: A Survey of Recent Evidence', Journal of Transport Economics and Policy, XIV, pp 37-52

NELSON J.P. (1982), 'Highway Noise and Property Values: A Survey of Recent Evidence', Journal of Transport Economics and Policy, XVI, pp 117-130

Non-Environmental Externalities

BOARDMAN H.G. and HOGAN W.W. (1988), 'Is an Oil Tariff Justified? An American Debate: The Numbers Say Yes', The Energy Journal Volume 9, No. 3, July, 7-29.

BURBIDGE J. and HARRISON A. (1984), 'Testing for the Effects of Oil-Price Rises Using Vector Autoregressions', International Economic Review, June, 25(2), 459-484.

GISSER M. and GOODWIN T.H. (1986), 'Crude Oil and the Macroeconomy: Tests of Some Popular Notions', Journal of Money, Credit and Banking, February, 18(1), 95-103.

HALL D. (1991), 'Oil and National Security', Department of Economics, California State University, Long Beach, *mimeo*.

HAMILTON J.D. (1985), 'Historical Causes of Postwar Oil Shocks and Recessions', The Energy Journal Volume 6, No. 1, January, 97-116.

HAMILTON J.D. (1983), 'Oil and the Macroeconomy Since World War II', The Journal of Political Economy Volume 91, No. 2, 228-248.

HUDSON E.A. and JORGENSON D.W. (1978), 'The Role of Energy in the US Economy', National Tax Journal, September, 31(3), 209-220.

HUDSON E.A. and JORGENSON D.W. (1978), 'Energy Prices and the US Economy 1972-1976', Natural Resources Journal, October, 18(4), 877-897.

MORK K.A. and HALL R.E. (1980), 'Energy Prices, Inflation and Recession 1974-1975', The Energy Journal, July, 1(3), 31-63.

SMEERS Y. (1991), 'Security of Supply as a Non-Environmental Externality on Networks', EC/US DoE Working Group, *mimeo*.

Non-Use Values

BENNETT J.W. (1984), 'Using Direct Questioning to Value the Existence Benefits of Preserved Natural Areas', <u>Australian Journal of Agricultural Economics</u>, Volume 28, Nos 2 and 3, pp. 136-150

BROOKSHIRE D, SCHULZE W.D. and THAYER M. (1985), 'Some Unusual Aspects of Valuing a Unique Natural Resource', University of Wyoming, *mimeo*

Radiation Damage

COOPER J. (1990), 'The United Kingdom Nuclear Fuel Cycle: the Radiological Impact', NRPB, Paper C410/050, Chilton.

FERGUSON R. (1991b), 'Environmental Costs of Energy Technologies: Routine Radiological Impacts of Nuclear Power', CEETES, University of Newcastle, *mimeo.*

FERGUSON R. (1991a), 'Environmental Costs of Energy Technologies: Accidental Radiological Impacts of Nuclear Power', Centre for Energy and Environmental Techno-Economic Studies, University of Newcastle, *mimeo.*

HARDING J. (1990), 'Reactor Safety and Risk Issues', Contemporary Policy Issues Volume VIII, No 3, July, 94-105.

JONES J.A. and WILLIAMS J.A. (1988), 'Assessment of the Radiological Consequences of Releases from Degraded Core Accidents from a Proposed PWR at Hinckley Point: Results Using MARC 1', NRPB-M152 NRPB.

JONES P. (1990), 'Social Costs of Energy', Atom, 403, May, 23-27.

NRPB (1986), 'Cost Benefit Analysis in the Optimisation of Radiological Protection', ASP 9, NRPB, Chilton, p. 6.

ROBB J. and CROFT J. (1991), 'Recent Perspectives on Optimisation of Radiological Protection', NRPB, Chilton, *mimeo.*

ROBB J. and WRIXON A. (1988), 'Revised Estimates for the Monetary Value of Collective Dose', NRPB - M157, Chilton, pp. 5.

ROBB J. (1990), 'Valuing Radiation Detriment for Optimisation Purposes', Radiological Protection Bulletin, No 110, March, 8-12.

ROCARD P. and SMETS H. (1992), 'A Socio-Economic Analysis of Controls on Land-Use Around Hazardous Installations', Geneva Papers in Insurance, forthcoming.

Recreational Losses

BOCKSTAEL N.E, McCONNELL K.E. and STRAND I. (1989), 'Recreation' in BRADEN J.B. and KOLSTAD C.D. eds, <u>Measuring the Demand for Environmental Improvement</u>, Urbana, Illinois, Institute for Environmental Studies, Chapter 8

CLAWSON M. and KNETCH J.L. (1966), 'Economics of Outdoor Recreation', <u>Resources for the Future Inc</u>, Washington DC

GREEN C. *et al* (1990), 'The Benefits of Coast Protection: Results from Testing the Contingent Valuation Method (CVM) for Valuing Beach Recreation', Flood Hazard Research Centre, Middlesex Polytechnic

KRUTILLA J. and FISHER A. (1975), 'The Economics of Natural Environments: Studies in the Valuation of Commodity and Amenity Resources', Johns Hopkins University Press, Baltimore

MOREY E. and SHAW W. (forthcoming), 'An Economic Model to Assess the Impact of Acid Rain: A Characteristics Approach to Estimating the Demand for and Benefits from Recreational Fishing', in SMITH V. and WITTE A. eds <u>Advances in Applied Microeconomics Theory</u>, Volume 8, JAI Press Inc, Greenwich, Connecticut

SMITH V.K. and KAORU Y. (1990), 'Signals or Noise? Explaining the Variation in Recreation Benefit Estimates', <u>American Journal of Agricultural Economics</u>, pp. 419-433

STRAND J. (1981), 'Valuation of Fresh Water Fish as a Public Good in Norway', Institute of Economics, University of Oslo, Oslo, *mimeo*

WILLIS K.G. and GARROD G.D. (1990), 'Valuing Open Access Recreation on Inland Waterways', <u>ESRC Countryside Change Initiative Working Paper 12</u>

WILMAN E.A. (1984), <u>'External Costs of Coastal Beach Pollution'</u>, Resources for the Future, Washington DC

Transmission

DECICCO J, BERNOW S. and BEYEA J. (1992), 'Environmental Concerns Regarding Electric Transmission in North America', Energy Policy, Volume 20, No. 1, January

MORGAN M. (1989), 'Electric and Magnetic Fields From 60 Hertz Electric Power: What Do We Know About the Health Risks?', Carnegie-Mellon University, Engineering and Public Policy Department, Pittsburgh

SAVITZ D, PEARCE N, POOLE C. (1989), 'Methodological Issues in the Epidemiology of Electromagnetic Fields and Cancer', Epidemiologic Reviews, Volume 11

US Office of Technology Assessment (OTA) (1989), Effect of Power Frequency Electric and Magnetic Fields, OTA-BP-E-53, Washington DC

UK Valuation Studies

'Commission on the Third London Airport (1971): <u>Report</u>', Her Majesty's Stationery Office, London, p. 230.

'Commission on the Third London Airport (1970): <u>Papers and Proceedings</u>' Volume VII, Her Majesty's Stationery Office, London, p. 440.

BENSON J.F. and WILLIS K.G. (1990), 'The Aggregate Value of Non-Priced Recreation Benefits of the Forestry Commission Estate', <u>Report to the Forestry Commission Estate</u>, Department of Town and Country Planning, University of Newcastle, Newcastle.

BURTON T.L. (1967), 'Windsor Great Park: A Recreation Study', <u>Wye College Studies in Rural Land Use</u> No 8, University of London, London.

BUTTON K.J. and PEARCE D.W. (1989), 'Infrastructure Restoration as a Tool for Stimulating Urban Renewal - The Glasgow Canal', <u>Urban Studies</u>, 26, pp. 559-71.

CHESHIRE P.C. and STABLER M.J. (1976), 'Joint Consumption Benefits in Recreational Site Surplus: An Empirical Estimate', <u>Regional Studies</u> 10, pp. 343-51.

COCKER A. *et al* (1989), 'An Evaluation of the Recreational and Amenity Benefits of a Flood Alleviation Scheme for Maidenhead', <u>Flood Hazard Research Centre</u>, Enfield.

COLENUTT R.J. (1969), 'Modelling Travel Patterns of Day Visitors to the Countryside', <u>Area</u> 1, pp. 43-7.

DASGUPTA A.K. and PEARCE D.W. (1972), '<u>Cost-Benefit Analysis: Theory and Practice</u>', Macmillan, London p. 270.

DEPARTMENT of the ENVIRONMENT. (1991), 'Policy Appraisal and the Environment', Department of the Environment, London, p. 67.

DURHAM COUNTY COUNCIL. (1971), 'Crimdon Benefit Study', Durham County Council, Durham.

ELSON M.J. (1973), 'Some Factors Affecting the Incidence and Distribution of Weekend Recreation on Motoring Trips', <u>Oxford Agrarian Studies</u> 2, pp. 161-79.

EVERETT R.D. (1979), 'The Monetary Value of the Recreational Benefits of Wildlife', <u>Journal of Environmental Management</u> 8, pp. 203-213.

GARROD G.D. and WILLIS K.G. (1991a), 'The Hedonic Price Method and the Valuation of Countryside Characteristics', <u>Countryside Change Working Paper</u> 14, University of Newcastle, Newcastle.

GARROD G.D. and WILLIS K.G. (1991b), 'The Environmental Economic Impact of Woodland: A Two Stage Hedonic Price Model of the Amenity Value of Forestry In Britain', Countryside Change Working Paper 19, University of Newcastle, Newcastle.

GARROD G.D. and WILLIS K.G. (1991c), 'Some Empirical Estimates of Forest Amenity Value', Countryside Change Working Paper 13, Countryside Change Unit, University of Newcastle, Newcastle.

GIBSON J.G. and ANDERSON R.W. (1975), 'The Estimation of Consumers' Surplus from a Recreational Facility with Optional Tariffs', Journal of Applied Economics 7, pp. 73-9.

GIBSON J.G. (1978), 'Recreation Land Use', in PEARCE D.W. ed. The Valuation of Social Cost, Allen and Unwin, London.

GIBSON J.G. (1972), 'The River Trent Recreation Study', in Recreation Cost-Benefit Analysis, Countryside Commission, London.

GIBSON J.G. (1974), 'Recreation Cost-Benefit Analysis: A Review of English Case Studies', Planning Outlook, Special Issue, Newcastle University, Newcastle.

GREEN C.H. and TUNSTALL S. (1991a), 'Is the Economic Evaluation of Environmental Goods Possible', Journal of Environmental Management, (in press).

GREEN C.H. et al (1990a), 'The Economic Evaluation of Environmental Goods', Project Appraisal 5, pp. 70-82.

GREEN C.H. et al (1990b), 'The Benefits of Coastal Protection: Results from Testing the CVM for Beach Recreation, Annual Conference of River and Coastal Engineers, Loughborough University, Loughborough.

GREEN C.H. and TUNSTALL S. (1991b), 'The Evaluation of River Water Quality Improvements by the Contingent Valuation Method', Applied Economics 23, pp. 1135-1146.

GREEN C.H., TUNSTALL S. and HOUSE M.A. (1989), 'Investment Appraisal for Sewerage Schemes: Benefit Assessment', in Laikari H. ed. River Basin Management V, Pergamon Press, Oxford.

GREEN C.H. and TUNSTALL S. (1990), 'The Amenity and Recreational Value of River Corridors', Paper given at the Conservation and Management Rivers Conference, University of York, York.

HANLEY N.D. (1989a), 'Valuing Rural Recreation Benefits: An Empirical Comparison of Two Approaches', Journal of Agricultural Economics 40, pp. 361-74.

HANLEY N.D. et al (1991b), 'Design Bias in CV Studies: The Impact of Information Changes', Working Paper 91/13, Stirling Discussion Papers in Economics, University of Stirling, Stirling.

HANLEY N.D. (1991), 'The Economic Value of Wilderness Areas', in Dietz F, van der Ploeg R, and van der Straaten J. eds. Economic Policy and the Environment, Elsevier, North Holland.

HANLEY N.D. (1989b), 'Problems in Valuing Environmental Improvement Resulting from Agricultural Policy Changes', in DUBGAARD A. and NIELSON A. eds. Economic Aspects of Environmental Regulation in Agriculture, Wissenschaftsverlag, Vauk Kiel, Kiel.

HANLEY N.D. (1988), 'Using Contingent Valuation to Value Environment Improvements', Applied Economics 20, pp. 541-49.

HANLEY N.D. and COMMON M.S. (1987), 'Evaluating the Recreation, Wildlife and Landscape Benefits of Forestry: Preliminary Results from a Scottish Study', Papers in Economics, Finance and Investment, No 141, University of Stirling, Scotland.

HANLEY N.D. et al (1991a), 'Heathland Conservation in Dorset', Report to the NCC, Department of Economics, University of Stirling, Stirling.

HARLEY D. and HANLEY N.D. (1989), 'Economic Benefit Estimates for Nature Reserves: Methods and Results', Discussion Paper 89/6, Department of Economics, University of Stirling, Stirling.

HM TREASURY (1991), 'Economic Appraisal in Central Government: a Technical Guide for Government Departments', HM Treasury, London, p. 92.

KAVANAGH N.J. and GIBSON J.G. (1971), 'Measurements of Fishing Benefits on the River Trent', in The Trent Research Programme, The Institute of Water Pollution Control.

MANSFIELD N.W. (1971), 'The Estimation of Benefits from Recreation Sites and the Provision of a New Recreation Facility', Regional Studies 5, pp. 55-69.

PEARCE D.W, MARKANDYA A, and BARBIER E. (1989), 'Blueprint for a Green Economy', Earthscan, London, p. 192.

PENNING-ROWSELL E. et al (1989b), 'Recreational Aspects of Coast Protection Benefits', Paper presented to the Conference of River and Coastal Engineers, Loughborough University, Loughborough.

PENNING-ROWSELL E. et al (1989a), 'Scheme Worthwhileness', in Institution of Civil Engineers, Coastal Management, Thomas Telford, London.

PENNINGTON G. et al (1990), 'Aircraft Noise and Residential Property Values Adjacent to Manchester International Airport', Journal of Transport Economics and Policy 24, pp. 49-59.

PRICE C, CHRISTENSEN J.B. and HUMPHREYS S.K. (1986), 'Elasticities of Demand for Recreation Site and Recreation Experience', Environment and Planning A 18, pp. 1259-63.

SMITH R.J. and KAVANAGH N.J. (1969), 'The Measurement of Benefits of Trout Fishing: Preliminary Results of a Study at Grafham Water', Great Ouse Water Authority, Huntingdonshire, <u>Journal of Leisure Research</u> 1, pp. 316-32.

TURNER R.K. and BROOKE J. (1988), 'A Benefits Assessment for the Aldeburgh Sea Defence Scheme', <u>Environmental Appraisal Group Report</u>, School of Environmental Sciences, University of East Anglia, Norwich.

USHER M.B. (1977), 'Coastline Management: Some General Comments on Management Plans and Visitor Surveys', in BARNES R. ed. <u>The Coastline</u>, John Wiley, Chichester.

WILLIS K.G. and GARROD G.D. (1990), 'Valuing Open Access Recreation on Inland Waterways', <u>Countryside Change Working Paper</u> 12, University of Newcastle, Newcastle.

WILLIS K.G. <i>et al</i> (1990), 'The Value of Canals as a Public Good: The Case of the Montgomery and Lancaster Canals', <u>Countryside Change Working Paper</u> 5, Countryside Change Unit, University of Newcastle, Newcastle.

WILLIS K.G. and GARROD G.D. (1991a), 'An Individual Travel Cost Method of Evaluating Forest Recreation', Journal <u>of Agricultural Economics</u> 42, pp. 33-42.

WILLIS K.G. and BENSON J.F. (1988), 'A Comparison of User Benefits and Costs of Nature Conservation at Three Nature Reserves', <u>Regional Studies</u> 22, pp. 417-28.

WILLIS K.G. and BENSON J.F. (1988), 'Values of User Benefits of Forest Recreation: Some Further Site Surveys', <u>Report to the Forestry Commission</u>, Department of Town and Country Planning, University of Newcastle, Newcastle.

WILLIS K.G. and GARROD G.D. (1991b), 'Landscape Values: A Contingent Valuation Approach and Case Study of the Yorkshire Dales National Park', <u>Countryside Change Working Paper</u> 21, University of Newcastle, Newcastle.

Visibility and Amenity

BROOKSHIRE D.S. and CROCKER T.D. (1981), 'The Advantages of Contingent Valuation Methods for Benefit-Cost Analysis', <u>Public Choice</u> Volume 36, pp. 235-252.

BROOKSHIRE D.S, d'ARGE R.C, SCHULZE W.D. and THAYER M.A. (1981), 'Experiments in Valuing Public Goods', <u>Advances in Applied Microeconomics,</u> ed. V.K. Smith, volume 1, pp 123-172, Greenwich, CT: JAI Press.

BROOKSHIRE D.S, d'ARGE R.C, SCHULZE W.D. and THAYER M.A. (1982), 'Valuing Public Goods: A Comparison of Survey and Hedonic Approaches', <u>American Economic Review</u> Volume 72, pp. 165-178.

BROOKSHIRE D.S, IVES B.C. and SCHULZE W.D. (1976), 'The Valuation of Aesthetic Preferences', <u>Journal of Environmental Economics and Management</u> Volume 3, pp. 325-346.

BROOKSHIRE D.S, THAYER M.A, SCHULZE W.D. and d'ARGE R.C. (1982), 'Valuing Public Goods: a Comparison of Survey and Hedonic Approaches', <u>American Economic Review,</u> Volume 72, pp. 165-178.

CHESTNUT L.G, ROWE R.D. and MURDOCH J.C. (1986), '<u>Review of Establishing and Valuing the Effects of Improved Visibility in Eastern US.</u>' Report for the USEPA contract no. 68-01-7033, US EPA, Washington DC.

FERGUSON R. (1991), '<u>Environmental Costs of Energy Technology</u>', Unpublished Manuscript, Newcastle Upon Tyne University.

FISCHOFF B. and FURBY L. (1987), '<u>A Review and Critique of Tolley, Randall, et al Establishing and Valuing the Effects of Improved Visibility in the Eastern U.S.</u>' ERI Technical Report 87-6. Eugene, OR: Eugene Research Institute.

FISCHOFF B. and FURBY L. (1988), 'Measuring Values: A Conceptional Framework for Interpreting Transactions with Special Reference to Contingent Valuation of Visibility', <u>Journal of Risk and Uncertainty</u> Volume 1, pp.147-184.

GALLAHER D.R. and SMITH V.K. (1985), 'Measuring Values for Environmental Resources Under Uncertainty', <u>Journal of Environmental Economics and Management</u> Volume 12, pp. 132-143.

GRAVES P.E, MURDOCH J.C, THAYER M.A. and WALDMAN D. (1988), 'The Robustness of Hedonic Price Estimation: Urban Air Quality', <u>Land Economics</u> Volume 64, pp. 220-233.

HYLLAND A. and STRAND J. (1983), '<u>Valuation of Reduced Air Pollution in the Greenland Area</u>', memo no. 12-83, Department of Economics, University of Oslo.

MENDELSOHN R. (1980), 'An Economic Analysis of Air Pollution from Coal-Fired Power Plants', Journal of Environmental Economics and Management Volume 7, pp. 30-43.

RANDALL A, IVES B.C. and EASTMAN C. (1974), 'Bidding Games for Valuation of Aesthetic Environmental Improvements', Journal of Environmental Economics and Management, Volume 1, pp. 132-149.

ROWE R.D, d'ARGE R.C. and BROOKSHIRE D.S. (1980), 'An Experiment on the Economic Value of Visibility', Journal of Environmental Economics and Management Volume 7, pp. 1-19.

SCHULZE W.D, BROOKSHIRE D.S, WALTHER E.G. *et al* (1983), 'The Economic Benefits of Preserving Visibility in the National Parklands of the Southwest', Natural Resources Journal Volume 23, pp.149-173.

SCHULZE W.D, CUMMINGS R.G, BROOKSHIRE D.S, THAYER M.A, WHITWORTH R.I. and RAHMATIAN M. (1983), 'Experimental Approaches to Valuing Environmental Commodities: vol 2', Draft report for Methods development in measuring benefits of environmental improvements, USEPA grant no CR 808-893-01, US EPA, Washington DC.

TOLLEY G.S. and FABIAN (1988), The Economic Value of Visibility, Mount Pleasant, MI: Blackstone Books.

TOLLEY G.S, RANDALL A, BLOMQUIST G. *et al* (1986), Establishing and Valuing the Effects of Improved Visibility in the Eastern United States, Report for USEPA contract no 807768-01-0, US EPA, Washington DC.

Water Pollution: General

BOCKSTAEL N.E, McCONNELL K.E. and STRAND I.E. (1987), 'Benefits From Improvements in Chesapeake Bay Water Quality', Volume II of Benefit Analysis Using Indirect or Imputed Market Measures, Report prepared for US Environmental Protection Agency, CR-811043-01-0.

BOCKSTAEL N.E, HANEMANN W.M. and KLING C.L. (1987), 'Estimating the Value of Water Quality Improvements in a Recreational Demand Framework', Water Resources Research, Volume 23, No 5, pp. 951-960.

CARSON R.T. and MITCHELL R.C. (1988), 'The Value of Clean Water: The Public's Willingness to Pay for Boatable, Fishable and Swimmable Quality Water', final draft report Resources for the Future.

FEENBERG D. and MILLS E.S. (1980), 'Measuring the Benefits of Water Pollution Abatement', Studies in Urban Economics, Academic Press, New York

MITCHELL R.C. and CARSON R.T. (1981), 'An Experiment in Determining Willingness to Pay for National Water Quality Improvement', Draft Report to the US Environmental Protection Agency, Washington DC.

MOREY E. and SHAW W. (forthcoming), 'An Economic Model to Assess the Impact of Acid Rain: A Characteristics Approach to Estimating the Demand for the Benefits from Recreational Fishing' in SMITH V. and WITTE A. eds Advances in Applied Microeconomics Theory, Volume 8, JAI Press Inc, Greenwich, Connecticut.

SMITH V.K. and DESVOUSGES W.H. (1986), 'Measuring Water Quality Benefits', Kluwer Nijhoff Publishing.

AARSKOG E.M. (1988), 'Willingness-to-pay for cleaning up the Inner Oslo Fjord', (in Norwegian), MSc thesis, Department of Economics, University of Oslo, Report No 871013-2, March, Centre for Industrial Research, Oslo.

AMUNDSEN B-T. (1987), 'Recreational Value of the Fish Populations in the Recreational Area Oslomarka', (in Norwegian), MSc thesis, Agricultural University of Norway.

BAAN P.J.A. (1983), 'Inventory Study of the Benefits of an Improved Water Quality', (in Dutch), Delft Hydraulics Laboratory, #R1853 - R83/001, July.

BAAN P.J.A. (1985), 'Inventory Study of the Benefits of Recovery and Protection of Soil Quality', (in Dutch, English summary), Delft Hydraulics Laboratory report #R2182/S618 - D85/004, December.

CARLSEN A.J. (1985), 'Economic Valuation of Hydroelectric Power Production and Salmon Fishing', in CARLSEN A.J. (ed) Proceedings - UNESCO Symposium on Decision Making in Water Resources Planning, 5-7 May, Oslo, p 173-182.

DALGARD M. (1989), 'Willingness-to-pay for Regulatory Actions Towards Water Pollution in the Drammen Fjord', MSc thesis, Department of Economics, University of Oslo Report 881108-2, August, Centre for Industrial Research, Oslo.

EWERS H.J. and SCHULTZ W. (1982), 'The Monetary Benefits of Measures for Water Quality Improvement - A Case Study of Lake Tegeler in Berlin', (in German), Umweltbundesamt Berichte 3/82, Erich Schmidt Verlag, Berlin

GREEN C.H. and TUNSTALL S.M, (1990a), 'The Amenity and Environmental Value of River Corridors', Flood Hazard Research Centre, Publication No 171, Middlesex Polytechnic.

GREEN C.H. and TUNSTALL S.M. (1990b), 'The Benefits of River Water Quality Improvement', Report from the Flood Hazard Research Centre, Middlesex Polytechnic (in press, Applied Economics).

GREEN C.H. and TUNSTALL S.M. (1990c), 'The Benefits of Coast Protection. Results from Testing the Contingent Valuation Method (CVM) for Valuing Beach Recreation', Flood Hazard Research Centre, Publication No 168, Middlesex Polytechnic.

HANLEY N. (1989), 'Problems in Valuing Environmental Improvements Resulting from Agricultural Policy Changes: The Case of Nitrate Pollution', Report, Department of Economics, University of Stirling.

HEIBERG A. and HEM K-G. (1987), 'Use of Formal Methods in Evaluating Countermeasures to Coastal Water Pollution. A Case Study of the Kristiansand Fjord, Southern Norway', Centre for Industrial Research, in SEIP H.M. and HEIBERG A. (eds) (1989), Risk Management of Chemicals in the Environment, Plenum Press, London

HEIBERG A. and HEM K-G. (1988), 'Regulatory Impact Analysis for the Inner Oslo Fjord. A Comparison of Three Different Methods', (in Norwegian), Report 88 0105-1, September, Centre for Industrial Research.

HERVIK A, RISNES M. and STRAND J. (1987), 'Implicit Costs and Willingness-to-pay for Development of Water Resources, in CARLSEN A.J. (ed) Proceedings - UNESCO Symposium on Decision Making in Water Resources Planning, 5-7 May 1986, Oslo, p 195-202.

HJALTE K, LIDGREN K, THELANDER A-L. and WELLS C. (1982), 'Economic Consequences of Water Quality Changes in Lakes', (in Swedish, English summary), March 1982 Report TEM University of Lund.

HÜBLER K-H. et al (1991), 'Economic Losses Resulting from Soil Pollution in the Federal Republic of Germany', forthcoming in the Report series from the Federal Environmental Agency, Berlin, English summary in WESTKAMP and SCHULTZ (eds) p 30-33.

39

KANERVA V. and MATIKAINEN (1972), 'The Economic Losses Caused by Water Pollution in Lake Saimaa', (in Finnish, English summary), Rakennustalouden laboratorio 7, Otaniemi marraskuu, Report from the Technical Research Centre in Finland.

KYBER M. (1981), 'Harmful Effects of Water Pollution on Recreation and their Estimation at an Inspection', (in Finnish, English summary), Research Notes 23/1981 Technical Research Centre of Finland.

MAGNUSSEN K. (1991), 'Valuation of Reduced Water Pollution Using the Contingent Valuation Method - Methodology and Empirical Results', Norwegian Agricultural Economics Research Institute, Paper presented at the second annual meeting of EAERE, 10-14 June 1991, Stockholm.

MAGNUSSEN K. and NAVRUD S. (1991), 'Valuing Reduced Pollution of the North Sea' (in Norwegian), Report to the Ministry of Environment, Noragric / Agricultural University of Norway and Norwegian Agricultural Economics Research Institute.

MÄNTYMAA E. (1991), 'Some New Ideas and Preliminary Results for Using the CVM in Measuring the Environmental Benefits of a Lake', University of Oulu, Research Institute of Northern Finland, Paper presented at the Autumn Workshop in Environmental Economics 29 September - 5 October 1991.

NAVRUD S. (1989), 'Estimating Social Benefits of Environmental Improvements from Reduced Acid Depositions: A Contingent Valuation Survey', in FOLMER H. and IERLAND van der E. (eds) Valuation Methods and Policy Making in Environmental Economics, Studies in Environmental Science 36: 69-102, Elsevier Science Publishers, Amsterdam.

NAVRUD S. (1991a), Norway, in BARDE J-P. and PEARCE D.W. (eds) 'Valuing the Environment, Six Case Studies', p 141-202, Earthscan Publications, London.

NAVRUD S. (1991b), 'Cost-Benefit Analysis of Liming Lakes, Two Case Studies', (in Norwegian), Report from the Directorate for Nature Management, in press.

NAVRUD S. (1991c), 'Cost-Benefit Analysis of Liming River Audna, An Extended Analysis', (in Norwegian), Report from the Directorate for Nature Management, in press.

RASMUSSEN T. et al (1991), 'Lost Income to the Fishing Industry in the Federal Republic of Germany Resulting from Environmental Pollution and Other Anthropogenically Related Impacts', forthcoming Report from the Umweltbundesamt.

SILVANDER U. (1991), 'The Willingness to Pay for Angling and Ground Water in Sweden', (in Swedish, English summary), Dissertations No 2 Swedish University of Agricultural Sciences, Department of Economics.

SPCA (1991), 'The North Sea Declaration: Nutrients: A Proposed Regulatory Plan to Reach the North Sea Declaration's Goal of Nutrient Emission Reduction, Combined with the Largest Possible Improvement in Local Water Quality', (in Norwegian), <u>Report from the State Pollution Control Authority</u> (SPCA), September.

TURNER R.K. and BROOKE J.S. (1988), 'A Benefit Assessment for the Aldeburgh Sea Defence Scheme, Environmental Appraisal Group Report', School of Environmental Sciences, <u>University of East Anglia</u>, Norwich.

WINJE D, HOMANN H, LÜHR H.P. and BÜTOW E. (1991), 'The Influence of Pollution in the Aquatic Environment on the Costs of Supplying Water in the Federal Republic of Germany', (in German), Report No 2/91 <u>Federal Environmental Agency</u>, Berlin, UFOPLAN No 101 03 110-08 (English summary) in WESTCAMP and SCHULTZ (eds) 1991, p 27-30.

WRC and FHRC (1989), 'Investment Appraisal for Sewage Schemes: The Assessment of Social Costs', Water Research Centre (WRC) and Flood Hazard Research Centre (FRHC), Project Report, WRC, Swindon.

Wildlife, Biological Diversity, Natural Habitat

BOYLE K.J. and BISHOP R.C. (1987), 'Valuing Wildlife in Benefit-Cost Analysis: A Case Study Involving Endangered Species', Water Resources Research, Volume 23, No 5, pp. 943-950

HAMMACK J. and BROWN G. (1974), 'Waterfowl and Wetlands: Toward Bioeconomic Analysis', Johns Hopkins University Press, Baltimore

IMBER D, STEVENSON G. and WILKS L. (1991), 'A Contingent Valuation Survey of the Kakadu Conservation Zone', Research Paper Number 3, February 1991, Resource Assessment Commission, Canberra

PORTER P. (1982), 'The New Approach to Wilderness Preservation through Benefit-Cost Analysis', Journal of Environmental Economics and Management, Volume 9, pp. 59-80

SEMPLES J, DIXON J. and GOWEN M. (1986), 'Information Disclosure and Endangered Species Valuation', Land Economics Volume 62, No 3

TRAVERS MORGAN ECONOMICS (1991), 'Mersey Barrage Feasibility Study - Economic Valuation: Waders and Wildfowl: Contingent Valuation Method', Travers Morgan, London

Printed in the United Kingdom for HMSO.
Dd.0295091, 12/92, C8, 3396/4, 5673, 222710.